THE STUDIA PHILONICA ANNUAL
Studies in Hellenistic Judaism

PROGRAM IN JUDAIC STUDIES
BROWN UNIVERSITY
BROWN JUDAIC STUDIES

EDITED BY

David Jacobson
Ross S. Kraemer
Saul Olyan

NUMBER 337
THE STUDIA PHILONICA ANNUAL
Studies in Hellenistic Judaism

EDITED BY
David T. Runia
Gregory E. Sterling
Hindy Najman

THE STUDIA PHILONICA ANNUAL
Studies in Hellenistic Judaism

VOLUME XV

2003

EDITORS:
David T. Runia
Gregory E. Sterling
Hindy Najman

ASSOCIATE EDITOR
David Winston

Brown University
Providence

THE STUDIA PHILONICA ANNUAL
Studies in Hellenistic Judaism

The financial support of
C. J. de Vogel Foundation, Amsterdam
Queen's College, Melbourne
University of Notre Dame
is gratefully acknowledged.

Copyright © 2003 Brown University
Copyright © 2007 Society of Biblical Literature

All rights reserved. No part of this work may be reproduced or transmitted in any form or by any means, electronic or mechanical, including photocopying and recording, or by means of any information storage or retrieval system, except as may be expressly permitted by the 1976 Copyright Act or in writing from the publisher. Requests for permission should be addressed in writing to the Society of Biblical Literature, 825 Houston Mill Road, Suite 350, Atlanta, GA 30329 USA

ISBN 1-930675-15-2 (alk. paper : cloth)
ISBN 978-1-58983-476-7 (alk. paper : paper)
ISSN: 1052-4533

Printed in the United States of America
on acid-free paper

THE STUDIA PHILONICA ANNUAL
STUDIES IN HELLENISTIC JUDAISM

EDITORIAL BOARD

EDITORS: David T. Runia, *Queen's College, University of Melbourne*
Gregory E. Sterling, *University of Notre Dame*

ASSOCIATE EDITOR: David Winston, *Berkeley*

BOOK REVIEW EDITOR: Hindy Najman, *University of Notre Dame*

ADVISORY BOARD

David M. Hay, *Atlanta* (chair)
Hans Dieter Betz, *University of Chicago*
Peder Borgen, *Oslo*
Jacques Cazeaux, *CNRS, University of Lyon*
Lester Grabbe, *University of Hull*
Ellen Birnbaum, *Harvard University*
Annewies van den Hoek, *Harvard Divinity School*
Pieter W. van der Horst, *Utrecht University*
Jean Laporte, *Paris*
Burton L. Mack, *Claremont*
Birger A. Pearson, *Escalon, California*
Robert Radice, *Sacred Heart University, Milan*
Jean Riaud, *Catholic University, Angers*
James R. Royse, *San Francisco*
Dorothy Sly, *University of Windsor*
Abraham Terian, *St. Nersess Armenian Seminary*
Thomas H. Tobin S.J., *Loyola University, Chicago*
Herold D. Weiss, *St. Mary's College, Notre Dame*

The Studia Philonica Annual accepts articles for publication in the area of Hellenistic Judaism, with special emphasis on Philo and his *Umwelt*.

Contributions should be sent to the Editor, Prof. G. E. Sterling, Associate Dean of the Faculty, College of Arts and Letters, 100 O'Shaughnessy, University of Notre Dame, Notre Dame, IN 46556, U.S.A. Please send books for review to the Book Review Editor, Prof. H. Najman, Dept. of Theology, University of Notre Dame, Notre Dame, IN 46556, U.S.A.

Contributors are requested to observe the 'Instructions to Contributors' located at the end of the volume. These can also be consulted on the Annual's website: http://www.nd.edu/~philojud. Articles which do not conform to these instructions cannot be accepted for inclusion.

The Studia Philonica Monograph series accepts monographs in the area of Hellenistic Judaism, with special emphasis on Philo and his *Umwelt*. Proposals for books in this series should be sent to Prof. David M. Hay, 1428 Airline Road, McDonough, GA 30252, U.S.A.

τὰ δὲ τούτου μόνου βέβαια, ἀσάλευτα, ἀκράδαντα, καθάπερ σφραγῖσι φύσεως αὐτῆς σεσημασμένα, μένει παγίως ἀφ' ἧς ἡμέρας ἐγράφη μέχρι νῦν καὶ πρὸς τὸν ἔπειτα πάντα διαμενεῖν ἐλπὶς αὐτὰ αἰῶνα ὥσπερ ἀθάνατα, ἕως ἂν ἥλιος καὶ σελήνη καὶ ὁ σύμπας οὐρανός τε καὶ κόσμος ᾖ.

Philo, *De vita Moysis* 2.14

But of Moses alone do the laws, firm, unmoved, unshaken, stamped as it were with the seals of nature herself, remain steady from the day they were written until the present; and the expectation is that they will continue to remain as immortal for the entire further age, so long as the sun, moon, and the entire heaven and cosmos exist.

Philo, *On the life of Moses* 2.14

LAWS STAMPED WITH THE SEALS OF NATURE

Law and Nature in Hellenistic Philosophy
and Philo of Alexandria

edited by

David T. Runia
Gregory E. Sterling
Hindy Najman

CONTENTS

David K. O'CONNOR, Introduction 1

ARTICLES

David SEDLEY, The *Nomothetês* in Plato's *Cratylus* 5
Paul A. VANDER WAERDT, The Original Theory of Natural Law 17
Phillip MITSIS, The Stoics and Aquinas on Virtue and Natural Law 35
Hindy NAJMAN, A Written Copy of the Law of Nature:
    An Unthinkable Paradox? 54
Gregory E. STERLING, Universalizing the Particular: Natural Law
    in Second Temple Jewish Ethics 64
Brad INWOOD, Natural Law in Seneca 81

REVIEW ARTICLE

Tessa RAJAK, The Ancient Synagogue 100

BIBLIOGRAPHY SECTION

D. T. RUNIA, E. BIRNBAUM, K. A. FOX, A. C. GELJON, H. M. KEIZER,
    J. P. MARTÍN, R. RADICE, J. RIAUD, D. SATRAN, T. SELAND, D. ZELLER,
    Philo of Alexandria: an Annotated Bibliography 2000 109
SUPPLEMENT: Provisional Bibliography 2001–2003 138

BOOK REVIEW SECTION

Y. AMIR [י. עמיר] (ed.), כובים האלכסנדרוני פילון [Philo of Alexandria:
    Writings]: vol. 4, part 1. *Allegorical Exegesis (Genesis 1–5)*.
    Reviewed by David SATRAN 149
Cristina TERMINI, *Le potenze di Dio. Studio su duvnami" in Filone di
    Alessandria.*
    Reviewed by David T. RUNIA 151
Manuel ALEXANDRE, Jr., *Rhetorical Argumentation in Philo of Alexandria.*
    Reviewed by Stanley E. PORTER 156
Jutta LEONHARDT, *Jewish Worship in Philo of Alexandria.*
    Reviewed by David M. HAY 158

D. T. Runia, *Filone di Alessandria nella prima letteratura cristiana.*
   Reviewed by Angela Maria Mazzanti 161
F. Petit, *La Chaîne sur l'Exode. I Fragments de Sévère d'Antioche; La Chaîne sur l'Exode. II Collectio Coisliana. III Fonds caténique ancien (Exode 1,1–15,21); La Chaîne sur l'Exode. IV Fonds caténique ancien (Exode 15,22–40,32).*
   Reviewed by David T. Runia 162
Folker Siegert, *Zwischen Hebräischer Bibel und Altem Testament: Eine Einführung in die Septuaginta. Register zur „Einführung in die Septuaginta": Mit einem Kapitel zur Wirkungsgeschichte.*
   Reviewed by James R. Royse 165
Joan E. Cook, *Hannah's Desire, God's Design: Early Interpretations of the Story of Hannah.*
   Reviewed by Judith H. Newman 169
John David Dawson, *Christian Figural Reading and the Fashioning of Identity.*
   Reviewed by Robin Darling Young 171
Peter Schäfer, *Mirror of His Beauty: Feminine Images of God from the Bible to the Early Kabbalah.*
   Reviewed by Gregory E. Sterling 177

News and Notes 181

Notes on Contributors 189

Instructions to Contributors 193

INTRODUCTION

DAVID K. O'CONNOR

The six papers gathered here were among those presented at a conference at the University of Notre Dame in the fall of 2001, 'The Law of Nature: Ancient Origins and Contemporary Debates.' The conference brought together scholars whose work would usually be rather separate, some focused on ancient philosophy, others more focused on ancient Jewish and Christian thought. These papers show something of how the work of each group can be enriched by the other. Two papers (by Gregory E. Sterling and Hindy Najman) explore Philo's own contributions to the tradition of natural law, while the other four papers focus on the relation between law and nature in Plato (David Sedley), the earlier Stoics (Paul A. Vander Waerdt and Phillip Mitsis), and Seneca (Brad Inwood).

Philo was part of a lively debate going on in Jewish and Christian religious communities as well as in philosophical circles influenced by Plato and Stoicism. His subtlety and originality come more clearly to light when we see him in this larger philosophical context. Taken together, these six papers highlight Philo's transformation of two central questions raised by the philosophical tradition. (1) Must the laws of any particular community be in principle inferior to the laws that would characterize the best or ideal political community, the one defining the standard of nature? For Plato, the ideal community is the *kallipolis*, for the Stoics, the *kosmopolis*, for both the only true home of the philosopher; but for Philo, the community that adheres gladly to Mosaic law. (2) Is law as such, whether actual or ideal, in principle inferior to the wisdom of the exemplary sage, so that wisdom rather than any law becomes the standard of nature? The exemplary sage is represented for philosophy by the figure of Socrates, for Philo by the patriarchs and by Moses.

Ambiguities in Plato set in motion the two questions about law and nature to which Philo was heir. The *Republic* poses the first question about the relation between particular regimes and the ideal. Plato's Socrates cautions Glaucon to expect from him an account of the best city that can only be approximated by any actual city, just as a painter might represent a human being more beautiful than any actual person (*Republic* 5.472d4–7). The best city would exist in a real country only by a divine dispensation

---

* The editors wish to thank Gonni Runia for her tireless and careful work on this volume. Thanks also go to our students, Brad Milunski, O.F.C. and Matthew Gordley for their editorial assistance.

(*theia tuchê*); it is a paradigm in heaven, so that whether it will ever exist anywhere does not matter (*Republic* 9.592a8–9, b2–4). Yet Socrates also insists, first to Adeimantus then to Glaucon, that the best city is somehow possible, and not a mere prayer (*Republic* 6.499c4–5, 7.540d1–2).

The second question is posed most starkly in the *Statesman*, where the stranger from Elea tries to soften his interlocutor's unconditional attachment to the rule of law to give free rein to expert knowledge (*technê*) (*Statesman* 293e7, 300c9–d2). The stranger insists that even the best laws cannot capture the statesman's insight into the demands of the particular case (the *kairos*), in the same way that the expertise of a physician will always exceed the perfection of any fixed medical regimen, no matter how skillfully set out (*Statesman* 295c7–296a2). From this perspective, laws at best are no more than imitations of the truth, embodied in writings as far as possible by those with expert knowledge; the true regime is ruled by expertise, not law (*Statesman* 300c5–7). Yet it remains unclear how close the analogy is between medicine, which can dispense with the voluntary participation of its patients if need be, and politics, where the distinction between ruling over voluntary subjects and involuntary ones can appear as the most basic moral distinction of all, separating the king from the tyrant (*Statesman* 276d8–13 with 292c5–7 and 293a6–9).

David Sedley's 'The *nomothetês* in Plato's *Cratylus*' brings out a neglected linguistic aspect of these Platonic origins. The *Cratylus* is devoted to the question of whether language is or can be natural. Language might appear a paradigm of something conventional. But the dialogue complicates this view by invoking the figure of the *nomothetês*, the lawgiver who establishes correct language. On this model, language is natural if and only if it is the product of craft expertise, *technê*. As Sedley puts it, 'The Socrates of the *Cratylus* sees linguistic lawmaking, properly practised, as achieving its success by mapping the words it generates onto the true nature of things' (14). Sedley concludes by pointing out a striking passage where both laws and names (*nomoi* and *onomata*, with Plato wanting the pun) are held to a standard of perfection: the only real names and laws are the true ones, the natural ones. Incorrect names, and laws, are not really names and laws at all. Socrates is using the notion of a lawgiver in a very broad application, thinking as much about establishing the technical vocabulary of a particular discipline, such as medicine or astronomy, say, as about the laws of a political community. But the political application is there, and invites us to consider how the lawgiver's expertise and insight can be embodied in actual written laws. Presumably there can be real disciplines, ones that successfully 'map' nature; but can there be real laws?

If language is the material, so to speak, in which the lawgiver inscribes the forms of his expertise, the issue immediately arises of how receptive this material can be. Does the lawgiver's own wisdom survive uncorrupted and undiminished in the laws he establishes? Or is there an essential superiority of the living and thinking lawgiver over the laws he leaves as reminders of the expertise he exemplified? These questions link the *Cratylus* to Plato's *Philebus* and *Statesman*, also engaged with the issues of the nature of technical knowledge and its relation to political authority. But perhaps a more surprising connection, at least as a source for debate about natural law, is with the *Phaedrus*, with its discussions of the relation between the authority of speech and of writing.

These Platonic issues reverberate throughout the debate about early Stoic conceptions of natural law between Paul A. Vander Waerdt ('The Original Theory of Natural Law') and Phillip Mitsis ('The Stoics and Aquinas on Virtue and Natural Law'). Vander Waerdt argues that the early Stoics, following the lead of their founder Zeno in his own *Republic*, strove to avoid Plato's ambiguities about law, nature, and wisdom by straightforwardly identifying natural law with the sage's right reason. They 'accept the Platonic view of the inadequacy of rules and laws to guarantee morally correct conduct,' and would argue that 'the code of laws which the Platonic Socrates elaborates for his best regime [in Plato's *Republic*] cannot itself constitute' natural law (34). The only truly lawful action is the morally perfect action of the sage, just as the only true laws in the *Cratylus* are the ones that get nature right. Mitsis argues that this model underestimates the importance of the Stoic insistence that the sage's actions conform to divine providence. Though the connection between the sage's reason and the structure of providence is rather obscure in the surviving texts, Mitsis suggests that their view probably had some affinities to those of Thomas Aquinas, for whom there was no tension between virtue and lawfulness. In other words, Mitsis suggests that Vander Waerdt has made Stoic providence, the gods' mode of world governance, less regular and lawlike than is plausible.

Brad Inwood ('Natural Law in Seneca') discovers a variety of uses of the notion of natural law in Seneca. The most important use, however, links natural law to mortality. Achieving a rational, dispassionate attitude toward death becomes the hallmark of the wisdom embodied in natural law. This can be seen as an illustration of the 'conformity to nature' in dispute between Vander Waerdt and Mitsis. Inwood suggests that for Seneca, even if providence is in itself regular and lawlike, our imperfect epistemic access to providence means we can grasp it only in an unsystematic, particularist way. He also discusses Seneca's interesting use of the example of Socrates to illustrate the rational attitude toward death. Seneca exploits 'the appeal of something like contract law in unfolding a model of practical rationality' (96), a model with connections to Plato's *Crito*.

Gregory E. Sterling ('Universalizing the Particular: Natural Law in

Second Temple Jewish Ethics') and Hindy Najman ('A Written Copy of the Law of Nature: An Unthinkable Paradox?') explore different facets of the creative ways in which these Platonic and Stoic questions entered Jewish thought. Sterling takes up the first question: how did Jewish thinkers and defenders such as Philo and Josephus understand the relationship between their own particular law code, inspired directly by God, and natural law? Sterling shows how the surviving texts indicate there was a substantial shared code among Diaspora Jews, and that this code played an important role in defending the Jewish community against charges that their laws were somehow misanthropic. But he concludes that these texts 'suggest that the equation [of natural law and Mosaic law] was made on an ad hoc basis, i.e., Jewish moralists used it when they thought appropriate but did not work out a full-scale or systematic analysis' (76).

Hindy Najman shows that Philo has a strikingly original approach to the issues clustered around the second Platonic question, of how law is related to the sage. Plato and the Stoics both saw a tension between the community and the best individual. They did not explore the possibility that is central to Philo, of sages, namely the patriarchs, who are themselves the living and thinking law of their communities. For Philo, this does not mean that the patriarchs exercise political authority without constraint by previously established law, as it would for Plato. Rather, the patriarchs are exemplars of obedience to the law. Their influence comes not from command, but from becoming originals that others copy or imitate. We latecomers are related to them by a spirit of emulation.

This is an essentially different kind of authority from the expertise celebrated by the Eleatic stranger. For the patriarchs' authority is not in competition with the law's authority. In particular, the exempla of the patriarchs' lives are so to speak the lens through which the law comes alive itself and reveals its meaning. By containing the narratives of the originals we strive to emulate, the law overcomes the criticisms leveled against all law in the *Statesman* and indeed against all writing in the *Phaedrus*: it becomes adaptable to new particular circumstances and learns to speak to new people. In a Platonic mood, one is tempted to say Philo discovered that Moses accomplished with the narratives of the patriarchs what Plato accomplished through the vivifying personality of Socrates: he overcame the typical limits of didactic writing and made wisdom spring into flame in our souls, as a living teacher might.

If it is too much to hope that these essays cause the reader to burst into flame, perhaps at least they will make you smolder, and invite a wider group of scholars to profit from Philo of Alexandria's distinctive contributions to the natural law tradition.

University of Notre Dame

THE NOMOTHETÊS IN PLATO'S *CRATYLUS*

David Sedley

In the fifth century B.C.E., law (*nomos*) and nature (*physis*) frequently functioned as antithetical terms. Yet at some time they came together, to permit the concept of natural law, and, albeit at a much later date, that of the laws of nature. There can be little doubt that a major early force in this reconciliation of the two concepts was Plato, whose *Gorgias* is much concerned with erasing the *nomos-physis* antithesis as exploited by Callicles with regard to justice. But my focus in the present article will be, rather than the *Gorgias*, another of Plato's contributions to that reconciliation, found in one of the most intractable passages of his dialogue the *Cratylus*.

The *Cratylus* is an exploration of the thesis, espoused by Cratylus, that names belong to their *nominata* 'by nature'. This naturalist thesis is from the start directly opposed to the rival position of the other interlocutor Hermogenes that names are merely 'conventional'. The terms of art for 'convention' in this context are *synthêkê* (agreement) and *thesis* (fixing, setting, imposition, coining): all that makes a name a name is the fact that is has been fixed, assigned, and agreed on, irrespective of any natural fit to its *nominatum*, so that no one name is inherently better than any other. Along with these terms, Hermogenes also finds it appropriate to invoke the word *nomos*: 'For it is not the case that any individual thing has a name naturally belonging to it, but it is due to the *nomos* and habit (νόμῳ καὶ ἔθει) of those who habitually so call them' (384d).

Thus it is that the *Cratylus* debate has long been recognized as an instance of the celebrated *nomos-physis* (custom-nature) opposition, indissolubly associated with fifth-century Sophistic thought. Moreover, there is a possibility that this application of the antithesis to names represents one of its earliest roles in ancient debate. Although its most familiar incarnation is in the late fifth-century debate about the values — are they context-relative or absolute and objective? — as early as the mid-fifth century we find Empedocles attributing names to *nomos*: according to his fragment 9, when people talk of things being born and dying, they are speaking incorrectly of what is really no more than mixture and separation; but, Empedocles adds, he himself will go along with the convention (*nomos*). Here we can already glimpse the antecedents of the thesis, espoused by Plato's Hermogenes, that names are a matter of mere convention and for that reason a poor guide to the nature of their *nominata*.

In the *Cratylus*, however, it quickly becomes clear that the *nomos-physis* opposition is neither simple nor clear-cut. For the account of names as natural (*physei*) which Socrates proceeds to develop relies on the assumption that they are the product of *thesis*. It simply adds to that assumption the further principle that when a name is imposed additional criteria must be applied in order to determine whether or not it is a 'correct' name: some names are more correct than others, and these correspond to the ones which are 'natural' in the sense that they capture the nature of their *nominata*. Thus the opposition underlying the debate, as Socrates constructs it, is not to be understood as one between *nomos* and *physis* as such, but as one between *mere* custom on the one hand, and custom founded on nature on the other.

Now although up to this point the actual term *nomos* has put in no more than a cursory appearance, it takes centre stage soon after, when Socrates develops an argument based on his favoured distinction between the maker and the user of an artefact. A shuttle is a tool for separating the strands of a web; and its user, the weaver, is the right expert to oversee the work done by the craftsman who makes a shuttle. Analogously, a name is a tool for teaching and for separating the strands of being; and its paradigmatic user, the teacher or dialectician, is the right expert to oversee the work done by the subservient artisan, in this case the linguistic specialist or name-maker. So far, Socrates' own argument. But whereas shuttle-making was a familiar craft, name-making was not. Thus no doubt it is that we can set about explaining the turn which Socrates' argument takes at 388d. Who, he asks, is it that passes names down to us? Hermogenes cannot answer, but Socrates himself suggests, to Hermogenes' approval, that it is law or custom, ὁ νόμος, that does so. We may note in passing that *nomos* is thus invoked to answer, not a 'What?' question, but a 'Who?' question. *Nomos* is, it seems, personified into the status of our original benefactor in linguistic matters, for it is *nomos* itself, and not mere legislators (*nomothetai*), that has the power to pass down a tradition to us. The personification of *nomos*, most familiarly as 'king', was well established by this date (cf. Pindar fr. 169a, νόμος ὁ πάντων βασιλεύς; and Hippias in Plato, *Prot.* 337d), and need cause no great surprise.

Nevertheless, it is to the *nomothetēs* — the expert who actually creates and disseminates names — that attention now turns. The following data quickly emerge.

1. A *nomothetēs* is an expert in his own field (388d4–6).
2. His job, or at any rate one of his jobs, is to create names (388e1–2, 388e7–389a2; cf. 428a–429b).

3. The creation of names by the *nomothetês* is not just something that happened once at some earlier point in human history, for the craftsman in question is throughout spoken of in the present tense. This, perhaps the least appreciated aspect of the portrayal, is in fact confirmed by a variant passage at 437d10 preserved solely in the Codex Vindobonensis and rightly recognized by the editors of the new Plato OCT volume 1 as an authentic variant from the pen of Plato. Here Socrates recapitulates the earlier discussion as follows: 'Didn't we recently agree that those who *at any given time* (ἑκάστοτε) assign names in the cities, whether Greek or barbarian cities, are *nomothetai* and practise the skill that has this power, namely the *nomothetic* skill?' He then immediately goes on to ask a question about those whom, among these, he singles out as the 'first' *nomothetai*. It could hardly be clearer that name-making *nomothetai* are assumed still to exist and function.

4. The *nomothetês* is, however, 'the rarest of craftsmen in the human race' (389a2–3).

5. Like any good manufacturer, the skilled *nomothetês* creates a name by focusing his mind on the Form or ideal of the artefact he is currently working on, and by embodying that Form as best he can in the materials at his disposal — which in this case we can take to be the sound-system of his own language.

6. At any rate in ideal circumstances, the *nomothetês* is envisaged not as functioning autonomously, but as taking orders from a superior expert, the dialectician, who is the archetypal *user* of the names he constructs.

Why does Plato's Socrates feel the need to postulate this bizarre-sounding expert? I have never read a convincing answer in the literature,[1] and fear I shall not be able to offer one now either. But if I cannot supply the answer, I hope I can at least shed some light on the nature of the question.

One interpretation can be dealt with straight away. On this first view, the reference is quite literally to legislators in the political sense of the word, and Socrates is assuming that only these legislators, at the time when the bulk of language came into being, had the power to impose new usages on the populace at large. Such an interpretation has, it is true, the possible

---

[1] Relatively little light is shed by two articles devoted to the question: N. Demand, 'The nomethetes of the *Cratylus*', *Phronesis* 20 (1975) 106–9; S. Churchill, 'Nancy Demand on the nomothetês of the *Cratylus*', *Apeiron* 17 (1983) 92–93. There is more to be learnt from R. Robinson, 'The Theory of Names in Plato's *Cratylus*', in his *Essays in Greek Philosophy* (Oxford 1969) 100–17, and from M. Schofield, 'The Dénouement of the *Cratylus*', in M. Schofield, M. Nussbaum (edd.), *Language and Logos* (Cambridge 1982) 61–81.

advantage of providing a target for later critics, like the Epicureans Lucretius and Diogenes of Oenoanda,[2] who ridicule the idea of the first names having been deliberately coined, asking how, at the likely time of the original emergence of language, anyone could have had access to the necessary political structures to impose linguistic norms on the masses, let alone exploited those structures when addressing a populace that did not already understand the language in which it was being addressed. Although it is certainly in the cards that the Epicureans should have thought this the correct interpretation of the *Cratylus*, it surely cannot be that Plato has in mind so overtly political a concept of *nomos*. Even if he were thought to conjecture that the earliest name-makers used their status as (literal) legislators in order to bring a nomenclature into currency, he cannot have thought that the equivalent function in his own day, that of generating neologisms, was still the preserve of legislators. Yet, as we have seen, the name-making function of *nomothetai* is assumed to survive in his own day. When Socrates calls the *nomothetês* 'the rarest of craftsmen', he can hardly be referring to political legislators, of whom there were undoubtedly plenty in contemporary Greek cities, but to the postulated linguistic legislators, the people who succeed in bringing neologisms into circulation. New words do enter the language, so *someone* must be devising and launching them. But how many of us have ever met him? Of course, anyone can create a neologism, as Plato himself frequently does, but that does not in itself bring a new word into currency. As if to make this very point, in the passage we are now considering Plato has Socrates introduce an apparent neologism, ὀνομάτουργος,[3] 'name-worker', then immediately drop it in favour of νομοθέτης, as if in recognition that the skill of *institutionalizing* a name is something far more than the simple ability to string meaningful sound together into new forms.

Rather than think of literal legislation, therefore, it seems better at this stage to associate the *nomos* component of *nomothetês* with *nomos* in the sense 'custom' or 'convention', and to assume it to be chosen at least partly in deference to Hermogenes' attribution of naming to mere convention. But at the end of this article I will be airing the suggestion that the other main speaker, Cratylus, has a more political understanding of the same term, and that this too is in due course exploited by Socrates.[4]

---

[2] For the passages see A.A. Long and D.N. Sedley, *The Hellenistic Philosophers* (Cambridge 1987) 19B–C.

[3] I am grateful to Charles Brittain for pointing this out.

[4] In case it should be thought that the term *nomothetês* can be used only of one who imposes *nomoi* in the literal sense 'laws', so interpreted as to exclude 'custom', see Plato *Pol.* 295a, where a *nomothetês* is described as imposing *nomos* (singular), explicitly including not only written laws but also ancestral customs.

Despite what we have seen to be Socrates' postulation of contemporary, as well as ancient, linguistic *nomothetai*, there does seem to be a recognisable use of the singular, ὁ νομοθέτης, to refer historically to the original namegiver. In the *Cratylus* this occurs at, for example, 404b, where Socrates rejects the familiar etymology of 'Hades' as 'unseen' (ἀϊδής) in favor of a derivation from εἰδέναι, to 'know', remarking 'it is far preferable to say that it was on the basis of knowing all fine things that Hades was so named by the *nomothetês*'.[5] This occasional usage might have been dismissed as insignificant, but for a striking, if isolated, parallel altogether outside the etymological context of the *Cratylus*. In the *Charmides*, at 175b, Socrates expresses to Critias his frustration at not being able to find a definition of *sôphrosynê* ('moderation'): 'But as it is we are defeated on all sides, and are unable to find what on earth the thing was to which the *nomothetês* assigned (ἔθετο) this name, *sôphrosyne*.' Few scholars have thought the *Charmides* to postdate the *Cratylus*, and even supposing that it does it seems very unlikely that Socrates' casual remark to Critias can have been intended to rely on prior acquaintance with the theory developed in the latter dialogue. Rather, we seem to have here evidence of an established assumption about the origin of language: we owe it to some anonymous *nomothetês*. And, if so, the ready and unargued assumption in the *Cratylus* that names were and still are assigned by one or more *nomothetai* will have to be explained as borrowing from that tradition.

Given the silence of our poetic and mythological sources about any such tradition, I am reluctant to infer that it was a popular one. A better bet might be that it was a product of the fifth-century etymological industry, a large-scale Sophistic enterprise[6] of which Plato's *Cratylus* is no more than an echo. For anyone seeking to etymologize the actual word ὄνομα — 'name' or 'word' — was only too likely to link its origin to νόμος, and thus to look for and emphasize ways in which naming is a kind of lawmaking.[7] I suspect, for this reason, that the lost Sophistic discussions of 'correctness of names' had come to postulate a role for one or more linguistic *nomothetai*, and that that is why Critias, Hermogenes and Cratylus are all familiar enough with the same assumption to endorse it without question.

What that tradition actually held is hard to reconstruct. At one extreme, to speak of one or more individuals as the originators of some human institution might be little more than a *façon de parler*. If I say to you, 'Where

---

[5] Other examples of the singular include '393e, 402b, e1, 404c2, 406b4, 407b3, 408a7, 416b3, 419a5.
[6] For recognition of this, see *Crat.* 391b–c, cf. 384b.
[7] Plato's own etymology of ὄνομα at *Crat.* 421a in terms of 'hunting for being' has a strictly localized purpose, to link ethical and logical vocabulary to constant change.

were you when they handed out the brains?', or remark of a historical figure, 'They don't make them like that any more', it would be unwise to interpret me as endorsing some bizarre form of creationism. Or, to switch to a less popularizing model, even subscribers to one or another version of the 'social contract' theory may speak in those terms without for a moment being misunderstood as holding that on some historic occasion an actual contract was drawn up and signed. Likewise, talk of the *nomothetês* who gave things their names could have been present in Sophistic thought as nothing more than a convenient fiction.

On the other hand, the assumption that language was a deliberate contrivance by early humans was virtually universal before Epicurus formulated an alternative explanation a generation after Plato's death. It therefore may have seemed to follow that some person or persons really did devise and propagate it; and indeed that very presupposition runs throughout the *Cratylus*.

But if it was an established practice, even outside Plato's writings, to call these people *nomothetai*, what sense of the word was in play? A small but valuable clue can be found in the Hippocratic treatise *De arte*, which has long been recognised as a product of Sophistic thought. In his introductory remarks, its author argues (chapter 2) that each of the arts spotlights some forms or essences (εἴδεα), and that the art's nomenclature itself reflects those same forms, rather than imposing them. This insistence that names are derivative from the forms of things and not vice versa is then secured with the further remark that the forms of things cannot grow (βλαστάνειν) from names because names are themselves 'legislations of nature' (φύσιος νομοθετήματα), while the forms are not legislations but growths (βλαστήματα).[8] The logic of this is obscure, so much so that it has even provoked emendation.[9] However, in outline the point seems intelligible enough: the way things are is a 'growth', i.e. objectively given in nature, while names are in some sense derivative. But does φύσιος νομοθετήματα indicate that names are enactments *by* nature (subjective genitive), as one might most naturally construe the Greek? This makes little immediate sense in the context. Or are names, alternatively, enactments imposed *on* nature (objective

---

[8] οἶμαι δ' ἔγωγε καὶ τὰ ὀνόματα αὐτὰς διὰ τὰ εἴδεα λαβεῖν· ἄλογον γὰρ ἀπὸ τῶν ὀνομάτων τὰ εἴδεα ἡγεῖσθαι βλαστάνειν καὶ ἀδύνατον· τὰ μὲν γὰρ ὀνόματα φύσιος νομοθετήματά ἐστι τὰ δὲ εἴδεα οὐ νομοθετήματά ἀλλὰ βλαστήματα.
[9] See DK II 339: Diels excised φύσιος, while Gomperz transposed it to after βλαστήματα. Further discussion in F. Heinimann, *Nomos und Physis* (Basel 1945) 157. A more orthodox formulation is no doubt that in Hipp. *Nat. hom.* 5: names are κατὰ νόμον assigned to body components in a non-overlapping way, and likewise φύσει the corresponding components have non-overlapping 'forms' (ἰδέαι).

genitive)?[10] This too is less than satisfactory, since it implies that naming somehow constrains nature, whereas the author's point is meant to be that names follow and reflect nature, rather than causally impacting upon it. It therefore seems more helpful to opt for a third interpretation of φύσιος νομοθετήματα: names are enactments *embodying* the facts of nature. That is, names follow and reflect nature in so far as they *codify* it. On any of the three accounts, but especially on the third, we have here as striking a symbiosis of *nomos* and *physis* as the *Cratylus* introduces when it assigns to a *nomothetês* the task of giving things their 'natural' names.

As for the notion of *nomothetêmata*, we can presumably exclude from the Hippocratic context any reference to literal legislation, as we have already seen reason to do in the *Cratylus*. But what then *is* the operative notion of *nomos*? Here are some possibilities.

(a) Custom or habit, as contrasted with nature. The Hippocratic corpus (for example, *Airs, Water and Places*) often exhibits this standard antithesis between *nomos* and *physis* as competing explanatory factors regarding human anatomy, pathology and the like. On such an account, what is emphasized by appealing to *nomos* is that names are arbitrary impositions on things, their form not dictated by the nature of reality. That was, of course, Hermogenes' idea in the *Cratylus* when he made *nomos* the principle of name assignment, and, as I have remarked, it has a longer history which already surfaces in fragment 9 of Empedocles. But both the author of the *De arte* and the Socrates of the *Cratylus*, by presenting linguistic *nomothetêmata* as themselves embodiments of nature, appear to be rejecting the entire antithesis.

(b) Codification. As a lawgiver encapsulates a complex body of conduct in a single enactment, so a name encodes the nature of its *nominatum* in a single string of sound.

(c) Rules. The essence of a language lies in a shared set of labelling rules to which all users tacitly subscribe, and in virtue of which they are able to understand each other. The notion of rules imposed on an entire population, as by a legislator, captures the required uniformity of practice.

(d) Distribution. The noun *nomos* is derived from the verb νέμειν, to 'distribute', as Plato was very well aware, given his own etymology of *nomos* in the *Laws* (714a5) as νοῦ διανομή, 'distribution of intelligence'. Perhaps then the linguistic *nomothetês* is above all, at

---

[10] Thus Guthrie, *The Sophists* (Cambridge 1971) 204, 'words are an attempt to impose legislation on nature'.

least in Plato's eyes, a distributor or assigner — either because he assigns names to things, or because he brings names into circulation among the public.

(e) Authority. Although names cannot be disseminated by political decree, the task requires a rare degree of authority among one's fellow citizens. The metaphor of a lawmaker is an appropriate one for bringing this out.

I do not at present see much merit in trying to choose between these options, since all may well play a significant part. However, I do now want to suggest that their cumulative significance can be further supplemented by focusing on the likely *context* of name-assignment. In the ancient Greek world, what sphere of activity would most readily come to mind as calling for name-assignment? The answer is almost certainly, the creation or development of a *technê* — a formal discipline, be it medical, rhetorical, musical, or whatever else. And it seems possible that it was in this context, involving as it typically did the construction of a systematic terminology, that the model of the legislator suggested itself. The clues I have accumulated so far are admittedly meagre, but for what they are worth here they are.

First, the Hippocratic *De arte*, in the passage I have already cited, is making its point, that names are mere *nomothetêmata*, in the context of generalizing about the *technai*, whose power to impart knowledge the author is emphasizing: the arts, he says, have 'acquired names' (τὰ ὀνόματα ... λαβεῖν) on the basis of the forms (εἴδεα) of things. Although this might refer to nothing more than the names of the arts themselves, 'medicine', 'rhetoric' etc., I see no reason why the author should confine himself to so restricted an observation, and it seems more appropriate to the context to suppose that he has in mind the entire terminology that each art has acquired: by legislating the nomenclature for their subject matter, arts do not change the nature of that subject matter, but simply reflect it.

The generation of a technical terminology is, after all, a procedure that naturally invites comparison to the formulation of a law code. This is supported by a text of Ptolemy, written many centuries later but closely echoing the debate of the fifth and fourth centuries BCE, especially the Epicurean discussion of the origin of language.[11] According to chapter 4 of Ptolemy's short treatise *On the criterion*, words originated as instinctive

---

[11] The importance of this passage was brought to my attention by Alexander Verlinsky in an important forthcoming paper on the Epicurean theory of the origin of language. For text and translation of the Ptolemy treatise, see the valuable collaborative edition included in P. Huby and G.C. Neale (edd.), *The Criterion of Truth* (Liverpool 1989) 179–230.

utterances, later organized into a proper system of communication. It was at a still later stage, however, that a quasi-legislative process (ὥσπερ νομοθετεῖν) was added, and by this Ptolemy turns out to mean the formal restriction of usage to one term per concept. This kind of 'legislation' he treats as typical of philosophers, not only here but also in chapter 7, where he speaks of those who 'legislate' as to how the term 'body' should be used, some ruling that it should designate perceptibles, others anything with the power to interact.

One connotation of the legislative metaphor thus turns out to be that of restriction. Political legislators determine conduct not just by prescribing but also by *limiting* what we are to do, and linguistic legislators, comparably, do not simply enable communication, but also impose semantic restrictions. Every imposition of a correct usage carries with it, explicitly or implicitly, the proscription of other, incorrect usages. A paradigmatic case of this procedure lies in the formulation of *technai*, with their rigid terminologies.

But is Plato himself party to this view? I think that he is, and some measure of support can be sought from an unexpected quarter, his *Philebus*. In the early part of this dialogue, Socrates recommends a method which he calls 'a gift to mankind from the gods', maybe transmitted, along with fire, 'through some Prometheus'. The gift of Plato's Prometheus is based on number in the following way: between the single genus from which a scientific investigation might start, and its infinite range of individual members, the true scientist will be concerned above all with systematic *enumeration* of the intervening kinds or species. Asked for an explanation, Socrates illustrates the method with three examples, all concerned with the classification of sounds. In the second and third of these cases (17b–18d) — the sciences of classifying, respectively, musical sound and alphabetic sound — Socrates puts enormous stress on the choices of terminology made by the ancestors who bequeathed us these disciplines. More specifically — although my discussion of this unnoticed feature will be reserved for elsewhere[12] — the terminology they chose can be etymologically decoded as designed to convey to us the all-important role of *number* in science.

The passage thus brings out a vital etymological strand in Plato's thought, even outside the confines of the *Cratylus*. For present purposes, however, what is most significant is that it is in creating terminology for the *technai* — both the names of the *technai* themselves and the vocabulary for classifying their subject matter — that our ancestors are seen to have

---

[12] 'Etymology as a *technê* in the *Cratylus*', in C. Nifadopoulos (ed.), *ETYMOLOGIA: Studies in Ancient Etymology* (Münster, forthcoming); and in my *Plato's Cratylus* (Cambridge 2003), where much of the material in the present article recurs.

manifested their superior understanding. While the legislative metaphor is this time absent, we do have here strong evidence of Plato's recognition that the codification of a *technê* provides an archetypal case of a vocabulary artfully constructed to embody and transmit vital truths. There is a parallel for this in the *Phaedrus* (244b-d), where Socrates etymologizes the names of two further *technai* — prophecy (*mantikê*) and augury (*oionistikê*) — as once again demonstrating the superior methodological understanding displayed by those of our ancient ancestors who gave these arts their names.

We can now, finally, return to the *Cratylus*. I have been suggesting that its legislative model of name-giving conveys, among many other things, the restrictive codification that is typical of the *technai*: the arts characteristically make it their business to distinguish right from wrong ways of designating the items in their chosen domain. This is very close to Socrates' own agenda in the passage of the *Cratylus* where he first introduces the *nomothetês* concept. His major contention there is — in opposition to the earlier view of Hermogenes that no name is inherently better than another — that there are a right *and a wrong* way of naming each thing. If his view is accepted, then the successful practice of ordinary linguistic naming is much closer to technical designations in the arts than Hermogenes supposed, in that both practices will consider it as important to exclude inappropriate names as to prescribe appropriate ones.

Not unlike the author of the *De arte*, the Socrates of the *Cratylus* sees linguistic lawmaking, properly practised, as achieving its success by mapping the words it generates onto the true nature of things. And it is because a proper linguistic code involves this human-made mapping of language onto nature that both authors, in speaking of linguistic legislation, pointedly bring into partnership the traditionally opposed concepts of *nomos* and *physis*.

I turn finally to a rarely noticed but deeply puzzling sequence of argument in the *Cratylus*. At 428e–429b Socrates, now in conversation with the linguistic naturalist Cratylus, extracts from him his opinion that names are not better or worse made, but that, if they are names at all, they are entirely correct. The conversation runs as follows:

> SOCR. Should we say that this too [i.e. name-making] is an expertise, with its own craftsmen?
>
> CRAT. Certainly.
>
> SOCR. Who are they?
>
> CRAT. The ones you said at the outset — the *nomothetai*.
>
> SOCR. Then should we say that this expertise too arises among people in the same way as other ones, or not? What I mean is something like this. Of painters, I take it, some are worse, others better?

CRAT. Certainly.

SOCR. Do the better ones make their own products — that is, pictures — superior, the worse ones inferior? And of builders likewise, do some make the houses they build superior, others inferior?

CRAT. Yes.

SOCR. What about *nomothetai*? Do some of them make *their* products superior, others inferior?

CRAT. This time, I don't think so.

SOCR. So you don't think that some laws (*nomoi*) are better, others worse?

CRAT. Certainly not.

SOCR. In that case apparently you don't think either that one *name* is worse made, another better?

CRAT. Certainly not.

SOCR. Then all names are correctly made?

CRAT. Yes — those that *are* names.

As we have seen, Socrates first secures Cratylus' willing endorsement of the earlier agreement between himself and Hermogenes that names are imposed by *nomothetai*. He then asks him whether some *nomothetai* do a better job than others. Cratylus' opinion is that they do not. His real ground for this opinion emerges in his next answer, which is much more emphatically and confidently stated: it is not the case, he insists, that some *nomoi* are better than others. By this he can only mean, as the later parallel treatment of names confirms, that only a well-made law is a law at all. I translate *nomoi* as 'laws' here because it is hard not to see in this unexpected plural at least some reference to laws in the familiar political sense. Yet it is only from Cratylus' confident assertion about *nomoi* that Socrates secures his equally confident further reply that *names too* are not better and worse.

What is puzzling here is that Cratylus should be expected to infer the infallibility of names from that of *nomoi*, as if the infallibility of *nomoi* were for him somehow a prior truth. His doctrine about names is that they belong by nature: hence, unless a name exhibits a perfect *natural fit* to its object, it is not that thing's name at all. Must we then take it that Cratylus was known by Plato to hold a corresponding view about laws in general?[13]

---

[13] S. Mouraviev, 'La première théorie des noms de Cratyle', in M. Capasso et al. (edd.), *Studi di filosofia preplatonica* (Naples 1985) 159–72, and 'Cratylos', in R. Goulet, *Dictionnaire des philosophes antiques* II (Paris 1994) 503–510, at 506–508, plausibly lists this as one of the doctrines implicitly assigned to Cratylus by Plato. In the former paper (p. 162) he defers his actual discussion of it a separate study, which, if it ever appeared, I have not managed to trace.

The view in question will presumably have been that, unless laws have a perfect *natural fit* to the world, they fail to be laws at all.

If Plato is in these lines echoing and building on a doctrine to which the historical Cratylus subscribed, we may start to wonder whether we have here stumbled upon an early antecedent of the doctrine of natural law. Cratylus, according to Aristotle (*Metaphysics* A 6, 987a32–b7), was the earliest philosophical influence on Plato. It might well pay dividends to ask whether a Cratylean doctrine on the naturalness of laws shows through in Plato's own discussions of law.[14] But that would be a topic for another article.[15]

University of Cambridge

---

[14] I suspect that a plausible case might be made for attributing it to Plato, e.g. on the basis of the *Crito*, although the closest his corpus comes to it may well be in the presumably spurious *Minos*.

[15] For comments, I am grateful to audiences at the Notre Dame conference on natural law, and at Cornell University (where some of this same material featured in my Townsend Lectures on the *Cratylus* in the fall semester 2001), as well as to Tony Long, my commentator at Notre Dame.

THE ORIGINAL THEORY OF NATURAL LAW

Paul A. Vander Waerdt

Our subject poses a curious, but neglected, problem whose clarification promises to illuminate the historical development of the natural law tradition, as well as the philosophical alternative it offers contemporary debate concerning the role of rules in structuring moral reasoning — one of the most controversial issues in contemporary moral philosophy. My purpose is to show that the early Stoic scholarchs who originated the theory of natural law develop a philosophically significant alternative, one dispensing entirely with rule-based moral reasoning, that has disappeared from the natural law tradition, despite its significance as a philosophical alternative within the ancient debate over whether, and if so how, law has a natural foundation and specification in human rationality.

As traditionally understood, the term 'natural law' (typically translating *nomos physeôs* or *lex naturalis*) designates a law, discernible by reason, which determines what is right and wrong by nature, and which is therefore valid everywhere, always and for everyone, independently of circumstance or local custom. Natural law theorists from Aquinas through Suarez, Grotius and Pufendorf down to the present, in which John Finnis and his colleagues in analytical jurisprudence are its most prominent proponents, have so consistently specified the moral content of natural law's prescriptions in terms of a code of norms, rules or precepts of conduct that one might easily assume that natural law theory presupposes a rule-based model of moral reasoning. This assumption, although so prevalent within the tradition that it tends not to be seen as requiring defense, might well be defended by interpretation of natural law theory's claim to provide universally applicable moral prescription: thus one could argue, on the

---

* My thanks to the organizers of the Notre Dame conference for the opportunity to present this final statement on the original form and motivation of Stoic natural law theory, the subject that formed the cornerstone of my research between 1987–1992, and to meet again treasured friends: Julia Annas, Donald Morrison, David K. O'Connor, David Sedley, Michael J. White, and above all my disputant Phillip Mitsis. This chapter and the reply by Phillip Mitsis, *infra*, build upon years of memorable discussion concerning the theory of natural law in antiquity, dating to my dissertation on 'The Stoic Theory of Natural Law' (Princeton 1989), supervised by Michael Frede with Brad Inwood as an external examiner. Other friends who contributed significantly to the development of my views on this subject include my Duke colleagues Diskin Clay and Michael Gillespie, and Harold Tarrant, who was my gracious host for a memorable visit at the University of Sydney during the antipodean winter of 1990.

basis of views dominant within this tradition, that (i) law can provide such prescription only if it is circumstance-independent, i.e., its validity does not depend upon the particular circumstances of its application; and (ii) such prescription must be formulated as rules if it is to be accessible, at least in principle, to all human beings by virtue of their rational nature.

My purpose is to show that a better understanding of the original form and motivation of natural law theory entails reconsideration of the traditional assumption that the only theoretical model available to the natural law theorist is a rule-based model of moral reasoning. Contrary to the assumptions encapsulated in (i) and (ii), law need not be circumstance-independent in order to provide universally valid moral prescription, nor need that prescription take the form of rules if it is to be accessible in principle to all human beings. The early Stoic scholarchs who originated the theory of natural law specifically rejected assumptions (i) and (ii) in the form these assumptions took in the Platonic theory of natural justice that they regarded as their principal rival within the Socratic tradition.[1] In developing a conception of natural law which presupposes rejection of the rule-based model now traditional, they argue that there is no class of exceptionless moral rules or hierarchy among rules which could by itself guarantee moral infallibility, the standard which they consider natural law must prescribe in order to meet the philosophical challenge in response to which they developed this theory. In place of a rule-based model, I shall argue, the Stoics propose a dispositional model of natural law which prescribes not the external characteristics of morally correct actions but rather the intentionalist features of the agent's motivation which guarantee that all his actions are morally infallible. These intentionalist features exemplify a conception of human rationality whose perfected form excludes moral rules, because only circumstance-dependent moral reasoning can account for the exceptions to which all moral rules are in some circumstances subject and so provide the required morally infallible guidance. The rule-based model of natural law which has become so prevalent in the tradition as to suppress recognition of the alternative model out of which it originated thus presupposes a central assumption concerning the nature of moral reasoning, the rejection of which importantly informed the original formulation of the theory. That so paradoxical a feature of the natural law tradition seems to have passed without notice in our age of historical

---

[1] As I have argued at length in 'Politics and Philosophy in Stoicism', *Oxford Studies in Ancient Philosophy* 9 (1991) 185–209 and in 'Zeno's *Republic* and the Origin of Natural Law', in P. A. Vander Waerdt (ed.), *The Socratic Movement* (Ithaca, New York 1994) 272–308, a companion to the present essay that includes full citation of the ancient evidence on some central issues discussed below, as well as further discussion of alternative views.

scholarship requires some explanation, if only to appreciate the obstacles which have impeded previous discussion of this subject.

The assumption that natural law theory must follow a rule-based model might appear to be confirmed, at least to one who regards the history of a philosophical theory as a suitable test of its resources, by the only two notable scholarly reconstructions of the early Stoic theory: both Gisela Striker and Phillip Mitsis celebrate the Stoics as the first philosophers to develop an entirely rule-based model of morality, and as responsible in this respect for the conceptual shift which divides typically classical from modern conceptions of morality.[2] This latter claim, quoted by Mitsis from Henry Sidgwick's *History of Ethics*, provokes the question of whether certain assumptions concerning human rationality which have made rule-based models so prominent in post-Kantian moral philosophy may not have obscured even among classical scholars the distinctive alternative afforded by the early scholarchs' conception of human rationality in relation to moral rules and natural law. Whether or not one regards the development of entirely rule-based models of moral reasoning as the appropriate basis on which to contrast typically classical from modern conceptions of morality, such considerations presumably explain why thinkers critical of the rule-based conception of morality and of law so characteristic of modern philosophy, and who are prepared to entertain the possible relevance and philosophical merits of pre-modern approaches, tend not to regard the Stoic theory in particular and the natural law tradition in general as obvious sources for reflection in formulating a significant alternative to the contemporary rule-based approach. The widespread assumption that the Stoics in certain significant respects anticipate the Kantian approach to moral reasoning thus helps to explain why they attract far less attention and respect than Aristotle does among contemporary philosophers who have found in him guidance in developing what they call 'virtue ethics'.

The contrast I shall develop between the early Stoics' model of natural law and the rule-based model now traditional will highlight one feature of their position among several that are immediately relevant to current debate. We aim to understand why the standard of moral infallibility to which they held natural law's prescriptions led them to reject the assumption of the later tradition that these prescriptions could be formulated in a

---

[2] G. Striker, 'Origins of the Concept of Natural Law', *Proceedings of the Boston Colloquium in Ancient Philosophy* 2 (1986) 79–94 (with a reply by B. Inwood, *ibid.*, 95–101), supplemented by 'Following Nature: A Study in Stoic Ethics', *Oxford Studies in Ancient Philosophy* 9 (1991) 1–73, at pp. 35–50; P. Mitsis, 'Natural Law and Natural Right in Post-Aristotelian Philosophy: The Stoics and their Critics', *ANRW* II.36.7 (Berlin 1994) 4812–4850, which is the most sophisticated alternative reconstruction of the early Stoic theory and its philosophical implications.

code of moral rules, and to develop a dispositional model of natural law which prescribes the intentionalist rather than merely extensionalist features of morally correct actions. To contrast this position with a rule-based model of natural law is not to deny that intentionalist considerations may feature prominently in the latter model, e.g., in determining how to apply moral rules in particular situations or which rule takes precedence in cases of apparent conflict. The contrast is rather between theories in which apparent exceptions to moral rules generally are explained in terms of appeal to higher-level rules and the Stoic position that all moral rules admit of exception, such that it is impossible to formulate an exceptionless or morally infallible canon of natural law except in intentionalist terms — which terms the Stoics regard as the sole criterion of moral evaluation in the case of any action extensionally characterized. In this respect the early Stoic theory provides an alternative model of how to specify the moral conduct prescribed by natural law which avoids the objections to which rule-based theories of moral reasoning are generally exposed and which represents the conception of natural law its original exponents considered the best response to the philosophical challenge they faced in developing it.

In exploring some central differences between these two models of natural law I have chosen to proceed by contrasting Aquinas' account of the primary and secondary precepts of natural law with Chrysippus' account of the prescription of natural law in his *On Law*.[3] Brief consideration of the Thomistic theory, perhaps the best-known rule-based model of natural law, will enable us to develop several representative, philosophically significant contrasts with the original theory of natural law that will apply, with minor modifications, to almost all subsequent Thomistic, early modern and contemporary versions of natural law theory.

In the Thomistic tradition, the model of moral reasoning which defines the content of natural law is specified by an elaborate code of primary and secondary precepts which guide human beings in their rational participation in God's eternal law.[4] Aquinas distinguishes (q. 92 a. 2) a single primary precept from three classes of secondary precepts, each of which is ranked according to the order of a human's natural inclinations. The secondary precept in each of these categories, Aquinas argues, can be derived from the universal, unchangeable and ineradicable primary precept to promote good and avoid evil. Now the distinction between primary and secondary precepts originated in an attempt, first attested for Roland of Cremona[5]

---

[3] Marc., *Inst.* 1 = *SVF* 3.314; Plut., *Stoic. Rep.* 1037c–1038a.
[4] *Sum. Theolog.* I.ii, q. 91 a. 2; cf. Suarez, *De Legibus* 1.3.6.
[5] *Summa Magistri Rolandi Cremonensis* III, q. 187, pp. 557–8 Cortesi.

and introduced for the same purpose by Aquinas,[6] to explain biblical practices, such as the patriarchs' polygamy, which were held to conflict with natural law — although much later Locke, characteristically in an unpublished diary entry, entertained the possibility that polygamy is fully compatible with natural law.[7] In any case, Aquinas clearly uses this distinction to structure moral reasoning through the application of moral rules to particular cases. He offers (q. 95 a. 2) two examples of the derivation of specific moral decisions from natural law, adducing (i) the injunction 'do not kill' as a conclusion derived from the primary precept that one should avoid doing evil; and (ii) the particular penalty for an evildoer as a specific application of the precept of natural law that the evildoer be punished. Aquinas' discussion of exceptional cases (where, e.g., the duty of repaying a loan admits of exception when the money would be used for a harmful purpose) makes it clear that exceptions to moral rules, as well as their application to unproblematic cases, are explained in terms of the hierarchy of primary and secondary precepts.

In contrast the early Stoics' model of natural law, I shall try to show, is one in which the moral content of law's prescriptions is specified through an account of the dispositional characteristics required to guarantee moral infallibility. It is this requirement of moral infallibility, I shall argue, that largely motivates their adoption of a dispositional rather than rule-following model of natural law. The founder of the Stoa, Zeno of Citium, appears to have regarded this requirement as a necessary condition of answering the conventionalist challenge — set forth most famously in Glaucon's speech in Plato's *Republic* 2 — to show that justice invariably benefits the agent, even when suffering the most extreme apparent harms. In offering his theory of natural law in his own *Republic* as an alternative to and improvement over the Platonic teaching on natural justice, Zeno argues that all moral rules are subject to exception in ways that render any rule-based model of moral reasoning continually exposed to moral error.[8] Defining *nomos* in a radically revisionary fashion as identical with the perfected rationality of the Stoic sage, whose disposition enables him infallibly to ascertain the natural course of action in every particular circumstance, rather than with a system of legislation or code of moral rules,[9] the Stoics

---

[6] *In 4 Sent.* d. 33, q. 1 a. 1; *Supplementum tertiae partis*, q. 65 a 1.
[7] *Atlantis*: see *Two Treatises on Government* with Laslett's note on II 81.
[8] See Vander Waerdt, 'Zeno's *Republic* and the Origin of Natural Law', esp. 299–301.
[9] See esp. Cicero, *Leg.* 1.18; Philodemus, *De Stoic.* 20.4 Dorandi; Diogenianus *ap.* Euseb., *Praep. ev.* 6.264b = *SVF* 3.324; Clem. Alex. *Strom.* 4.26 = *SVF* 3.333; Diogenes of Babylon *ap.* *P.Herc.* 1506 col. 8; D. Obbink and P.A. Vander Waerdt, 'Diogenes of Babylon: The Stoic Sage in the City of Fools', *Greek, Roman & Byzantine Studies* 32 (1991) 355–396; some new readings are proposed by Obbink in 'The Stoic Sage in the Cosmic City', in K.

develop a 'canon of justice and injustice'[10] whose moral content is specified not by a code of moral rules but by application of the sage's infallibly correct right reason to particular circumstances. The Stoic theory which came in the course of antiquity to be known as the theory of natural law thus recognizes no 'natural laws,' in the sense of exceptionless moral rules, at all; it prescribes that one act in accordance with a certain carefully delineated rational disposition, rather than with a specified code of moral rules; and it seeks to promote moral infallibility not by characterizing classes of actions as morally correct or incorrect according to their external characteristics, but rather by defining the disposition out of which an agent must act to perform morally correct actions. The early Stoics' dispositional model of natural law, with its exclusive focus on the agent's motivation rather than the specification of rules to guide him in performing morally correct actions, thus differs quite radically from the rule-based models of natural law which tradition has taught us to take for granted.

Aquinas' rule-based model of natural law, albeit modified in diverse and significant ways, has prevailed down to the contemporary efforts of Finnis and others to provide an account of the principles of practical reason which specify the content of natural law without appealing to divine revelation or providential theology. This model has prevailed despite fundamental modifications in the scope and purpose of natural law theory in the early modern period. Even before Hobbes openly rejected the teleological assumptions on which classical and Christian natural law rests, Grotius responded to the challenge posed by contemporary skeptics who appropriated Carneades' brilliant but utterly irrelevant arguments against the Stoic theory of natural law, as preserved in *De Republica* 3, by attempting to found natural law solely upon the doctrine of man's sociality, a criterion for which he claims universal agreement and therefore invulnerability to skeptical counter-attack. In narrowing so considerably the conception of human nature on which to base his precepts of natural law, Grotius revised its scope and purpose in such a fundamental way that its original objective of guiding human beings in achieving their natural perfection and fulfillment disappears from view. His heir Pufendorf, exploiting the implications of Grotius' notorious *etiamsi daremus non esse Deum* argument,[11] goes so far as to hold that all the precepts of natural law, even including man's duties towards God,[12] are no more than subsumptions under the fundamental natural law, that 'every man ought to do as much as he can to cultivate and

---

Ierodiakonou (ed.), *Topics in Stoic Philosophy* (Oxford 1999) 178–195.
[10] Chrysippus *ap*. Marcian *Inst*. I = *SVF* 3.314.
[11] *De jure*, Proleg. 11; cf. Suarez, *De leg*. 2.6.
[12] *De officio hominis* 1.3.13.

preserve sociality' (1.3.9) — hence everything that promotes sociality, he concludes, belongs to natural law. This conception of natural law, as Leibniz pointed out in his 1706 essay 'On the Opinions of Pufendorf', differs fundamentally from its classical and Christian antecedents in eliminating as a central concern of natural law theory the development of other kinds of virtue and duty, regulation of the agent's intentions or motives, and the perfection of trans-political or -social human impulses and aspirations. Whether or not this early modern revision of the scope and intention of natural law theory rests upon an adequate understanding of, or argument against, classical natural law theory, it is clear that Grotius' heirs accepted without dissent the rule-based model of natural law which had become canonical.

During this period, the succession of natural law theorists who undertook to develop a version of the theory that would be invulnerable to Carneadean challenges and independent of natural theology regularly turned to our ancient sources for the Stoics for guidance in enumerating and classifying the precepts consistent with their conception of natural law. The absence of any Stoic account of the precepts of natural law appears merely to have occasioned regret or surprise rather than a reconsideration of the assumption that the morally infallible conduct prescribed by Stoic natural law could be achieved through adherence to a specifiable code of moral rules. Thus Pufendorf, when celebrating Grotius as the founder of natural law theory in his influential essay 'On the Origin and Development of Natural Law' (1678), maintained that 'the Stoics made some claims which, somewhat emended, would apparently have been easily developed into a body of natural jurisprudence, but they were neglected, and only the dogmas of Aristotle admitted to the schools.' Similarly a self-professed Stoic such as Adam Smith, who specifies as the criteria for perfectly virtuous conduct adherence to 'the rules of perfect prudence, of strict justice, and of proper benevolence' (*Theory of Moral Sentiments* 6.3.1), could complain that the 'ancient moralists' had made no 'attempt towards a particular enumeration of the rules of justice.' This assumption that the Stoics too must have adopted a rule-based model of natural law has been accepted without question by all modern scholars known to me save one, Brad Inwood.[13]

Yet our evidence for the early Stoa, I want now to argue, unequivocally establishes that this assumption is false. To explain fully why the early Stoics regard any rule-based model of natural law as inadequate would require a complete exposition of how their theory — in contrast to the

---

[13] See Inwood, *Proceedings of the Boston Colloquium in Ancient Philosophy*, 95–101 and, most extensively, 'Rules and Reasoning in Stoic Ethics', in Ierodiakonou (ed.), *Topics in Stoic Philosophy* (Oxford 1999) 95–127.

early modern versions we have been considering — guides human beings in attaining their highest moral and rational perfection in a world whose every detail has been ordained by divine providence. The theory is complex, and our evidence for it extremely fragmentary and beset with difficulties of interpretation. Our best introduction to the Stoic theory, I suggest, is provided by two *testimonia* concerning Chrysippus' *On Law*, interpretation of which in light of well-attested and uncontroversial features of Stoic ethics will enable us to see why the early Stoics hold that *nomos* must be identical with perfected human rationality, rather than with a code of laws or moral rules, if it is to provide a canon of moral conduct which attains the standard of infallibility they believe is necessary to answer the philosophical challenge to which their theory represents a response.

* * *

Chrysippus began his *On Law* as follows:

> Law is the king of all things, both human and divine. It ought to preside over the noble and the base, as ruler and as guide, and thus be the canon of justice and injustice, prescribing to animals which are by nature political what they should do, and prohibiting them from what they should not do.[14]

Among the several features of this text which help to clarify the contours of the Stoic theory, let us focus strictly on one, how *nomos* serves as the source of moral prescription for 'political animals'. The function of law as here specified is fully consistent with the formal definition of natural law quoted in Cicero's *Leg.* 1.18–19, but *nomos* in this passage appears to refer not only to the sage's right reason, but also, inasmuch as it is said to govern divine as well as human things, to its second, related sense as the causal nexus of fate, i.e., the sequence of causes whereby Zeus has willed all that happens in the Stoics' providentially ordered world down to the smallest detail. The sage's right reason consists precisely in his apprehension of the causal nexus of fate as it applies to his particular circumstances, such that he understands why it accords with nature for him to act in a certain manner in a particular time and place. It is right reason understood in this very particular sense as the sage's apprehension of what accords with nature in any given circumstance which constitutes the morally infallible 'law' or canon of justice and injustice which Chrysippus here undertakes to expound.

There is no clear indication in the exordium of *On Law*, however, how we are to understand the content of the moral conduct prescribed by this

---

[14] Marcian, *Inst.* 1 = *SVF* 3.314.

canon of justice and injustice or what form of moral reasoning political animals must employ in order to comply with this canon. These are the questions we must clarify if we are to understand the model of natural law here presupposed. The convergence between Chrysippus' formulation here and the formal definition of natural law as perfected right reason applied to conduct makes it clear that the sage's right reason provides the prescription which links political animals to Zeus' will and enables them to attain their natural end of rational consistency with nature. But we must not presuppose that the Stoics understand human rationality, let alone the perfected rationality of the sage, in such a way as to assume that such prescription necessarily takes the form of rules. To the contrary, if we turn now to consider the content of the moral conduct natural law prescribes, we will find decisive reasons to reject this presupposition. We will then be in a position to see why the Stoics reject a rule-based in favor of a disposition model of natural law.

The formal definition of natural law as right reason as applied to conduct, prescribing what political animals should do, and proscribing what nature forbids, obviously admits of various interpretations, depending upon how one specifies the content of the moral conduct that natural law or right reason enjoins. That is the issue raised but not explained by Chrysippus at the beginning of his *On Law*, when he identifies *nomos* as the canon of justice and injustice.

To set the stage for consideration of how Chrysippus developed this issue, we have to introduce a technical distinction in Stoic ethics between appropriate acts (*kathêkonta*) and virtuous acts (*katorthômata*).[15] *Kathêkonta* are actions which reason prevails upon us to do in accordance with nature's arrangements and which, once done, admit of a rational defense. They promote what is 'appropriate' to a being's natural constitution or 'consistent' with its life, beginning with its initial impulse towards self-preservation and expanding, in the case of rational beings, to encompass the wide range of activities suitable to his social and rational nature. *Kathêkonta* thus are 'measured' (Arius 86.12–16) by the 'preferred indifferents' which have 'value' (*axia*) with respect to human nature and which constitute the 'material' (*hylê*) of virtue. What transforms these indifferents into *kathêkonta* and *katorthômata* is the agent's 'selection', which in turn depends upon the stage in his rational maturation: moral progressors who select from the indifferents in accordance with reason perform the former, while those few if any sages who have arrived at their natural perfection select the latter. Accordingly, it follows that only the agent who has reached the natural

---

[15] For citation of the evidence for this distinction, see Vander Waerdt 'Zeno's *Republic* and the Origin of Natural Law' 274–276.

apex of his rational maturation, such that all his non-rational impulses have been eradicated or transformed into rational ones,[16] is capable of performing the morally correct actions, the *katorthômata*, prescribed by natural law. One consequence of this rational maturation is that the sage's actions, in contrast to those of everyone else, have come to possess a fixity and firmness which guarantees their infallible consistency with nature (see esp. Chrysippus' account of the moral progressor who has reached the farthest point in his rational maturation but not yet attained wisdom[17]).

This dispositional difference corresponds to the moral difference between *kathêkonta* and *katorthômata*. From the perspective of morality, *kathêkonta* may be either virtuous or vicious, depending upon the agent's disposition: if he possesses the sage's rational disposition, which guarantees the infallible consistency between his actions and nature, then his *kathêkonta* are virtuous — they are *katorthômata*; on the other hand, if he lacks this rational disposition, then his actions are vicious from the standpoint of morality even if they do, in any given instance, accord with nature. *Katorthômata* thus represent a restricted class of *kathêkonta*; they are 'perfect *kathêkonta*' and include all the virtues and indeed 'everything done according to right reason';[18] they are actions done out of a rational disposition which ensures that the agent will act consistently with nature and so infallibly attain his goal of happiness. The distinction between *kathêkonta* and *katorthômata* thus corresponds to a stage in man's natural maturation (attained only by the sage) in which his non-rational impulses are entirely transformed into rational ones, such that the sole motivation of his action is to uphold the rational order and harmony that pervades all nature in accordance with Zeus' provident design.

Now, the question we need to consider is this: does natural law prescribe *kathêkonta* or rather a restricted class of them, the 'perfect *kathêkonta*' known as *katorthômata*? The answer to this question is crucial in understanding Chrysippus' conception of natural law. If natural law were to prescribe the former, then it would be largely identical with the moral rules which guide morally imperfect human beings in performing appropriate actions in accordance with nature's design, even though they lack the rational disposition which would enable them to perform these actions virtuously. Natural law so understood would provide a canon of justice and injustice achievable by all or most mature human beings, not just by the sage. In this case, the content of natural law would be specified by a

---

[16] Cicero, *Fin.* 3.17–25. See M. Frede, 'On the Stoic Conception of the Good', *Topics in Stoic Philosophy* (Oxford 1999) 71–94.
[17] Chrysippus ap. Stobaeus, *Ecl.* 5.906.18–907.5 = *SVF* 3.510; cf. Seneca, *Ep.* 75.8–18.
[18] Arius 96.18–97.14; cf. 85.18–86.12, 93.14–8: 'a *katorthôma* is a *kathêkon* which possesses all the measures or is a perfect *kathêkon*.'

determinate set of moral rules whose correctness is not entirely dependent upon the agent's mental disposition. This interpretation of the Stoic position would assimilate it to the rule-based model of natural law so familiar. Nearly all modern scholars have assumed without argument that the original Stoic theory also took this form, and Phillip Mitsis has published a long article attempting to defend this interpretation against the quite different reconstruction I have offered.[19]

If natural law prescribes *katorthômata*, on the other hand, then it will have a far more restricted scope, since only the Stoic sage, with his perfectly rational and consistent disposition, is capable of performing *katorthômata*.[20] The canon of justice and injustice established by natural law would, accordingly, be achievable only by the sage. (While this consequence might surprise in view of the evidence we have so far considered, Zeno clearly restricts citizenship in his regime governed by natural law to sages, just as Chrysippus admits them alone to participation in the megalopolis or cosmic city.) In this second case, natural law would correspond not to a set of rules, since the sage's right reason cannot be so codified, but to a certain mental disposition which enables the agent to determine infallibly, in any particular circumstance, what course of action accords with nature. The moral content of natural law would be circumstance-dependent, and specified by the mental disposition with which the sage performs the 'perfect *kathêkonta*' prescribed by natural law.

In determining whether natural law prescribes *kathêkonta* or *katorthômata*, then, we decide which of the two models the original exponents of the theory of natural law adopted. While all writers on the subject known to me have, with one exception, attributed to them the traditional rule-based model, I want to argue that the evidence establishes unequivocally and unambiguously that the second interpretation of the Stoics' formula is correct, i.e., that natural law prescribes *katorthômata*, that in so doing it enjoins a standard of conduct achievable only by the Stoic sage, and that the moral reasoning which enables him to ascertain Zeus' will cannot be codified in moral rules.

The most important testimony comes from a passage which certain philological considerations indicate derives from Chrysippus' *On Law*.[21] In the immediate sequel Plutarch attempts to expose alleged inconsistencies in the Stoic position, which has led Mitsis to attempt to discount this testimony altogether, but the sole part of the passage on which we need rely is

---

[19] P. Mitsis 'Natural Law and Natural Right in Post-Aristotelian Philosophy' 4812–4850.
[20] Cicero, *Fin.* 4.15; cf. Arius 96.10–6, 102.4–10.
[21] Plutarch, *Stoic. Rep.* 1037c–d = *SVF* 3.520.

the opening quotation, on whose accuracy the ensuing objections depend and which there is no legitimate ground to question.

> They say: 'Virtuous action is the prescription of law; moral error is its proscription.' Hence law proscribes many things for the base, but prescribes nothing, for they are incapable of virtuous action.[22]

This text, I want to argue, specifies the content of the moral conduct natural law prescribes as the 'canon of justice and injustice' announced in the exordium of *On Law*. Chrysippus states that *nomos* prescribes *katorthômata* and prohibits *hamartêmata*, and it is no exaggeration to say that on the correct interpretation of this sentence rests our understanding of the alternative posed by the original form of natural law theory. Since the latter class in standard Stoic usage encompasses everything done contrary to right reason, Chrysippus' formulation effectively stipulates that *only* actions performed out of the sage's rational disposition, i.e., only *katorthômata*, accord with natural law.[23] The issue then is whether this stipulation entails the claims I put forward in sketching the second interpretation of the Stoic position, most notably that it precludes the traditional view of Stoic natural law as prescribing a specific class of actions or code of moral rules. Clearly, in proscribing *hamartêmata*, Chrysippus rules out the possibility that natural law may enjoin conduct which falls short of the sage's morally infallible conduct, and in taking perfected rationality rather than the rationality ordinary human beings share as the standard required by natural law he

---

[22] My construction of the Greek differs from that of most commentators (e.g., von Arnim in *SVF* 3.520) in taking the *dio* clause as introducing an inference by Plutarch rather than as continuing his quotation from Chrysippus. My reasons are as follows (i) *nomos* as Chrysippus understands it is identical with the sage's right reason rather than a code of positive legislation which is aimed at restraining the base, as Plutarch's cnticism in this passage mistakenly presupposes. Chrysippus may of course have broached the question of whether *nomos* in this sense also proscribes certain kinds of conduct on the part of the base, but (ii) we can be pretty certain that Chrysippus holds that *all* action which falls short of a *katorthôma* should be proscribed, not just 'many things' (the *hamartêmata* which Chrysippus proscribes are all actions not motivated by the sage's right reason: see below). Moreover, (iii) the Stoics do recognize that the law's explicit prohibitions contain implicit proscriptions (1037d-e). Finally, (iv) while Chrysippus would agree that the base are incapable of *katorthômata*, he could still hold that natural law in some sense 'commands' *katorthômata* even among the base, inasmuch as that law is intended to serve as a standard of conduct to which all should naturally aspire.

[23] For the meaning of the distinction between *katorthômata* and *hamartêmata*, see Arius Didymus (93.14–18, 96.18–97.3, 113.18–23), whose frequent references to this distinction show that it was a standard one: offering a list of characterizations on each side (behaving prudently, moderately, ... on the one hand, and foolishly, immoderately, ... on the other), he draws the distinction in terms of whether or not the action is in accordance with *orthos logos*. This makes it clear that law proscribes *all* action not motivated by the sage's unique rational disposition.

differs sharply from his Thomistic and early modern heirs. But we need to consider further the character of *katorthômata* in order to understand why no code of moral rules guarantees the standard of moral infallibility which Chrysippus' dispositional model provides.

To understand Chrysippus' position we need to introduce a further refinement in our account of the relation between *katorthômata* and *kathêkonta*. According to Stoic doctrine, every virtuous action embodies both intentional and extensional features and so may be characterized from two different perspectives. In its intentional aspect it is (i) a *katorthôma*, 'a purely formal principle' which provides an adverbial specification of the motivation with which the action in question is performed, e.g., prudently, moderately, justly. In its *extensional* aspect it is (ii) a *kathêkon*, an objective description of the content of the action performed, e.g., returning a deposit. Put crudely, (i) specifies *how* a virtuous action is performed, i.e., the agent's disposition in performing it, (ii) *what* the action is, i.e., its descriptive specification.

Now this distinction is of crucial importance in understanding how *katorthomata* constitute the content of the moral conduct prescribed by natural law. For it is a well-attested Stoic doctrine that the descriptive content of a *kathêkon* can vary according to the circumstances; so, e.g., to treat friends in accordance with their worth may involve returning a deposit in some circumstances but not in others, e.g., when doing so would harm the depositor,[24] just as health is usually but not always preferred over illness (D.L. 7.108–109 might appear to suggest that some *kathêkonta* are invariably appropriate, but see the discussion below). To borrow an example from Ariston which is fully consistent with orthodox Stoic doctrine, if it were necessary for healthy men to serve a tyrant and in so doing to be executed, and sick men were released from service and therewith destruction, 'on such an occasion the sage would choose sickness over health. In this way health is not unconditionally preferred.'[25] As this example demonstrates, *kathêkonta* are circumstance-dependent. Although it has been claimed on the basis of some late doxographical texts that there is a class of *kathêkonta* which does not admit of exception in the light of circumstances, one glance at the examples adduced shows quite clearly that this position is not consistent with that of Chrysippus.

If no class of actions is always *kathêkon*, then we can rule out the possibility that the same action, considered descriptively according to its extensional specification, can invariably constitute the morally virtuous course of action. The Stoics are clearly committed to the view that the same type of

---

[24] Cicero, *Fin.* 3.58–59; Philo, *Cher.* 14–15 = *SVF* 3.513.
[25] Ariston *ap.* Sextus, *Adv. Math.* 11.61–64 = *SVF* 3.122.

action may be a *kathêkon*, and hence vicious from the standpoint of morality, or a *katorthôma*, hence virtuous, depending upon whether or not the agent acts out of a perfected rational disposition which guarantees the agent's moral infallibility.

An example will help to illustrate why the Stoics hold that only the intentional characteristics of correct actions can hold without exception. The promotion of one's health over illness might be thought an especially promising candidate for a preferred indifferent which is 'unconditionally preferred', but it too admits of exception in certain circumstances. Thus, while good health is preferred both for its own sake and for what follows from it (D. L. 7.106–7), Chrysippus tells us that under some circumstances he would choose to be ill:

> But if I knew that it is now fated for me to be ill, I would direct my impulse even to that. For the foot, too, if it were intelligent, would direct its impulse even to being muddied.[26]

The circumstances in which Chrysippus' illness accords with nature presumably are those in which a discrepancy arises between what ordinarily promotes Chrysippus' personal well-being and what promotes the well-being of the world in which he lives. This occasional divergence between the individual's nature and cosmic nature, which Chrysippus treats in *On Nature* 1,[27] is one reason that no code of exceptionless 'natural laws' could be formulated which could guide the individual in achieving his natural perfection. However inscrutable the goodness of illness may be to ordinary human beings, one cannot formulate a moral rule to the effect, 'promote health over illness', by adherence to which a non-sage can invariably adopt the morally correct course of action; to the contrary, anyone who follows such a precept without variation always risks falling into moral error because he has no way of determining when justified exceptions to it are necessary to remain consistent with nature. Chrysippus went so far as to argue that Plato's inclusion of health in the classification of goods in *Republic* 2 annulled all the virtues,[28] and there can be no doubt that the Stoic insistence that no rules of conduct are immune to exception in special circumstances represents one of their motivations in identifying *nomos* with the sage's right reason. He alone is able to recognize when exceptions to generally accepted moral rules accord with nature, and consequently he alone is immune to moral error.

As the example of health shows, then, the extensional characteristics of *kathêkonta* by themselves are insufficient to guarantee the moral infallibility

---

[26] Plutarch, *Stoic rep.* 1050a; cf. Epictetus, *Diatr.* 2.6.9 = *SVF* 3.191.
[27] Chrysippus *ap.* Plut., *Stoic. rep.* 1050a = *SVF* 2.937.
[28] Chrysippus *ap.* Plut., *Stoic. rep.* 1040d = *SVF* 3.157.

of an agent's action, and it is precisely moral infallibility that Chrysippus establishes as his standard in stipulating that natural law proscribes *hamartêmata*.

What is needed to establish an infallible canon of justice and injustice is a specification of the intentional features of the agent's disposition which ensures that he invariably performs these *kathêkonta* in rational consistency with Zeus' provident will. It is precisely this rational disposition, as we saw above, which transforms *kathêkonta* into *katorthômata*. The intentional features of a virtuous action, accordingly, guarantee its moral infallibility in a way no description of its extensional specification can. These intentionalist features, in contrast to the extensionalist features of a virtuous action, can be specified in a manner that does not admit of exception: the adverbial specification, e.g., of behaving 'prudently' or 'justly' is always the correct motivation of virtuous actions even though the descriptive characteristics of these actions, i.e., what actions are in fact prudent or just, vary in accordance with circumstances. Arius Didymus offers an extended list of the adverbial specifications in question, concluding the list: 'everything done in accordance with right reason.'[29] These distinctions help to explain why Chrysippus holds that *katorthômata*, and only *katorthômata*, constitute the canon of justice and injustice prescribed by natural law. If this law is to provide an infallible standard of moral conduct, it cannot merely prescribe the extensional characteristics of actions, given that these actions under certain circumstances admit of exception. It must rather prescribe their intentional characteristics, i.e., the rational disposition which makes these actions infallibly correct from a moral point of view. Accordingly, when Chrysippus states that natural law prescribes *katorthômata*, he is not describing a class of actions described extensionally which an agent must perform in order to act in accordance with nature. He is rather describing the rational disposition which the sage must bring to the performance of these actions. So, in terms of the distinctions just drawn, natural law prescribes only the intentional features of virtuous actions.

Since all *katorthômata* are also *kathêkonta*, the agent who acts in accordance with natural law will of course perform actions which admit of extensional description. In fact, this agent will in the vast majority of particular cases perform preferred *kathêkonta*, departing from them only when the special circumstances of a particular case require him to violate them, e.g., by choosing illness over health, as required by the occasional discrepancy between the rational determinism of nature and man's individual nature. This discrepancy entails the potential moral fallibility of all *kathêkonta* and

---

[29] Arius Didymus, 96.20–22 = *SVF* 3.501.

ensures that actions characterized extensionally can never meet the moral standard prescribed by the Stoic theory of natural law.

This conclusion is also supported by the well-attested early Stoic evidence that the sage's right reason gives him special warrant to break common rules and prohibitions. In his *Republic* Zeno held that 'the sage will even taste of human flesh under special circumstances' (or 'under stress of circumstances' as the Loeb translates it, *kata peristasin*: D.L. 7.125; cf. 7.188–89 for Chrysippus), and there is abundant evidence that Chrysippus and Cleanthes entertained the appropriateness not only of cannibalism but also of incest as well as the community of women and children. While the Stoics' critics took them to be recommending these practices in their own name, I have argued elsewhere that they intended rather to demonstrate that even moral rules or prohibitions which might be thought to have universal sanction in fact admit of exception.[30] In certain 'special circumstances', there is reason to suppose, these practices may well prove to accord with nature — as, e.g., when incest between a father and daughter, who are the last representatives of the human race and are stranded together on an isolated island, is necessary to secure the preservation of the race. While none of our evidence explicitly concerned with *kathêkonta kata peristasin* specify what conditions must obtain to give rise to 'special circumstances', my proposal that we link this class of *kathêkonta* with divergences between the common nature and human nature, which Chrysippus cites as grounds for overriding the preferred indifferent of health, has the advantage of providing clear criteria for the appropriateness of this class.

Now if this interpretation is correct, and the class of these *kathêkonta kata peristasin* represent test-cases of potentially immutable moral prohibitions, then we have prima facie evidence that the early Stoics hold that all such moral rules or prohibitions, at least in principle, admit of exception. And the account developed above of the relation between intentionalist and extensionalist aspects in Stoic thinking on virtuous action provides a clear philosophical motivation for their position — unique in the natural law tradition — that natural law prescribes only the intentionalist features of correct actions while eschewing any description of their externalist characteristics.

* * *

The question inevitably arises of why the early Stoics considered moral infallibility the standard which their theory of natural law had to meet. Were they willing to accept any possibility of moral error in its prescription, after all, they need not have restricted this canon to *katorthômata* which

---

[30] See Vander Waerdt 'Zeno's *Republic* and the Origin of Natural Law.'

only sages, who are said to be as rare as the Ethiopians' phoenix, are capable of performing. They could have construed their distinction between *katorthômata* and *kathêkonta* as Aquinas employs his distinction between primary and secondary precepts, accounting for the problem of justified exceptions while retaining the sages' infallible moral reasoning as grounds to maintain the claim that natural law provides universally applicable guidance in achieving human perfection. They could have regarded occasional moral error as a reasonable concession to the utility of moral rules in promoting natural law, and so advanced a theory whose form, scope and intention would resemble that of their philosophical heirs far more closely than in fact it does. The historical fact that the rule-based model of natural law into which the Stoics' theory was transformed as early as the first century B.C. proved so successful that the original form of the theory has vanished entirely from philosophical discussion only increases the puzzle.[31]

To understand why moral infallibility is the standard the early scholarchs adopt in developing their account of the prescription of natural law, we must turn briefly to consider the specific philosophical problem which their theory aimed to solve. So far we have focused mainly on Chrysippus because our meager fragments of his *On Law* best illustrate why the early Stoics rejected a rule-based model of natural law. But much our most extensive evidence for the Stoic theory in fact comes from the famous *Republic* of Zeno of Citium, founder of the Stoa. The 'main point' of this work, as Plutarch helpfully informs us, is 'that we should not dwell in cities or demes, each one marked out by its own principles of justice, but we should regard all human beings as our fellow-demesmen and -citizens, and there should be one way of life and order, like that of a herd grazing together and nourished by a common law.'[32] In sketching the way of life consistent with natural law Zeno depicts, in what Plutarch characterizes as 'a dream or image of a philosopher's well-regulated regime', a polity of sages whose moral perfection makes possible the abolition of all positive laws, social classes and other instruments of social compulsion, as well as temples, gymnasia and currency. Numerous anti-Platonic features of Zeno's doctrines suggest that his central purpose, as I have argued elsewhere, is to provide a more precise and consistent answer than Plato had succeeded in giving in his own *Republic* to the challenge posed by conventionalism, the thesis widely held among fifth century Greek sophists and stated most powerfully by Glaucon at the beginning of *Republic* 2, that

---

[31] I have offered some remarks on this transformation in 'Philosophical Influence on Roman Jurisprudence? The Case of Stoicism and Natural Law', *ANRW* II.36.7 (Berlin 1994).
[32] Plutarch, *Alex.* 329a–b.

law and justice originate solely in human agreement and that they are not in any meaningful sense specified by man's rational nature.

When one recognizes that Zeno first put forward the theory of natural law as a contribution to the debate among Socrates' heirs over how best to answer Glaucon's challenge, it readily becomes clear why moral infallibility assumes such importance in their theory. The early Stoics, I propose, accept the Platonic view of the inadequacy of rules and laws to guarantee morally correct conduct, and their position that natural law is identical with the sage's right reason merely draws out its logical implications. For if the challenge posed by conventionalism is to prove that justice invariably benefits the agent, even when suffering the most extreme apparent harms, then the standard adopted to demonstrate its natural basis in human rationality must be infallible, i.e., it must not admit of exception. By this standard, the Stoics could easily have argued, the code of laws which the Platonic Socrates elaborates for his best regime cannot itself constitute the standard demanded by conventionalism; it is the 'knowledge of good and evil' which his philosopher-guardians alone possess that provides a guarantee of moral infallibility. Translated into Stoic terms, it is only the sage, morally infallible by virtue of his perfectly rational and consistent disposition, whose right reason provides the canon of justice and injustice demanded by Glaucon's challenge. If in developing his theory of natural law Zeno aimed to develop a better answer than Plato's to the same challenge, it is not difficult to see why only morally infallible conduct, i.e., *katorthômata*, could suffice as the prescription of natural law. The extensive controversy concerning Zeno's discussion of cannibalism and incest in the *Republic*, which he apparently considered as test-cases of immutable moral prohibitions, provides strong evidence in support of the hypothesis that the original form of natural law theory was decisively informed by the particular terms in which the challenge of conventionalism and Plato's previous attempt to develop an adequate statement of the Socratic position were cast.

San Francisco

THE STOICS AND AQUINAS ON VIRTUE AND NATURAL LAW

PHILLIP MITSIS

I wish to begin with a few general observations about the natural law tradition and the striking thesis defended by Paul Vander Waerdt and Brad Inwood about its origins in antiquity. In Vander Waerdt's more extreme formulation, the early Stoics, whom he believes originated the theory of natural law, dispensed 'entirely with rule-based reasoning' and proposed a 'dispositional model of natural law which prescribes not the external characteristics of morally correct actions but rather the intensionalist features of the agent's motivation which guarantee that all of his actions are morally infallible.'[1] Natural law, in this view, is strictly isomorphic with the perfected rational disposition of the sage, and it prescribes nothing over and above just what such a perfectly virtuous agent should be internally disposed to do on any given occasion. Thus, at the heart of the thesis is the claim that the theory of natural law originates as a kind of radically particularist moral theory that does not presume to offer moral guidance of a general nature and that has as its exclusive focus the inner virtuous dispositions of moral agents engaged in discrete episodes of moral choice. Presumably, one might think that in principle it would be possible to derive more general, law-like prescriptions for moral actions from the reasoning behind them or from the rational and moral dispositions that engender them. But the claim here is that both moral reasoning and moral dispositions themselves are not susceptible of law-like analysis and that they are

---

* I am indebted to Norman Kretzmann for first introducing me to these issues and for many years of subsequent conversation. Paul Vander Waerdt and Brad Inwood have been defending an opposing view to the one set out here about Stoicism for so long and so ably that the present paper may seem to reflect merely a bad case of intellectual stubbornness. In any case, I wish to thank them for their friendship and intellectual indulgence. I am also extremely grateful to Scott MacDonald for comments on an earlier version of this paper, and to audiences at Columbia, Oxford, London, Geneva, Bern, Kyoto, and Notre Dame for many helpful observations.

[1] This volume, p. 18. Inwood's fullest statement is to be found in B. Inwood, 'Rules and Reasoning in Stoic Ethics', in K. Ierodiakonou (ed.), *Topics in Stoic Philosophy* (Oxford 1999) 95–127. He argues for a 'more procedural understanding of moral 'law'' wherein ''law'' represents the prescriptive force behind the correct moral choice of the ideal moral reasoner, the sage, whatever the content of that choice might be on a given occasion.' (96–97). Thus, his account differs from Vander Waerdt's in important ways. I will be discussing various aspects of both accounts as I go along.

manifested in a series of discrete behaviors that themselves are immune to more contentful general analysis. One is probably more likely to associate the kind of radical particularism claimed here for the Stoics with intuitionist theories of moral epistemology, rather than with their own relentless emphasis on rationality, but the thesis yokes together other strange philosophical bedfellows. Another crucial assumption in this thesis about the origins of natural law is its postulation of a strong link between moral infallibility and particularism. It holds that since any non-vacuous moral rule or general recommendation inevitably falls prey to exceptions, the moral deliberations of infallible moral agents cannot be guided by generalizations at any level. Again, one might be more used to associating claims about the inevitable failure of moral generalizations with theories that display a heightened emphasis on the indeterminacy of moral choice and the inexactness of the moral domain, and hence, presumably, on the consequent fallibility of moral agents. But perhaps the greatest paradox of all is the central claim of the thesis itself. Surely, it is *prima facie* a little paradoxical to claim that the tradition of natural law begins as a theory rooted in the assumption that moral reasoning is not law-like, and that when we are faced with forming our moral attitudes or acting morally, natural law can offer no contentful recommendations beyond the immediate moment. Why, one might plausibly wonder, appeal to a conception of *law*, if the aim is to endorse a radical particularism about moral choice and action?

To be sure, these claims about origins are only part of a larger and more complicated historical story. The purely intentionalist or internalist account of natural law and morality that originates in the early Stoa gives way, in Vander Waerdt's view, to a more rigid, rule-based theory under various philosophical and social pressures.[2] Indeed, by the time of Cicero, perhaps, and of Aquinas, certainly, and then in all accounts of natural law thereafter, the tradition transforms its notion of law from an intentionalist into an externalist one, and its focus shifts from the virtuous inner dispositions of the wise to the delineation of hierarchical sets of rules governing the external behavior of all men. In a deep sense, Vander Waerdt's overall assessment of the natural law tradition is one of depressing decline, both in its substance and in the expectations it has of its audience. It begins as a theory that attempts to ground in nature the kinds of rational motivations and

---

[2] The historical basis for this claim is set out with great power and learning in P. Vander Waerdt, *The Stoic Theory of Natural Law*, Ph.D. Dissertation (Princeton 1989), idem, 'Politics and Philosophy in Stoicism', *Oxford Studies in Ancient Philosophy* 9 (1991) 185–211, idem, 'Zeon's Republic and the Origins of Natural Law', in idem (ed.), *The Socratic Movement* (Ithaca, New York 1994) 272–308 and idem, 'Philosophical Influence on Roman Jurisprudence? The Case of Stoicism and Natural Law', in *ANRW* II. 36.7 (Berlin 1994) 4851–4900.

dispositions we plausibly appeal to in explaining individual moral actions and that arguably are crucial for explaining accounts of the development and perfection of virtue. It declines into a theory that eliminates concern for virtue *per* se and with it, the regulation of agents' motivations and intentions. It thus settles for the mere stipulation of external behaviors and thereby abandons the project of cultivating our virtuous political and social impulses.[3] As a consequence, what it offers is merely an abstract and rigid code of external conduct that cannot but fail to capture the particular nuances of a moral life characterized by wisdom and virtue. Sadly, one might note, this seems an especially ironic outcome for the theory given its origins in the Stoics' fundamental belief that virtue alone is what is valuable; indeed, presumably one of the primary reasons they held virtue to be uniquely valuable is precisely because it requires the autonomous cultivation of one's inner psychological states which, in their view, are in no way dependent on the vagaries of externals.

In all stories of decline and fall, of course, there can be a kind of conceptual clarity and sense of historical inevitability that makes for compelling and exciting reading. But at the risk of playing Bishop Spadeworth to Vander Waerdt's Gibbon, I want to argue that the truth about the natural law tradition is considerably more complicated and that the basic elements that sustain it are there from the beginning and continue to persist, certainly at least through the formulations of Aquinas. One of the questions I therefore will be asking is why the tradition of natural law was able to offer viable philosophical alternatives for so many for so long, and especially for those who took themselves to be concerned with virtue and its cultivation. Moreover, since I see neither strong conceptual shifts nor decline, I do not think that we need to be on the lookout for any good or bad emperors in the story. No Stoic, even those for whom we have more evidence of an interest in delineating law-like rules of behavior, ever gave up a commitment to the inner criteria of virtue. Nor, arguably, did Aquinas. Accordingly, although such a Spadeworthian history of natural law may be more conceptually tangled and certainly less exciting, it perhaps will turn out to be more uplifting in the end, since, after all, it is a history depicting both unceasing virtue and the abiding empire of law.

It might be useful to begin with Aquinas, not only because his account is more familiar, but also because Vander Waerdt's understanding of Thomistic theory, I believe, is to a certain extent shaping his reading of the entire development of the tradition. Of necessity, I must be aggressively schematic, but it seems to me that Vander Waerdt's account relies on taking the so-called Treatise on Law (and so the most famous passages on natural

---

[3] See P. Vander Waerdt, p. 23 with the quotation from Leibniz (1706).

law) in isolation from the rest of Aquinas' discussion of ethics proper. This is important, since it leads him, I think, into a parallel mistake about the relation between natural law and virtue in the early Stoa. In any case, although it might often go unremarked, it is quite obvious that Aquinas' discussion of law follows upon an extended account of ethical theory or more precisely, if you will, virtue ethics. He discusses moral goodness (questions 1–17), morally right actions (questions 18–21), and the states of human beings that are essential to moral goodness and the performance of morally right actions — these include the passions (questions 22–48), habits in general (questions 49–54), virtue (questions 55–70) and vice (questions 79–81). Aquinas' discussion of ethics thus begins with an account of happiness and concludes with problems of virtue.

In introducing the Treatise on Law, Aquinas says that having treated of the *intrinsic* principles of human action, i.e. those of ethics proper, he is now going to talk about *external* principles. But this does not mean, of course, that his views about intrinsic and external principles are unrelated. What he has in mind in the Treatise on Law is primarily real law of that sort that imposes external constraints on moral agents. He is at most tangentially interested in Kantian-style moral laws or what we might characterize as *moral* precepts that agents use to govern their moral conduct. Indeed, Aquinas says 'Properly speaking, no one imposes a law on his own actions, since personal moral judgments about what one ought to do are not laws, strictly speaking.' (q. 93.5)[4] Yet, within the Treatise on Law, one can also find abundant evidence of the intentional requirements of Aquinas' wider moral theory. He says, 'A man can bring law to bear on those things which he can judge. But a man's judgment cannot be about interior motivations.[5] Nevertheless it is required for the perfection of virtue that a man be right (*existat rectus*) in both sorts of acts.' (91.4).

This requirement, not surprisingly, serves as an important element in Aquinas' claim that there is a need for divine law. Such divine dictates about our inner states can be found, for instance, in the Sermon on the Mount in which we learn that it is not only wrong to kill, but also to hate, not only to steal, but to covet, etc.

Clearly, the fact that Aquinas' central moral theory gives such a prominent place to virtue is itself evidence that he takes the internal states of

---

[4] For fuller discussion, see N. Kretzmann, 'Lex Iniusta Non Est Lex', *The American Journal of Jurisprudence* 33 (1988) 99–122 and idem, 'Warring Against the Law of My Mind', in T. Morris (ed.), *Philosophy and the Christian Faith* (Notre Dame, Indiana 1988) 172–95.

[5] I am indebted to Scott MacDonald for discussion of these passages. With him, I take Aquinas' reference here to *motibus* 'that are hidden' to be making a distinction between internal motivations and external behavior.

agents to be crucial for moral evaluation. A virtue, for Aquinas, just is a disposition of the agent toward the right ends. Choice (*electio*) is therefore essential to morally right actions. At the same time, however, one might ask how these features of Aquinas' moral thinking, which can be characterized as being straightforwardly intentionalist, are supposed to fit with the picture of externally imposed natural laws that we find in the Treatise on Law. The question is central for Aquinas' account of natural law and also absolutely parallel, I would argue, to a key question facing the Stoics — how to connect their intentionalist moral psychology, theory of virtue, and account of moral evaluation with a set of divine and externally imposed natural requirements.

In the case of Aquinas, the connection between these two elements seems to be roughly the following. He often says that morally right action is 'action in accordance with right reason.' This formula for Aquinas arguably includes both externalist and intentionalist considerations. It is externalist because action in accordance with right reason is just that action that divine reason and natural law dictate. But the reasoning, as Aquinas says, is in the agent performing the action, and the agent's following right reason in this case is a manifestation of the agent's soul — that is his virtue — disposing him to follow reason in general.

However successful Aquinas' attempt to bring internalist and externalist elements together in one account, it seems to me that the early Stoics face a parallel problem in trying to reconcile the demands of their intentionalist accounts of virtue and happiness with what are taken to be external commands of a divine and providential reason. The same holds for the later Stoic tradition and, indeed, for natural law theorists well into the early modern period. Indeed, at no time, until very late in the tradition, does natural law become a theory focused exclusively on following a set of externally imposed commands. By the same token, it would be a mistake, however, to treat the early Stoic view as a purely intentionalist one since it is quite clear that, for them, the laws of nature emanate from divine reason — and hence are externally imposed requirements. It seems to me that something goes wrong with Vander Waerdt's claim that natural law for the early Stoa is solely about dispositions. Clearly, as for Aquinas, dispositions and the reasoning that is in moral agents are an important part of the story for the early Stoics. But we have equally compelling evidence that natural laws for the Stoics are just that — laws of nature that are not entirely reducible to a series of particularist manifestations of the inner dispositions of moral agents, however infallible.

One long-standing problem in the interpretation of Stoic moral theory has been how one connects evidence from their theories of virtue and happiness to their claims about nature and the divine. If one focuses on the Stoics' accounts of virtue and happiness, one can surely find abundant evidence for their emphasis on an agent's inner dispositions.[6] It is sometimes tempting to suppose that this is the whole story about their moral theory, and to then infer, as I believe Vander Waerdt does, that everything of moral importance that can be said about the sage's perfected rational disposition appears in texts that describe the workings of virtue. Once one makes this step, however, it is easier to slide into a view that takes natural law to be 'dispositional'. But it seems to me that the Stoic view of moral action is in many ways no more 'dispositional' than that of Aquinas, since it is clear that the sage's reasoning is also in accordance with what are viewed as externally imposed divine requirements.

Given Aquinas' extensive discussion of both law and virtue, we would be compelled, even without the kinds of explicit indications that he offers, to attempt to piece together theses two aspects of his theory. The fragmentary nature of Stoic texts perhaps makes it easier to lose sight of these twin demands on action in accordance with reason. A famous passage from Diogenes Laertius, however, reports the following claim of Chrysippus — a claim that in many ways, I think, prefigures the Thomistic linkage between internalist and externalist requirements and between virtue, happiness, and natural law:

> Therefore, living in agreement with nature comes to be the end, which is in accordance with the nature of oneself and that of the whole, engaging in no activity forbidden by universal law, which is right reason pervading everything and identical to Zeus, who is the director of the administration of existing things. And the virtue of the happy man and his good flow of life are just this: always doing everything on the basis of concordance of each man's guardian spirit with the will of the administrator of the whole. (D.L. 7.88, trans. Long and Sedley, 63C)

The Stoics, of course, are innocent of the kinds of voluntarist and rationalist debates that this picture of God lets itself in for by the time of Aquinas and they have a monistic moral psychology free from tensions between reason and the will. But when the Stoic sage is said to act in accordance with 'right reason' or to be following the will of Zeus, this is meant by the Stoics to capture, in much the same way as it is in Aquinas' theory, both internalist and externalist criteria. Vander Waerdt is surely right to argue that the

---

[6] Here I simplify, since even in Stoic texts that some have taken to give strictly internalist accounts of the perfection of one's internal states and virtues, there still remain difficult questions about the kinds of roles that externalist considerations play in structuring agents' reasoning and impulses toward their own good. See, e.g. M. Frede, 'On the Stoic Conception of the Good', in K. Ierodiakonou (ed.), *Topics in Stoic Philosophy* (Oxford 1999) 71–94.

correct moral action of a sage mandated by nature's divine reason expresses the sage's internal rational disposition arising from his virtuous state of soul. There is little doubt as well that, to borrow a turn of phrase from Aquinas, the reasoning is in the agent performing the action. But the sage's action is also in accordance with right reason and is of the sort that right reason and divine law dictate. Thus, to claim as Vander Waerdt does, that the early Stoic theory of natural law is dispositional is only part of the story. The full story includes externalist demands as well as an account of the relation of those demands to individual virtuous dispositions.

It might be objected at this point, of course, that whatever the origin and nature of the commands of right reason, at least the actual content of its demands remains strictly dispositional, in the sense that nature's commands for the early Stoics are about internal states of agents rather than about particular actions or external behaviors. I take it that this is an important linchpin in Vander Waerdt's claims about Stoic particularism and, as far as I can make out, one reason for this is because he takes there to be a fairly straightforward connection between dispositional accounts and moral particularism. But, of course, there may be other routes to moral particularism. One might claim, for instance, that natural law merely gives a series of particular injunctions about moral actions (in the sense of external behaviors) on an ongoing basis. In other words, the claim that we can rely on no general rules to guarantee that we act infallibly does not mean we can only appeal to dispositions to guarantee such infallibility. Conversely, appealing to dispositions to explain moral actions does not necessarily require a commitment to particularism. One might argue that moral dispositions or the reasoning behind such dispositions are susceptible of general analysis and thus exhibit law-like features that we can use to predict the types of actions to which they give rise. Thus, one cannot merely assume a straightforward connection between moral particularism and an interest in virtuous dispositions. Note as well, that for both Vander Waerdt and Inwood, the commands of natural law cannot be about the kinds of generalized dispositions we find, say, in Aquinas, not to hate or not to covet.[7] They must turn out to be commands aimed at getting an individual in particular circumstances into a discrete psychic state that is causally linked to a particular action. It is not clear to me what philosophical sense, if any, can be made of this claim, but if we are to attribute it to the early Stoics and connect their interests in moral dispositions to any specific theory of particularism, it seems to me that we at least need some textual warrant. But here, the dispositional theory of natural law runs into difficulty.

---

[7] Inwood 'Rules and Reasoning' 95–127, for instance, argues that a general injunction to, say, act prudently, would be vacuous.

Vander Waerdt's treatment of the evidence from Chrysippus' *Peri Nomou* well illustrates our problem, since in his account[8] there is not only, I would argue, a troubling elision of externally imposed divine commands, but also an assumption that the actual content of those commands is necessarily dispositional. At the same time, it seems to me that the evidence is neutral, to say the least, with respect to questions of moral particularism generally.[9] Let us begin with the exordium of Chrysippus' *Peri Nomou*.

> Law is king of all things divine and human. It must preside over what is honorable and base, both as ruler and as guide, and in virtue of this it must be the standard (*kanon*) of justice and injustice, prescribing to animals whose nature is political what they should do, and prohibiting what they should not do. (Marcian *Inst.* I = Long and Sedley 67R, adapted)

The claim that Chrysippus formulates a 'dispositional' theory of natural law strikes me as problematic for several reasons. In this initial passage, which is admittedly programmatic, there is nothing to give a hint that the content of the injunctions of natural law is either about dispositions or, for that matter, about moral particulars. The early Stoics, just as Aristotle before them, have a well-articulated distinction between actions and their underlying intentions. Indeed, their ethical theory rather relentlessly stresses, some might say to the point of implausibility, the claim that the only thing that matters from the point of view of moral evaluation is the intention from which an action is performed. But these worries about what, following Aquinas, we might call the intrinsic principles of human action are hardly in evidence here. Chrysippus does not claim that natural law prescribes to animals whose nature is political *how* and *how not* they should perform actions or with what sorts of inner attitudes. He maintains that natural law prescribes *what* they should and should not do. Given the centrality of intentions in their theory of virtue and also their fondness for invoking their own technical distinctions and vocabulary even in the most programmatic contexts, we should be wary of assuming the kind of neat folding of these externalist concerns into the requirements of ethics proper as postulated by Vander Waerdt. This is not to claim, of course, that Chrysippus' view of natural law is unconnected to his views of moral action. Far from it, since it would be a foolhardy to venture such a claim about a school that prides itself on the systematic unity of all of its philosophical positions. But the fact that particular Stoic views are connected does not mean that we cannot discern different philosophical motivations from separate areas of their thought coming into contact. Nor does it mean that we should merely

---

[8] This volume, pp. 24–31.
[9] This volume, p. 28.

run these separate motivations together or elide them. Of course, the question of how smoothly such motivations fit together is another matter. But at least at first glance, it seems implausible to suggest that this passage is concerned with the intrinsic principles of human action and not with the workings of an externally imposed law.

Moreover, Chrysippus' claim that natural law prescribes what we should do, is at best ambiguous between more general recommendations and those aimed solely at particular occasions. I say at best ambiguous, since it seems to me that only someone in the grips of a particularist theory could take this passage to preclude general law-like recommendations. But since such an interpretation cannot be entirely ruled out at this point, we need to turn to what is perhaps the crucial move of the dispositionalist interpretation.

In claiming that natural law enjoins only dispositions, Vander Waerdt invokes the Stoic distinction between *katorthômata* and *kathêkonta*, which is meant to pick out the crucial difference between actions that arise from the proper moral intentions and those that may not. He further claims that natural law enjoins only *katorthômata*. The sole passage, or better, sentence he relies on for this claim comes from a passage in Plutarch (*De Stoic. Repug.* 1037c–d = *SVF* 3.520) whose aim is meant to show inconsistencies in the Stoic position. Here is Vander Waerdt's reconstruction of the passage in question:

> They say: 'Virtuous action is the prescription of law; moral error is its proscription. Hence law proscribes many things for the base, but prescribes nothing, for they are incapable of virtuous action.

How can natural law prescribe virtuous actions for all animals that are political, Plutarch objects, since the vicious are incapable of virtuous action? Plutarch, I take it, is concerned with what becomes a standard objection to natural law theory, and for which there is an equally standard response. Natural moral laws are unlike physical laws and therefore can be disobeyed. Thus, their prescriptions are equally for the vicious as well as for the virtuous, even if the former do not obey them. However, even if we grant to Vander Waerdt that the passage reflects a Chrysippean claim that natural law enjoins only *katorthômata* (which I think is deeply problematic on textual grounds[10] and also threatens to make *kathêkonta* somehow anomalously natural), it still fails to show that the Stoic account is narrowly dispositionalist in the way that he suggests.

---

[10] Since I have discussed this passage at length elsewhere (P. Mitsis, 'Natural Law and Natural Right in Post-Aristotelian Philosophy. The Stoics and Their Critics', *ANRW* II. 36.7 (Berlin 1994) 4812–4850), I will refrain from repeating my reasons for rejecting it as good evidence for the Stoic position.

Katorthômata are actions that are undertaken with the right rational intention and have the right focus on the good. Yet, even if natural law were held to enjoin only *katorthômata,* the most that this would show is that natural law for the early Stoics enjoins actions that are performed out of the right moral intentions. It does not follow that the injunctions of natural law themselves are solely about inner states or the dispositions producing those perfect actions. If I return a deposit with the right moral intention and my action is in accord with right reason, I have performed a perfect action (*katorthôma*). But I have not merely lit up a particular inner bulb. I have performed an action and my action also has an external dimension. This intuitively plausible feature of morally correct actions is reflected in the Stoic claim that all *katorthômata* are also *kathêkonta.*

Part of the reason Vander Waerdt goes astray here, perhaps, is because of a related set of issues concerned with the Stoic response to the external failure of particular actions. Suppose, for instance, that I intend to return a deposit, and it is the morally right thing to do, but I am prevented from doing so by something out of my control. What is the moral status of my action? For the Stoics, such an action, even if it fails in achieving its external aim, is still entirely successful from the moral point of view. Accordingly, one might be tempted to conclude from this Stoic doctrine that successful moral actions can only be identified by focusing on their underlying intentions. Let us grant, for the moment, Vander Waerdt's claim that the infallible sage is the paradigmatic moral agent acting in accordance with nature's commands and that natural law only gives injunctions for successful *moral* actions (*katorthômata*). This still does not get us to his conclusion that *katorthômata* are internal dispositional states, however, or that the content of nature's commands is entirely dispositional. If natural law enjoins that a sage return a deposit and this is a perfect action (*katorthôma*), he might manage to return the deposit or he might be prevented from doing so by events out of his control. His injunction from nature, however, if it is in the form of an injunction to perform a *katorthôma,* is to perform an action. The fact that the external object of the action is attained or not is strictly a matter of indifference. But this further feature of our evaluation of the action does not show that the action itself is not part of what is enjoined by nature, however successful or unsuccessful it may be in attaining its external aim. This is because *katorthômata* are not merely dispositions; they are actions carried out from the right moral motives. Attention to the inner motivation of an action and indifference to an action's external success does not commit the Stoics to the claim that actions themselves are merely dispostions to act. Thus, a sage obeys a moral injunction to act, not merely to get himself into a particular moral mood. Of course, it might seem odd, in the light of these claims, to say that whether the sage manages to return a deposit or not, he is performing the very same moral action (*katorthôma*). But the oddity stems here, not from the Stoics inability to distinguish dispositions from actions, but from the extremity of the moral perspective they espouse and their belief that success or failure in attaining the external aim of actions does not serve to individuate those actions, at least from a moral point of view. Thus, I do not believe that the evidence of Chrysippus' *Peri Nomou* can support the so-called dispositionalist theory of natural law, even if we grant the problematic claim that natural law only enjoins *katorthômata*.

A related worry that leads Vander Waerdt to this characterization of *katorthômata* as mere instances of dispositions is connected to a second major set of issues involving the problem of apparent exceptions to laws. In some circumstances we might think it morally wrong to return a deposit. How can proponents of natural law account for such seeming exceptions to what we take as standard moral demands? Do they, Vander Waerdt asks, make room for exceptions by somehow linking them to dispositions or by appealing to higher order rules? I myself think this is a false dichotomy, since I think the Stoics link externalist and internalist demands in their theory. They, as it were, do not follow rules without virtuous motivations and their virtuous motivations are linked to rationally ordered laws. However, in order to begin answering this question, we need to backtrack a bit and look more generally at how the question of exceptions arises in Stoic texts. Here we will be forced to take a brief doxographical detour, since I believe that both Vander Waerdt and Inwood[11] have used this evidence in a way that is deeply anachronistic for the early Stoa and generally misleading for later Stoics as well. But they are by no means alone in this, since the form that their discussion takes is to be found in modern scholarship at least as early as 1852 in Zeller.[12]

Our problem begins with how we are to understand a series of shocking reports (well, shocking at least to Zeller and to those with similar nineteenth century sensibilities) suggesting that the early Stoics somehow countenanced cannibalism and incest. I wish to begin by leaving this claim about early Stoicism rather vague initially, since Zeller, on the basis of a report in Diogenes Laertius (7.121), went on to restrict these practices to sages in special circumstances (*kata peristasin*). Inwood and Vander Waerdt take on board a similar reading of the evidence and use it to establish their claim that there are no universal or substantive injunctions of natural law, since

---

[11] Inwood 'Rules and Reasoning' 102–103.
[12] E. Zeller, *Die Philosophie der Greichen in ihrer geschichtlichen Entwicklung*, vol.3 (Leipzig, 1852).

all types of appropriate actions (*kathêkonta*) are subject to exception. Their star cases of such exceptions are the sage's practice of cannibalism and incest *kata peristasin*. It is more likely, however, that this doctrine of actions *kata peristasin* reflects later attempts to account for doctrines of the early Stoa that had become embarrassing to later Stoics, much in the same way, say, that Aquinas was faced with explaining the polygamy of patriarchs in the Bible. In the case of the Stoics, the Bible in question is Zeno's *Republic*, and the incest and cannibalism apparently condoned there[13] are the sources of subsequent embarrassment.

In any case, one can hardly fail to notice that incest and cannibalism are the two practices discussed in early Stoic writings that particularly fired the imagination of the doxographers. Zeller, arguably mirroring the moves that a later Stoic apologist might be forced to make, seems particularly anxious to neutralize the ancient charges that the Stoics condoned such practices — thus, the prominence he gives to D.L. 7.121 and the doctrine of actions in special circumstances. In the case of incest, for instance, he adduces a passage from Origen (*SVF* 2.743) which reports that the Stoics allowed incest only in the extraordinary circumstances of the wise man and his daughter being the last two humans on earth. This allows him to come to the comforting conclusion that incest for the Stoics was at most a theoretical possibility available to the sage only in very special circumstances. But the attempt to account for this evidence as a kind of desert island thought experiment quickly founders on the consideration that incest is built into the very structure of Zeno's *Republic* because of his doctrine of the communal sharing of women (D.L. 7.131). Nor do we have any evidence to suggest that Zeno attempted to erect any barriers to incest in the way that Plato does in his own account of the community of women in the *Republic*. Sextus, moreover, has preserved a quotation, possibly from Zeno's *On Listening to Poetry* (*PH* 3.205 = *SVF* 1.256) in which Zeno discusses the relationship between Oedipus and Jocasta. Incest, he says, is merely a matter of rubbing different parts of the body and is therefore indifferent. Zeno's comment seems to reflect a cynic attitude toward the practice of incest of the sort exemplified in the cynic mock tragedy *Oedipus* that apparently made light of incest. At the very least, whatever Zeno was thinking of in this passage, it is does not seem to be of the theoretical prospect of the wise man and his daughter being the last humans on earth.

At the same time, however seriously we take Origen's desert island example, incest for Zeno would still remain, even in such special circumstances, a matter of physical rubbings that are indifferent from a moral

---

[13] This is an inference, but I believe a good one, about Zeno's *Republic* from reports about Chrysippus' *Republic* and from other testimonies about Zeno.

point of view. Indeed, it is hard to manufacture for the Stoics any special kind of moral imperative of the sort that seems to lie behind Origen's desert island justification. This is because, for a Stoic, there would be no moral imperative to ensure the continuation of the human race (assuming this, and not just a desire for sex, is the underlying justification for incest in Origen's report). One might argue that a Stoic would consider that insuring the survival of the human race is at least an appropriate action. But notice, this still would hardly fit the model of exceptions to rules endorsed by Vander Waerdt and Inwood, since in committing incest, the sage would be substituting one type of appropriate action for another, not merely breaking a moral rule without any appeal to another. I want to return to this issue shortly, since it raises a deeper difficulty for understanding Stoic view about apparent exceptions to moral rules. But first we need to finish our doxographical detour.

If it is in any way difficult to gauge the extent of Zeno's commitment to incest in the *Republic*, Chrysippus seems to have treated the practice with a kind of cynic insouciance. Also, given his flair for logical completeness, he apparently made clear that he thought that 'sexual intercourse with mothers or daughters or sisters' . . . has 'been discredited without reason.' (Plutarch, *De Stoic. Repug.* 1044F–1045A = *SVF* 3.753, trans. Long and Sedley 67F). Sextus, who for his own reasons, obviously thought it meet to focus on a practice that might create moral quandaries, reports that Chrysippus viewed incest as an indifferent, in no way restricting it to special circumstances (*PH* 1.160; 3.205; 3.246–48). On the one hand, of course, Sextus might have an interest in attributing this practice to the Stoics. Yet, at the same time, it seems plausible to infer from his evidence that Chrysippus is defending a practice that is a fairly straightforward consequence of a central arrangement of Zeno's *Republic* and the community of women. Thus, I think we have little reason for supposing that incest is a practice limited by the early Stoics to special circumstances. Rather, I would argue, the attempt to characterize it as an action *kata peristasin*, if not the whole notion of action *kata peristasin* itself, is a later attempt to come to grips with doctrines of the early Stoic patriarchs that later proved embarrassing.

A parallel argument can be made for cannibalism, the particular practice restricted in D.L. 7.121 to special circumstances. Again, reports about the early scholarchs' views suggest more of a desire on their part to register a cynic shock than to come to grips with a theoretical casuist objection to a standard moral rule. Take, for instance, the following bits from Chrysippus' *Republic* reported by Sextus:

> If from the living person a part should be cut off which is edible, we should not bury it or dispose of it in some other way, but consume it, so that from our parts a new one may be generated. (*PH* 3.247= LS 67G)

And Sextus continues:

> In his books *On proper function*, he says explicitly concerning the burial of parents: 'When parents die, we should use the simplest methods of burial, as though the body, like the nails and the teeth or hair, were nothing to us and we give no care or attention to anything like that. So too, if the flesh is edible, people should use it, as they should one of their own parts such as a severed foot and the like. (*PH* 3.247–8 = LS 67G)

Chrysippus' endorsement of cannibalism no doubt reflects a cynic desire to shock, but it also tumbles naturally out of a central and abiding Stoic claim given voice to in this passage. We should treat our bodies and those of others as though they 'were nothing to us' and we should 'give no care or attention to anything like that.' In other words, it is hardly to such practices that we should look for a Stoic account of exceptions to *moral* rules. Not only would such an account be anachronistic for the early Stoa, but also more importantly, it misconstrues the very context in which the question of exceptions to moral rules might even arise for a Stoic. In these particular cases, it seems, the Stoics are keen to show that some normal societal practices, especially those that often generate the strongest sense of taboo, have no moral basis once one comes to the realization that nothing of moral importance attaches to an external entity such as the body. It is a matter of indifference where one rubs one's bodily parts, just as it is a matter of indifference if one eats one's own severed foot. And as long as one continues to view such actions with moral repugnance, one cannot be said to be free of a fool's attachment to externals. If anything, rather than provoking a quandary about its moral permissibility in special circumstances, cannibalism seems to have provided for Chrysippus an occasion for expanding our views about what might be included in our pursuit of health. This hardly betokens a worry about the justified breaking of a moral rule; rather, it enlarges our horizons about what new foods might help fulfill the proper function of maintaining our health.

Even leaving aside for the moment questions of its provenance, if we look at how the notion of action *kata peristasin* actually arises in Diogenes, it hardly seems designed to bear the heavy theoretical weight loaded on to it by Inwood and Vander Waerdt. Diogenes reports a distinction between *kathêkonta aneu peristaseôs* and *kathêkonta kata peristasin* (D.L. 7.109), i.e. proper functions not depending on circumstances and proper functions depending on circumstances. An example of the first class is looking after one's health; of the second, maiming oneself.[14] We generally look after our

---

[14] I would argue, e.g. that cannibalism is moved from the first class into the second by later apologists.

health, but we sometimes might need to maim ourselves either to preserve our health or in the pursuit of some other goal. For an example of the latter, think, for instance, of the great Roman patriot Mucius Scaevola thrusting his arm into the fire in letter after letter of Seneca to demonstrate his courage and love of his fatherland. The first thing to notice about this distinction, however, is that it cannot capture, nor do I think it was designed to capture, any worries about the justified breaking of a *moral* rule. If an agent is faced with maiming himself to preserve his health, he is faced with a non-moral technical question about something, which, to the Stoic, is a matter of indifference, his bodily health. Moreover, we might say that in submitting to being maimed, he is most likely following rules for maintaining his health. There is no need to insist on this latter claim, however, since in any case, he is being presented with a problem of health, not of breaking a moral rule.

On the other hand, if he maims himself for the fatherland, like Mucius, this too presents for the Stoic no dilemmas about the breaking of a moral rule. To the contrary, it exemplifies the virtuous choice of an individual who places the needs of his country over his own health or life. It is a choice, that is, of virtue over a non-moral good. Stoic texts teem with examples of those who place virtuous goals above their life, health, wealth, etc., and although it is not always clear exactly how specific cases actually are meant to demonstrate choices of moral over non-moral goods, this is clearly the conclusion that Stoics draw from them. Of course, we still need to understand how Stoics understood agents choosing moral over non-moral paths and the role that internalist and externalist considerations play in such choices. But for now, at least, I hope to have shown that both Inwood and Vander Waerdt, in attempting to use this body of evidence to support their claim that Stoics deny that there are universal or substantive natural moral rules, have mistaken both its terms and its historical context.

Of course, this does not mean that one cannot take this distinction of action *kata peristasin* and attempt to generate an apparent moral dilemma for the Stoic. Mucius has a duty to protect the fatherland and also to honor his father. What if he must sacrifice his father *kata peristasin* in order to protect his fatherland? One reason I would resist such a move here, however, is that I think there is a better place, and one more faithful to its historical context, to raise such questions in Stoicism.[15]

So far my argument has been mostly negative and I can hardly claim to have shown that the Stoics think that nature does provide contentful rules that offer a rational structure for moral thought and virtuous action. But it

---

[15] P. Mitsis, 'Seneca on Reason, Rules and Moral Development', in J. Brunschwig and M. Nussbaum (edd.), *Passions and Perceptions* (Cambridge 1993) 285–312, here 304–310.

might be helpful, at this point, to give a few brief indications[16] about how one might do so. Let me begin by flagging two key points of disagreement with the Vander Waerdt/Inwood view that speak to this issue. One involves the structure of moral reasoning itself and the extent to which the virtues are thought by the Stoics to be structured by law-like principles. The second involves the nature of the gulf that separates the deliberations of sages from those of ordinary deliberators.

If I have one ongoing complaint about the Vander Waerdt/Inwood project, it is that it slights what to my mind is the best evidence for the role of rules in Stoic thinking, and that is our reports of the debates between Aristo and orthodox Stoics over the usefulness of general and particular moral recommendations. Moreover, it strikes me that for anyone who takes that debate seriously, Vander Waerdt's claim that the early Stoics dispensed with rule-based reasoning appears to accurately capture the view of really only one early Stoic and that is the defrocked renegade Aristo. Even if we grant that our evidence for this early debate is in some way filtered through Cicero's and Seneca's own concerns, it seems undeniable that the early Stoics were keen to defend the usefulness of rules against the anti-rule arguments of Aristo. Exactly how this debate went is a matter of controversy; but what seems beyond controversy is that we would do better to look to Aristo and not to orthodox Stoicism for defense of a theory that dispenses with rule-based reasoning. Inwood, too, even with his new 'heuristic model' of moral rules, seems to let his Stoic wise man lurch uncomfortably between Aristo's intuitionism and something approaching the kind of evaluative attitude now standardly attributed to Aristotle's *phronimos*. In Inwood's still staunchly particularist account, rational principles, which he believes are non-prescriptive, provide a general evaluative background for the sage's reasoning. But it is hard to see how, if this were indeed the orthodox Stoics' view, they could hope to attribute to the wise man a kind of knowledge that is identical with divine rationality and the prescriptions of divine law itself. One major strength of Vander Waerdt's reading is his insistence that we take seriously Stoic claims about the confluence between the wise man's perfected rational disposition and nature's prescriptions, hence about the identity of the wise man's knowledge and nature's law. The Stoics' model of rationality, I would argue, must offer moral principles that provide more than a mere evaluative

---

[16] Given the number of years our debate has gone on and the number of pages it has generated, I will limit myself to a few salient points. Those interested may consult the works listed in notes 2 and 3 and Mitsis (1993) for fuller discussion. These issues are helpfully discussed by Charles Brittain in 'Rationality, Rules, and Rights' *Apeiron* 34.3, (2001) 247–267.

background; they should be prescriptive, external, and determinate, if the sage's reasoning in accordance with them is in any way to approach the mind of God.

My second disagreement with the Vander Waerdt/Inwood view stems from how we are to understand differences between the moral deliberations of sages and the non-wise. The historical shift that Vander Waerdt describes from virtue to rules becomes encapsulated as a timeless divide between sage and non-sage in Inwood's account. He postulates a two-track system of moral deliberation in which sages dispense with rules, while non-sages rather slavishly rely on them. I say slavishly, since it seems that only the wise could ever be justified in breaking them. Such a view leads to a number of absurd consequences since, for instance, it would make the Stoic industry of urging on us exempla such as Mucius unintelligible, especially on Inwood's own theory, since a non-sage could hardly be justified in maiming himself for his country. Moreover, rather than creating a more flexible view of Stoic rules, Inwood's heuristic account threatens to consign sages merely to a kind of Aristonian indeterminacy while dooming non-sages to an objectionable — even for non-sages — moral unadventurousness.

Let me deal with the second disagreement first. I take the disjunction between virtue and rules and externalist and internalist justifications underlying either purported historical shifts or two-track systems of deliberation to be unhelpful and also unnecessary. Two of the central objections of orthodox Stoics to Aristo, at least as reported by Seneca, precisely depend on denying a two-level track for sages and non-sages. One is conceptual and attempts to show that any argument that denies rules must assume the existence of a further rule (see *Ep. Mor.* 95.60–61.) This is a general feature of rational thought and language and one that obviously applies to sage and non-sage alike. Reasoning is structured by rules and that is that. It is conceptually inescapable. Second, orthodox Stoics claim that knowing the fundamental doctrines or principles of morality (decreta) is not enough to insure correct moral action; one also needs more determinate moral rules to pick out the morally salient situations to which they apply (cf. Seneca, *Ep. Mor.* 94.32). This applies to those who are wise and those who are not equally. Indeed, this is one of the sources of dispute with Aristo and arguably grounds the whole orthodox Stoic project of picking out *kathêkonta*. So again, I think, whether in its historical or timeless version, the Vander Waerdt/Inwood assumption of what amounts to an unbridgeable gulf between virtue and rules smacks more of Aristo than of orthodoxy.

Let me close with a few comments about the structure of the wise man's reasoning and its relation to both virtue and natural law. The kinds of connection between virtue and natural law that I suggested were first developed by Stoics can be seen in very general outlines in the texts from Chrysippus that I began with. But there is an important passage in Diogenes Laertius (D.L. 7.125–126), which gives us a glimpse, though unfortunately only a glimpse, of some of the deeper connections Stoics saw between virtue and rational nature writ large. This passage shows one key way that nature provides us with external rational principles to structure virtuous actions. Diogenes reports that as part of an argument defending the unity of the virtues, various Stoics claimed that the virtues have *koina theoremata,* or common principles. Chrysippus and Hecato did so in works on the virtues and Apollodorus made the same claim in his book on the natural philosophy of the early school. The fact that this doctrine about the *koina theoremata* of virtue shows up in works of natural philosophy as well as of ethics proper should not occasion surprise, given the general connections we have witnessed between internalist and externalist concerns. Presumably, the way one comes to know such *theorêmata* is through reasoning, since as we find out in Diogenes' introduction to his summary of Stoic ethics, one comes to know all things through reasoning in ethics (*dia tês en logois theôrias,* D.L. 7. 83) including how laws have given order to various actions (*hopôs dietaksan hoi nomoi epi tois ergois).*[17] Diogenes relates a further important clue about the structure of virtue from Hecato's *Peri aretôn* (D.L. 7. 90). Hecato argued that prudence and justice, for instance, are based on *theôrêmata* and that they both have a structure that consists of principles (*sustasis ek theôrêmatôn*). It seems plausible to claim, on the evidence so far, that the virtues have a rational structure of connected principles that can be grasped by reasoning. Such principles also give a rational way of classifying actions.

In turning to D.L. 7.126, we find the intriguing report that the man who is virtuous is able to grasp these *theôrêmata* and also to act. Diogenes then proceeds to offer a taxonomy of more determinate types of actions connected to the *theôrêmata* of the four cardinal virtues. Each virtue, he reports, has its own determinate focus for the Stoics. Justice, for instance, has as its particular subject matter actions involving the just distribution of goods. Justice also has further determinate subcategories such as equality and fairness. When we turn to prudence, *phronêsis,* we find that it too is comprised of a *sustasis theôrêmatôn* whose principles have as their special focus actions that should be done and those that should be avoided. Harking back to the exordium of Chrysippus' *Peri Nomou,* we can hardly fail to

---

[17] The text is problematic. I am trying to offer a bland and general translation. However strongly we take this passage, it is hard to deny, though, that there is a claim about the rational structure of laws and their connection to actions.

notice an overlap between the functions of *phronêsis* and the injunctions of divine, rational law. This, perhaps, should come as little surprise, since I promised at the beginning that this would be a story of both virtue and law — though story is perhaps a little grand for what turns out to be only a glimpse of what the Stoics thought. But this glimpse is not entirely negligible. It suggests that the Stoics believe that internally, the virtues are structured by a set of determinate rational principles (*theôrêmata*) that prescribe[18] what we should do and avoid; at the same time, these principles and their prescriptions are also in accord with divine reason and its injunctions about what we should and should not do. Such principles are both internal features of virtue and thus of our rational dispositions, but they are also in accordance with divine reason. (cf. D.L. 7.93, *kat' orthon logon*). Conceived of in this way, we may be in a better position to understand two puzzles about the Stoics: why it is they can insist that sages can think like gods and that we ordinary fools can sacrifice ourselves for our countries.

New York

---

[18] Cf. D.L. 7.126. In introducing these issues, Diogenes is tantalizingly vague on just how we are to conceive this connection between theoretical principles and actions: *ton gar enareton theôrêtikon t'einai kai praktikon tôn poiêteôn*. However, it becomes clear in the course of the passage that lower level principles have prescriptive force, e.g. *ta de poiêtea kai hairetea esti kai hupomenêtea* ...

A WRITTEN COPY OF THE LAW OF NATURE: AN UNTHINKABLE PARADOX?

Hindy Najman

In the writings of Philo of Alexandria, we witness a major turn in the history of the concept of the law of nature.[1] The law of nature becomes intimately linked to the written law revealed by God, the Law of Moses.[2] Philo's recasting of both Greek philosophy and Jewish tradition sets the scene for centuries of development, not only within Judaism, but also within Christianity and Islam.

As with any conceptual revolution, it is all but impossible to bring the Philonic turn clearly into view. To those who inherit Philo's sense of God as creator, lawgiver and source of revelation, the unity of natural law and revealed law[3] can seem obvious. But, if one tries to think oneself into the position of Philo's Hellenistic predecessors and contemporaries, such a

---

[1] In early Greek philosophy, nature and law were contrasting terms, whose competing merits were the subject of an important controversy. For an excellent discussion of this debate with extensive primary sources see R. D. McKirahan, Jr., 'Chapter 19: The NOMOS-PHYSIS Debate', in *Philosophy Before Socrates: An Introduction with Texts and Commentary* (Indianapolis and Cambridge 1994) 390–413. There is one reference to natural law in Plato's *Gorgias* 483A7– 484C3. See G. Striker, 'Origins of the Concept of Natural Law', in *Essays on Hellenistic Epistemology and Ethics* (New York 1996) 212. However, as Striker argues, Gorgias uses the term as a deliberate paradox, on the assumption that nature itself, of course, has no normative import for human actions whatsoever. H. A. Wolfson claims that Philo borrows Aristotle's concept of nature. See his discussion in *Philo: Foundations of Religious Philosophy in Judaism, Christianity, and in Islam*, 2 vols. (Cambridge, Massachusetts 1947) 1:332–347. However, it seems quite clear that Philo's concept of nature and of natural law is derived from later Stoic philosophy. On this point see Striker, 'Origins of the Concept of Natural Law', 209–220.

[2] S. G. Sowers, *The Hermeneutics of Philo and Hebrews: A Comparison of the Interpretation in Philo Judaeus and the Epistle to the Hebrews*, Basel Studies of Theology 1 (Richmond, Virginia 1965) 44–49; M. Niehoff, *Philo on Jewish Identity and Culture*, TSAJ 86 (Tübingen 2001) 247–266; D. M. Hay, 'Philo of Alexandria', in D. A. Carson, P. T. O'Brien, M. A. Seifrid (edd.), *Justification and Variegated Nomism: Volume I, The Complexities of Second Temple Judaism*. WUNT 2.140 (Tübingen 2001) 357–379, esp. 373–378; H. Najman, 'The Law of Nature and the Authority of Mosaic Law', *SPhA* 11 (1999) 55–73; F. Calabi, *The Language and the Law of God: Interpretation and Politics in Philo of Alexandria*, South Florida Studies in the History of Judaism 188 (Atlanta 1998) 31–78, esp. 36–43.

[3] In the case of Philo of Alexandria, revealed law is synonymous with the Law of Moses.

unity not only fails to be obvious, it seems incoherent, paradoxical. As I will explain, the revolutionary character of Philo's move seems to me to be one factor underlying the debate between Phillip Mitsis and Paul Vander Waerdt continued in this volume.[4] If Philo's move is revolutionary, as I am suggesting, how is it possible, not merely to think in post-revolutionary or in pre-revolutionary terms, but to *clarify* Philo's move, to render it intelligible? I want first to explain more precisely why Philo's position seems paradoxical. Then I will seek, not to remove the paradox — for that, I believe, cannot be done — but rather to exhibit some of the inner logic of Philo's thinking.

Philo writes within the context of what is now called Middle Platonism,[5] and his conception of the law of nature seems indebted to both Platonism and Stoicism.[6] To see the paradoxical character of Philo's linkage of the law of nature with the written law revealed by God, we need to recall a presupposition that Philo's philosophically educated readers would very likely have made. The presupposition is that the law of nature, in accordance with which we should live, is necessarily an unwritten law, which transcends the written laws of any human *polis*.[7] In his discussion of the exemplary legislator Lycurgus, Plutarch writes:

> None of his laws were put into writing by Lycurgus, indeed, one of the so-called 'rhetras'[8] forbid it. For he thought that if the most important and binding principles which conduce to the prosperity and virtue of a city were implanted in the habits and training of its citizens, they would remain unchanged and secure, having a stronger bond than compulsion in the fixed purposes imparted to the young by education,

---

[4] See P. A. Vander Waerdt, 'Zeno's Republic and the Origins of Natural Law', in P. A. Vander Waerdt (ed.), *The Socratic Movement* (Ithaca and London 1994) 272–308 and J. G. Defilippo and P. T. Mitsis, 'Socrates and Stoic Natural Law,' in *The Socratic Movement*, 252–271. See also their essays in this volume.

[5] For some helpful discussions on the relationship between Middle Platonism and Philo of Alexandria, see D. T. Runia, 'Was Philo a Middle Platonist? A Difficult Question Revisited' *SPhA* 5 (1993) 112–140; G. E. Sterling, 'Platonizing Moses: Philo and Middle Platonism' *SPhA* 5 (1993) 96–111; J. Dillon, *The Middle Platonists: 80 B.C. to A.D. 20* (Ithaca 1996); *idem*, 'A Response to Runia and Sterling' *SPhA* 5 (1993) 151–155; T. H. Tobin, 'Was Philo a Middle Platonist? Some Suggestions' *SPhA* 5 (1993) 147–150; D. Winston, 'Response to Runia and Sterling' *SPhA* 5 (1993) 141–146.

[6] H. Koester is surely incorrect when he suggests that Philo originated the notion of natural law. See his article, 'ΝΟΜΟΣ ΦΥΣΕΩΣ: The Concept of Natural Law in Greek Thought', in J. Neusner (ed.), *Religions in Antiquity: Essays in Memory of Erwin Ramsdell Goodenough*, SHR 14 (Leiden 1968) 540. For a refutation, see R. A. Horsley, 'The Law of Nature in Philo and Cicero' *HThR* 71 (1978) 35–59, especially 56ff.

[7] See my essay, 'Philo of Alexandria on the Law of Nature and the Law of Moses', 55–73.

[8] On *rhetras* see *Lyc.* 13.6, where Plutarch says that Lycurgus understood the *rhetras* to be divine oracles.

which performs the office of a law-giver for every one of them ... Indeed, he assigned the function of law-making wholly and entirely to education.[9]

Already in Sophocles' *Antigone*, a sharp contrast is drawn between the written law of the *polis* and the unwritten law.[10] Closer to the time of Philo, when the unwritten law has come to be called the law of nature, we find Cicero drawing the contrast as follows:

> I see that because custom is so corrupted such behavior is neither thought dishonorable nor forbidden by statute and civil law. It is, however, forbidden by the law of nature. For there is a fellowship that is extremely widespread, shared by all with all (even if this has often been said, it ought to be said still more often); a closer one exists among those of the same nation, and one more intimate still among those of the same city. For this reason our ancestors wanted the law of nations and the civil law to be different: everything in the civil law need not be in the law of nations, but everything in the law of nations ought also to be a part of civil law. We, however, do not have the firm and lifelike figure of true law and genuine justice: we make use of shadows and sketches. I wish we would follow even those! For they are drawn from the best examples of nature and truth.[11]

Here, the law of nature is distinguished from the laws of particular nations. The distinction concerns both normative status and epistemic access. First, the law of nature has superior normative status. It constrains the laws of particular nations, but they do not constrain it. Second, there seems to be no special problem gaining epistemic access to the laws of particular nations, which are presumably embodied, not only in custom, but in written statutes. But gaining epistemic access to the law of nature is problematic. At best, we can know 'shadows and sketches' of the law of nature. Those are 'drawn from the best examples of nature and truth' — that is, presumably, from the exemplary lives of those who are virtuous and wise. But we do not know the originals. We know nature and truth only through those whose lives copy them. The reason for Cicero's epistemic contrast between laws of particular nations and the law of nature may perhaps be that natural virtue and wisdom can be exemplified by living actions, but

---

[9] Plutarch, *Lyc.* 13.1–2.
[10] Sophocles, *Ant.* 450–460: 'For me it was not Zeus who made this proclamation, nor was it Justice who dwells with the gods below who established these laws among humans. And I did not suppose that your proclamations had power enough that you, a mortal, could prevail over the gods' unwritten and secure practices. For they live not just now and yesterday, but always forever. No one knows when they appeared. I did not out of fear of the will of any man intend to pay a penalty before the gods for transgressing them.' This translation is taken from R. D. McKirahan, Jr., *Philosophy Before Socrates: An Introduction with Texts and Commentary* (Indianapolis and Cambridge 1994) 409.
[11] This passage is cited from the translation of Cicero found in M. T. Griffin and E. M. Atkins, (edd.), *Cicero: On Duties*, Cambridge Texts in the History of Political Thought (Cambridge 1991) 125–126.

can never be reduced to any set of norms that might be transcribed into a written code of law.

Now, some passages in Philo might suggest that he shares this presupposed contrast between the unwritten laws of nature on the one hand and written laws on the other. Thus Philo emphasizes that the intelligible originals, through which God created the material world, can never be adequately represented in language (*Opif.* 4):

> In celebrating the beauty of the thoughts contained in this creation account, no one, whether writing poetry or prose, can do them true justice. They transcend both speech and hearing, for they are greater and more august than what can be adapted to the instruments of a mortal being.[12]

If the originals cannot be adequately represented in language, then of course, they cannot be adequately represented in writing. So it is no surprise to find that Philo says of the patriarchs, whom he portrays as living in accordance with nature, that they 'followed the unwritten law' (*Abr.* 4–6):

> These (patriarchs) are such men as lived good and blameless lives, whose virtues stand permanently recorded in the most holy scriptures, not merely to sound their praises but for the instruction of the reader and as an inducement to elicit emulation; for in these men we have laws endowed with life and reason, and Moses extolled them for two reasons. First he wished to show that the enacted ordinances are not inconsistent with nature; and secondly that those who wish to live in accordance with the laws as they stand have no difficult task, seeing that the first generations before any at all of the particular statutes was set in writing followed the unwritten law with perfect ease, so that one might properly say that the enacted laws are nothing else than reminders of the life of the ancients, preserving to a later generation their actual words and deed. For they were not scholars or pupils of others, nor did they learn under teachers what was right to say or do: they listened to no voice or instruction but their own: they welcomed conformity with nature, holding that nature itself was, as indeed it is, the most venerable of statutes, and thus their whole life was one of happy obedience to law.

For it would seem that, if a life of virtue is a life in accordance with nature, and if the originals of nature cannot be adequately represented in writing, then the law followed by the virtuous is of necessity unwritten.

Now we are ready to hear how paradoxical Philo must sound to his contemporaries. For his central theme is that a unique status must be accorded to one collection of written laws, the Law of Moses, which is the law of a

---

[12] The quotations in English from the writings of Philo of Alexandria are taken from PLCL. The only exception are passages taken from Philo's essay *De opificio mundi*, are taken from D. T. Runia, On the Creation of the Cosmos: Introduction, Translation and Commentary, Philo of Alexandria Commentary Series 1 (Leiden 2001). I have, in certain cases, modified the Colson translation on the basis of the Greek in consultation with the critical edition of PCW.

particular nation. These laws are unique. They remain 'firm, unshaken, immovable, stamped as it were, with the seals of nature herself' (*Mos.* 2.14):

> But Moses is alone in this, that his laws, firm, unshaken, immovable, stamped, as it were, with the seals of nature herself, remain secure from the day when they were first enacted to now, and we may hope that they will remain for all future ages as though immortal, so long as the sun and moon and the whole heaven and universe exist. Thus, though the nation had undergone so many changes, both to increased prosperity and the reverse, nothing — not even the smallest part of the ordinances — has been disturbed; because all have clearly paid high honor to their venerable and godlike character.

Now, in his account of creation, Philo uses the metaphor of stamping with a seal to express the relationship between original and copy (*Leg.* 1.47).

> Before the particular and individual mind there subsists a certain original as an archetype and pattern of it, and again before the particular sense-perception, a certain original of sense perception related to the particular as a seal making impression is to the form which it makes.

Philo's claim, then, is that the laws of Moses are copies of the laws of nature. Indeed, he says elsewhere that they are 'likenesses and copies of the patterns enshrined in the soul' (*Mos.* 2.11), and that 'the laws [are] the most faithful copy of the world-polity' (*Mos.* 2.51-2). But here lies the paradox. How is it so much as possible for the written laws of a particular nation to be copies of the laws of nature? Philo seems to share, in large part, a framework of thought with Cicero and others. Yet there is simply no room in Cicero's thinking for a written copy of the laws of nature.

The difficulty of finding conceptual room for Philo's position seems to be one factor underlying the debate between Mitsis and Vander Waerdt. According to DeFilippo and Mitsis, 'The Stoic theory of natural law ... assumes ... that the divine order of nature legislates a system of moral laws that provides a normative structure for human conduct.'[13] However, Vander Waerdt sees here the risk of anachronism. He argues that,

> the early Stoics clearly do not conceive of natural law as being constituted by a code of moral rules comparable, for instance, to Aquinas' code of primary and secondary precepts. To the contrary, they advance a dispositional rather than a rule-following model of natural law, and a correspondingly different account of the content of the moral conduct prescribed by it: in their theory, it prescribes not a determinate class of actions but a certain rational disposition with which one is to act, namely, the perfectly rational and consistent disposition which enables the sage to apprehend and act in accordance with the provident order of nature.[14]

---

[13] Defilippo and Mitsis, 'Socrates and Stoic Natural Law,' 265.
[14] Vander Waerdt, 'Zeno's Republic and the Origins of Natural Law,' 275-276.

Underlying Vander Waerdt's argument is the question: how could the early Stoic conception of the law of nature be expressed by a code of precepts, since the early Stoics conceive the law of nature as unwritten and as embodied in the life of the sage? The question is not, I suggest, only interpretive. It is also conceptual. For early Stoic texts seem to leave no room for the idea of a code of precepts, a code that could be enshrined in a written text, which has the authoritative status of a copy of the law of nature. Underlying the debate between Mitsis and Vander Waerdt, then, is the question of how to make sense of Philo's revolutionary move.

An initial answer to the question is that, for Philo, the law of nature and the Law of Moses have the same source. Both are legislated by God. Thus, for example, John Martens contrasts Philo's position with Cicero's:

> Philo could not admit that the Mosaic law was only a shadowy sketch of true law. God gave the law to Moses; God also created the world and with it the law of nature. The law of Moses, divinely given, could in no way contradict the law of nature, divinely implanted in the world at creation.[15]

Now, this answer certainly has some validity. It is clearly important to Philo to emphasize that God is the source of both the law of nature and the Law of Moses. He makes this point in two main ways. First, as we can see in the two passages below (*Opif.* 3 and *Mos.* 2.48) Philo sees it as one of the main reasons why Moses prefaces the law with an account of creation that might otherwise be out of place (*Opif.* 3):

> The beginning is, as I just said, quite marvelous. It contains an account of the making of the cosmos, the reasoning for this being that the cosmos is in harmony with the law and the law with the cosmos, and the man who observes the law is at once a citizen of the cosmos, directing his actions in relation to the rational purpose of nature, in accordance with which the entire cosmos also is administered.

> *Mos.* 2.48:
> He did not, like any prose-writer, make it his business to leave behind for posterity records of ancient deeds for the pleasant but unimproving entertainment which they give; but, in relating the history of early times, and going for its beginning right to the creation of the universe, he wished to show two most essential things: first that the Father and Maker of the world was in the truest sense also its Lawgiver, secondly that he who would observe the laws gladly welcomes conformity with nature and lives in accordance with the ordering of the universe, so that his deeds are attuned to harmony with his words and his words with his deeds.

Second, Philo takes pains to show, not only that the laws of Moses have a moral purpose even when that purpose is not obvious, but also that the laws of Moses are structurally similar to the created cosmos. Hence, for

---

[15] J. W. Martens, 'Philo and the 'Higher' Law', *SBLSP* (1991) 317.

example, the importance of numerological analyses, such as Philo's account of the role of the decad in both natural and Mosaic law.[16]

However, it is simply not enough to say, with Martens, that God is the source of both natural and Mosaic law. Martens himself infers only that 'the Law of Moses ... could in no way contradict the natural law.' But what needs to be clarified is how the Law of Moses could be a *copy* of the natural law, so that fulfilling the former is at the same time fulfilling the latter! We might say, perhaps, that the omnipotent creator can make it the case that the Law of Moses is a copy of the law of nature. But this is to say that God can do even what is — or seems to be — conceptually impossible. If we can say no more than this, then it would seem that we have located a point where communication simply breaks down between, on the one hand, Philo and those who believe in an omnipotent creator, and, on the other hand, those who do not believe in an omnipotent creator. Those on one side of the Philonic revolution have no standard of intelligibility in common with those on the other side.

But I think that we can say more than this. One might think that there are two exclusive alternatives: either conceive the law of nature as a code of rules which can be written down, or else conceive it as exemplified by the disposition of the sage. But these are not exclusive alternatives for Philo. In two ways, the Law of Moses is more than a code of rules. First, it includes the lives of the patriarchs. Second, it is the Law of Moses, an expression of the life of Moses. Both the patriarchs and Moses are portrayed by Philo as sages living in accordance with nature. Thus, although to be sure the Law of Moses is written, it is not reducible to a code of precepts. For the precepts it contains must be understood in the context of the exemplary lives they express.

In Philo's view, the patriarchs exemplify the possibility of leading a virtuous life even if one does not have access to the written Law of Moses (*Abr.* 16):

> Great indeed are the efforts expended both by lawgivers and by laws in every nation in filling the souls of free men with comfortable hopes; but he who gains this virtue of hopefulness without being led to it by exhortation or command has been educated into it by a law which nature has laid down, a law unwritten yet self-taught.

In a striking phrase, Philo says that the patriarchs were not merely obedient to law; they were 'laws endowed with life and reason' (*Abr.* 5). Similarly, Philo says that Abraham was 'himself a law and an unwritten statute' (*Abr.* 276).[17] The point is that the patriarchs are sages, who have

---

[16] See *Decal.* 20–23.

[17] This phrase should be compared with Plutarch's later interpretation of a verse from

fully internalized the disposition to live in accordance with nature. So the lives of the patriarchs *are* the law of nature and have the normative force of law.

For two reasons, Philo says, did Moses include the lives of these living laws in the Pentateuch (*Abr.* 5):

> First he wished to show that the enacted ordinances are not inconsistent with nature; and secondly that those who wish to live in accordance with the laws as they stand have no difficult task, seeing that the first generations before any at all of the particular statutes was set in writing followed the unwritten law with perfect ease, so that one might properly say that the enacted laws are nothing else than reminders of the life of the ancients, preserving to a later generation their actual words and deeds.

This last phrase is of great importance for my argument. Philo says that the enacted laws — that is to say, the laws given by God to Israel through Moses — may be properly regarded as reminders of the lives of the patriarchs, indeed as nothing else. In other words, if read in accordance with Philo's instruction, the lives of the patriarchs and the laws of Moses turn out to be equivalent. Now, since the lives of the patriarchs embody the law of nature, it follows that the enacted laws of Moses also embody the law of nature. But this implies that the status of the laws of Moses, as copies of the laws of nature, would have remained unclear if not for the fact that the laws of Moses are situated within the context of the lives of the patriarchs and their descendants. Thus, the laws of Moses cannot be reduced to a code. They are expressions of the 'actual words and deeds' of sages.

But this is not all. It is also of the utmost importance to Philo that God gave the laws to Israel through Moses, whose own life is also included in the Pentateuch.[18] Philo wrote not one but two treatises on the life of Moses,

---

Pindar. When Pindar describes law as 'the king of all', Plutarch explains that law rules even a king: 'not law written outside him in books or on wooden tablets or the like, but reason endowed with life within him, always abiding with him and watching over him and never leaving his soul without its leadership.' See *Mor.* 780C. Compare Philo's description of a king in *Mos.* 2.4: 'the king is a living law and the law is a just king.'

[18] See, e.g., Philo's explanation of Moses' description of his own death (*Mos.* 2.291–92): 'But most wonderful of all is the conclusion of the Holy Scriptures, which stands to the whole law-book as the head to the living creature; for when he was already being exalted and stood at the very barrier, ready at the signal to direct his upward flight to heaven, the divine spirit fell upon him and he prophesied with discernment while still alive the story of his own death; told ere the end how the end came; told how he was buried with none present, surely by no mortal hands but by immortal powers; how also he was not laid to rest in the tomb of his forefathers but was given a monument of special dignity which no man has ever seen; how all the nation wept and mourned for him a whole month and made open display, private and public, of their sorrow, in memory of his vast benevolence and watchful care for each one of them and for all. Such, as

and he clearly thought that the laws of Moses could not be fully appreciated without a proper understanding of Moses himself.[19] As Philo sets out to show, Moses is the philosopher-king called for in Plato's *Republic* (*Mos.* 2.2; *Republic* 5.473D). Indeed, using the very terminology applied to the patriarchs, Philo describes Moses as 'a law endowed with life and reason' (*Mos.* 1.162). Again, the point is that Moses is a sage. So his life *is* the law of nature and thus, has the normative force of law.

It follows that, although the Law of Moses certainly includes rules and precepts, it cannot be reduced to a code. The rules must be read as expressions of the virtuous lives of the patriarchs and of Moses. When they are read in this way, Philo claims, one will see that, just as the virtuous lives are themselves the law of nature, so are the rules. Indeed, one might argue that, if one were to abstract the rules from the lives of the sages, in order to form a code, then one would run the risk of obscuring the true significance of the rules.

At this point, one might say that only one aspect of the Philonic paradox has been addressed. The paradox is that Philo regards the Law of Moses as a written copy of the law of nature, but the law of nature is unwritten and so cannot be reduced to a code of rules that could be written down. I have argued that Philo does not regard the Law of Moses as reducible to a code of rules. Instead, the rules have weight insofar as they direct us towards the virtuous life of the sage who has internalized right reason. But it still remains the case, one might say, that the Law of Moses is supposed to be a *written* copy of the law of nature. Why does Philo think it is possible to have a written copy of a law that he himself calls unwritten?

Again, I do not think that this paradox can be entirely removed. But something can be said to illuminate the inner logic of Philo's revolutionary move. Just as the Pentateuch contains rules but is not reducible to a code of rules, so too the Pentateuch is written but is not reducible to a piece of writing. For it must be read within what we might call *an interpretive community*.[20] This is a community which inherits and transmits interpretive traditions — what Philo calls the 'traditions of the fathers' — and which is

---

recorded in the Holy Scriptures, was the life and such the end of Moses, king, lawgiver, high priest, prophet.'

[19] E. R. Goodenough discusses the question of the intended audience for Philo's two essays on Moses in 'Philo's Exposition of the Law and His De Vita Mosis', *HThR* 26 (1933) 109–125. Although I disagree with Goodenough's claim that *De vita Mosis* is written for a gentile audience, I agree that these two essays on Moses should be considered as part of Philo's exposition of the Pentateuch. See also, G. E. Sterling, 'Philo and the Logic of Apologetica: An Analysis of the *Hypothetica*', *SBLSP* (1990) 412–30.

[20] On the concept and development of interpretive community in Christian Ethics see J. Porter, *Natural and Divine Law: Reclaiming the Tradition for Christian Ethics* (Grand Rapids 1999) esp. 212–224; cf. also 187–244, 259–268, 303–318.

also actively engaged in producing new interpretations. Thus Philo says that scripture must be read along with the instruction of a priest or elder, and he says that he himself always combines his own ideas with the traditions he has heard. To abstract the Pentateuch from the life of the interpretive community of Israel, one might argue, would run the risk of obscuring the true significance of the Pentateuch. Indeed, part of the motivation for Philo's authorial productivity may be precisely to make more widely available the interpretive context within which he thinks the Pentateuch should be read, while emphasizing the importance of the Jewish community that provides that context through its interpretive life.

I hope that my emphasis on the intimate linkage between the laws of Moses and the lives of the biblical figures whom Philo considers sages, and on the intimate linkage between the written text of the Pentateuch and the life of the interpretive community of Israel, sheds some light on the inner logic of Philo's revolutionary move. As I have also suggested, however, the paradoxical character of that move cannot be entirely alleviated. Now what must seem paradoxical is the claim that precisely one written text can have exactly this significance, that a written text can be regarded as God's revelation to a community whose life should center around the reading, interpretation and implementation of that text. In short, what must seem paradoxical is the idea of scripture itself. For, although I have argued that neither the rules in the Pentateuch alone nor the writtenness of the Pentateuch alone are sufficient to explain the sense in which Philo thinks the Pentateuch gives us epistemic access to the law of nature, it is still revolutionary with respect to Greek thought to suggest that a written text should play a fundamental role in giving us that access.[21]

University of Notre Dame

---

[21] Many thanks to P. Franks, D. K. O'Connor, J. Porter, G. E. Sterling, J. Strugnell and D. Winston for their helpful suggestions.

UNIVERSALIZING THE PARTICULAR: NATURAL LAW IN SECOND TEMPLE JEWISH ETHICS

GREGORY E. STERLING

One of the features that Graeco-Roman authors noted about Jews was their *diversitas morum*. The observations began with the earliest commentators on the Jews and extended throughout the Hellenistic and Roman periods. Hecataeus of Abdera, whose account of the Jews was essentially positive, wrote that Moses 'established sacrifices quite different from those among other peoples as well as (a different) lifestyle. As a result of his own expulsion (from Egypt) he introduced a certain asocial (ἀπάνθρωπος) and misoxenic (μισόξενος) lifestyle.'[1] Hecataeus' observation became a standard criticism among later Egyptians authors who castigated the Jews at every turn: Apollonius Molon,[2] Lysimachus,[3] and Apion[4] all criticized Mosaic legislation. The practice was not, however, restricted to Egyptian opponents. Greek authors such as Diodorus Siculus,[5] Cassius Dio,[6] and Philostratus[7] all remarked on Jewish μισόξενα νόμιμα. Roman authors also condemned the strange ways of the Jews: Juvenal[8] and Tacitus both found fault with them. The latter summarized the view of pagan elites in the blistering statement: 'the customs of the Jews are ridiculous (*absurdi*) and vulgar (*sordidi*).'[9]

Jewish authors were keenly aware of this perception and attempted to overturn it in numerous ways. They often downplayed the distinctive

---

[1] Diodorus Siculus 40.3.4. For text and commentary see M. Stern, *Greek and Latin Authors on Jews and Judaism*, 3 vols. (Jerusalem 1974–84) 1:26–35, §11 (hereafter abbreviated *GLAJJ*). Ethnographers typically gave aetiological explanations, as Hecataeus does here.
[2] Josephus, *c. Ap.* 2.145. Cf. also 2.148 (*GLAJJ* 1:154–55, §49).
[3] Josephus, *c. Ap.* 2.145 (*GLAJJ* 1:387, §161).
[4] Josephus, *c. Ap.* 2.125 (*GLAJJ* 1:414, §174).
[5] Diodorus Siculus 34–35.1.2; 34–35.1.4 (*GLAJJ* 1:182–83, §63).
[6] Cassius Dio 37.17.2 (*GLAJJ* 2:349–53, §406).
[7] Philostratus, *Vit. Apoll.* 5.33 (*GLAJJ* 2:340–42, §403).
[8] Juvenal, *Sat.* 14.96–106 (*GLAJJ* 2:102–07, §301).
[9] Tacitus, *Hist.* 5.4.1–5.5, esp. 5.5.5 (*GLAJJ* 2:17–63, esp. 18–19, 25–27, §281). For summary accounts of these criticisms see J. N. Sevenster, *The Roots of Pagan Anti-Semitism in the Ancient World*, NovTSup 41 (Leiden 1975) 89–144 and L. H. Feldman, *Jew and Gentile in the Ancient World: Attitudes and Interactions from Alexander to Justinian* (Princeton 1993) 123–76.

features of Jewish mores,[10] used an *interpretatio Graeca* to present their customs,[11] or, more specifically, defended their legislation by appealing to reason.[12] The last of these raises the question of the use of natural law among Jews of the Second Temple period. Did Jewish authors identify Jewish laws with natural law in an attempt to win respectability for Mosaic legislation? The obvious place to begin trying to answer this question would be to examine the works of authors who are openly indebted to philosophy, e.g., Aristobulus, Philo of Alexandria, Wisdom of Solomon, 4 Maccabees. Several of these authors make unambiguous use of natural law.[13] I would, however, like to explore a set of common ethical traditions that are attested by three different Jewish authors. These traditions permit us to ask whether there was a popular perception of natural law among Jews of this period, and, by extension, among those to whom they made their case.

A Common Ethical Tradition

We begin with the question of whether there was a common ethical tradition among Diaspora Jews of the Second Temple period. There are three epitomes of the law that have a number of striking similarities. Eusebius of Caesarea was the first to notice the agreements between the summary of the law in Philo's *Hypothetica* and Josephus' *Contra Apionem*. The similarities led him to juxtapose their two summaries of Mosaic legislation and to introduce the Josephan text with these words: 'Philo wrote the preceding. Josephus narrated an account similar to his in the second book of his work *Concerning the Antiquity of the Jews*.'[14] Modern scholars have concurred with the bishop's judgment and added a third work to the comparison: the maxims of Pseudo-Phocylides.[15]

Philo's epitome appears in his enigmatic *Hypothetica*, a work that I have argued was composed in the context of the pogrom in Alexandria and Philo's preparations to lead the Jewish embassy to Rome.[16] The summary

---

[10] In contrast to the *halakhot* among the Dead Sea Scrolls, there is relatively little material emphasizing purity concerns among the summaries of the law found in Diaspora authors.
[11] E.g., Pseudo-Phocylides recast the laws as sapiential instruction from a well known Greek figure.
[12] E.g., Pseudo-Aristeas.
[13] E.g., see the essay of Hindy Najman on Philo of Alexandria. in this volume
[14] Eusebius, *Praep. ev.* 8.7.21.
[15] The most important recent discussion of this material is K.-W. Niebuhr, *Gesetz und Paränese: Katechismusartige Weisungsreihen in der frühjüdischen Literatur*, WUNT 2.28 (Tübingen 1987) 6–72, esp. 31–72.
[16] G. E. Sterling, 'Philo and the Logic of Apologetics: An Analysis of the *Hypothetica*',

appears in the first of the two fragments that Eusebius has preserved of the work.[17] The laws fall into two bodies of material: the epitome proper and a treatment of the Sabbath.[18] Philo organized the epitome proper into five groups of laws that are set apart through transitional phrases.[19] The first lists twelve capital case laws.[20] The second also lists capital offenses but expands the form to include both case laws and apodictic laws articulated by (negated) infinitives.[21] The basic structure of this unit is a household code.[22] The third group contains 'unwritten customs and practices' as well as written laws. It consists almost entirely of negated infinitives and lacks any reference to penalties.[23] The most dominant aspect of this unit is the presence of the laws of Buzyges (on which see below). The fourth and fifth groups both contain two negated infinitives each and like the third do not list penalties, except for a final threat.[24]

There appear to be several criteria for the structure of this law code. The larger organization of the laws into five groups could reflect the structure of the Pentateuch. At least this became a common practice attested by a range of material: the Psalter and the *Megillot* in the OT; *1 Enoch* among the pseudepigrapha; Matthew's discourses in the NT; and *Pirqe 'Aboth* among later rabbinic sources. Unfortunately, our excerpt does not provide any explicit connection between the Pentateuch and the summary. We should also note that the five units do not correspond to the Pentateuch. It is possible that an explicit point of comparison was made in the text which Eusebius has not preserved, although it is unlikely that the bishop would have omitted such a reference. On the other hand, we should note that the other examples of this pattern also lack explicit comparisons. It is difficult for me to believe that a commentator like Philo would not have recognized the analogy. If we turn to the subunits within the epitome we find that Philo has grouped laws on the basis of the penalty, the form of the law (case law or [negated] infinitive), the source, and thematic concerns. Beyond these formal observations, it is difficult to find a pattern.[25]

SBLSP (1990) 412–30.

[17] Eusebius, *Praep. ev.* 8.6.1–7.20 and 8.11.1–18.

[18] Eusebius, *Praep. ev.* 8.7.1–9 and 8.7.10–20, esp. 11–14, respectively.

[19] Eusebius, *Praep. ev.* 8.7.1, 3, 6, 8, 9.

[20] Eusebius, *Praep. ev.* 8.7.1–2. Note that there are two subunits, each set off by a statement of the penalty (§§1, 2).

[21] Eusebius, *Praep. ev.* 8.7.3–4. The infinitives are in § 3 and the case laws in § 4. As with the first group, the penalty is stated at the end of each subunit.

[22] On the code in this text see J. E. Crouch, *The Origin and Intention of the Colossian Haustafel*, FRLNT 109 (Göttingen 1972).

[23] Eusebius, *Praep. ev.* 8.7.6–8a. Only two of the infinitives are positive.

[24] Eusebius, *Praep. ev.* 8.7.8b, 9.

[25] For details on this code see my forthcoming *Philo of Alexandria,* Hypothetica, *Philo*

Eusebius must have been struck by the similar contents of Josephus' code.[26] Josephus' description of the law in *Contra Apionem* shares twenty-one laws in common with Philo's *Hypothetica* or 60% of the laws in Philo's epitome, a significant percentage of agreement. At times this agreement extends beyond the concept to include sequence. Sometimes the two concur in incorporating laws that are unattested in the Torah, e.g., the laws of Buzyges (§ 211). The most impressive agreements are in the section detailing the penalty for violating the law (§§ 215–17). The common assignment of capital penalties to infractions against the law that the same writers do not elsewhere consider to be capital crimes is noteworthy (see below).

The two codes differ principally in form. Josephus has attempted to offer a systematic summary. Like Philo, he appears to use five editorial frames for his sections. Unlike the rather vague headings in Philo, he explicitly states the theme of the following laws in the frame.[27] He arranged the sequence of his units to reflect systematic thought: God (§§ 190–98), marriage (§§ 199–208), foreigners (§§ 209–10), kindness (§§ 211–14), and the penalties (§§ 215–17) and rewards (§§ 218–19) of violating or keeping the law. The fivefold nature of this arrangement is less clear than it is in Philo. This is due to the fact that Josephus created subunits within the larger units which he also introduces with some type of generalizing observation.[28] This is part of his effort to be systematic. Josephus does, however, imitate the sequence of the Pentateuch in his final unit by placing the penalties and rewards in the same position as Deuteronomy. The historian also differs from Philo by describing the laws rather than listing them. He does not give a series of infinitives functioning as imperatives or case laws; rather, he tends either to offer a description of Jewish beliefs in the indicative or to cast the laws in *oratio obliqua*.

Pseudo-Phocylides differs from both his fellow Alexandrian and the historian in Rome. Unlike Philo and Josephus, he did not compose a summary of the laws in a polemical setting but offered sapiential instruction to the Jewish community.[29] The teacher transformed the laws of the

---

of Alexandria Commentary Series (Leiden).
[26] The entire account of the Jewish constitution is in *c. Ap.* 2.145–219; however, the summary proper is in 2.190–219. On the *Contra Apionem* see L. Feldman and J. R. Levison (edd.), *Josephus' Contra Apionem: Studies in its Character and Context with a Latin Concordance to the Portion Missing in Greek,* AGJU 34 (Leiden 1996).
[27] Josephus, *c. Ap.* 2.190, 199, 209, 211, 215.
[28] Josephus, *c. Ap.* 2.193, 205, 217. I consider these secondary units since Josephus either returns to the announced main theme after these units or alludes to the main theme suggesting that these are subordinate units in a larger unit.
[29] On Pseudo-Phocylides see P. W. van der Horst, *The Sentences of Pseudo-Phocylides: With Introduction and Commentary,* SVTP 4 (Leiden 1978); idem, 'Pseudo-Phocylides',

Pentateuch into proverbial sayings. The result is that the 230 lines of Pseudo-Phocylides' hexameter present Jewish ethics in a form that would have been acceptable to 'any right-minded man in antiquity' — as Pieter van der Horst put it so poignantly.[30] Like Josephus, this author appears to have organized the material thematically, although less systematically.[31] The result is that there is little agreement in the sequence of the topics between the two. There are, however, a number of laws that are shared in common among all three authors: Pseudo-Phocylides has fifteen laws in common with Philo and seventeen with Josephus. The three share thirteen laws or thirty-four percent of Philo's code, together.

How should we explain the similarities and dissimilarities? I have set the common material out in a chart to help us clarify the specific details. The chart lists material that is common to at least two of the three authors. I assume that there was other material that was common property, but for the purpose of our investigation only the common material will be examined. I have also listed the texts from the Torah upon which the law is based. It is not always evident that the author is drawing directly from the biblical text; in some cases the biblical text may only serve as inspiration for a formulation that is quite different. While we might be tempted to restrict common material to laws that have no basis in the Torah since authors could draw from the biblical text independently, this would be too restrictive. Most — although by no means all — laws in Second Temple summaries or *halakhot* were based on Torah legislation: the issue is selection not dependence on the biblical text.

OTP 2:565–82; M. Küchler, *Frühjüdische Weisheitstraditionen: Zum Fortgang weisheitlichen Denkens im Bereich des frühjüdischen Jahweglaubens*, OBO 26 (Freiburg/Göttingen 1979); and W. T. Wilson, *The Mysteries of Righteousness: The Literary Compoosition and Genre of the Sentences of Pseudo-Phocylides*, TSAJ 40 (Tübingen 1994). On the ethics in Pseudo-Phocylides see J. J. Collins, *Between Athens and Jerusalem: Jewish Identity in the Hellenistic Diaspora*, The Biblical Resource Series (Grand Rapids 2000²) 168–74.

[30] Van der Horst, *The Sentences of Pseudo-Phocylides*, 64.

[31] I see the following clusters: 9–21, justice; 22–30, generosity; 42–47, money; 48–50, integrity; 59–69b, moderation; 70–75, envy; 97–121, death; 122–31, speech; 132–52, avoidance of evil; 153–74, work; 175–206, marriage; 207–17, children; 218–27, larger family unit. Wilson, *The Mysteries of Righteousness*, argues for a more formal structure. He suggests that vv. 9–131 are structured on the basis of the cardinal virtues (75–118): 9–54, justice; 55–96, moderation; 97–121, courage; and 122–31, wisdom. It is, however, difficult to see how all of the material subsumed under these virtues fits.

COMMON ETHICAL INSTRUCTION IN GREEK-SPEAKING JUDAISM

Law	Biblical Text	Philo, Hypoth. 7	Josephus, c. Ap. 2	Ps.-Phocylides
Sexual Offenses				
Sex in Marriage for Procreation Only			199	189
Homosexuality	Lev 20:13 (cf. 18:22)	1	199, 215	3, 190–92, 213–14
Adultery	Lev 20:10; Deut 22:22	1	199, 201, 215	3, 177–83
Rape	Deut 22:22–29	1	200, 201, 215	198
Violations of Person and Property				
Abuse of Slave	Exod 21:20–27	2	215	225–26
Theft	Exod 20:15//Deut 5:19 (cf. Lev 19:11, 13)	2	216	6, cf. also 18
Impiety against God, Parent, Benefactor	Lev 24:15–16	2	217	(80)
Haustafel				
Wife Subordinate to Husband	Gen 3:16	3	201	
Parents Govern Children/	Deut 21:18–21	3		207–09
Honor Parents	Exod 20:12//Deut 5:16		206, cf. 217	8
Honor of Elders	Lev 19:32		206	220–22
Property Rights				
Do not take what you have not deposited		6	208, cf. 216	
Theft	Lev 19:11, 13 (cf. Exod 20:15//Deut 5:19)	6	208, cf. 216	18, cf. also 6
Care for Others/ Laws of Buzyges				
Do not deny Fire		6	211	
Do not deny Water		6	211	
Give Food to Poor and Indigent	Lev 25:35	6	211	22–30, 109
Burial Practices / Laws of Buzyges				
Do not Deny Burial		7	211	99
Do not Disturb Graves		7		100–01

Human Reproduction				
Do not Sterilize Men		7		187
Abortion	Exod 21:21–22 (LXX)	7	202	184
Infanticide			202	185
Sex with Pregnant Wife			202	186
Do not Mistreat Animals		7	213	
Economic Honesty				
Unjust Scales	Lev 19:36 (cf. Deut 25:13, 15)	8	216	15
False Standards of Measurement	Lev 19:35 (cf. Deut 25:14)	8	216	14
Do not Divulge Secrets of a Friend		8	207	
Treatment of Animals				
Do not Empty a Nest	Deut 22:6	9	213	84–85
Do not Reject Pleas of an Animal	Deut 22:1–2	9	213	

The most impressive finding of this exercise is the presence of clusters of laws, i.e., a group of laws that appear together — occasionally even in the same sequence — in several of the texts. By cluster I mean a group of laws that have a common thematic unity. I have used two criteria in determining a cluster: first, several distinct laws must appear in relatively close proximity to one another not scattered in various places; and second, the collection of these laws in close proximity must occur in at least two of the three authors. I find nine such clusters. The first cluster contains laws dealing with sexuality: homosexuality,[32] adultery,[33] and rape.[34] It is possible that we could add a fourth, the restriction of sexuality to marriage for the purpose of procreation, although the meaning of the line in Pseudo-Phocylides is ambiguous.[35] The second cluster addresses violations of a person or her or his property: abuse of a slave,[36] theft,[37] and impiety.[38] The agreements between Philo and Josephus in the first two sections are particularly striking, although they do not have the same sequence. The third section is a household code: husband wife relationships,[39] parents and

---

[32] Philo, *Hypoth.* 8.7.1; Josephus, *c. Ap.* 2.199, 201, 215; Pseudo-Phocylides 3, 190–92.
[33] Philo, *Hypoth.* 8.7.1; Josephus, *c. Ap.* 2.199, 201, 215; Pseudo-Phocylides 3, 177–83.
[34] Philo, *Hypoth.* 8.7.1; Josephus, *c. Ap.* 2.200, 215; Pseudo-Phocylides 198.
[35] Josephus, *c. Ap.* 2.199; Pseudo-Phocylides 189.
[36] Philo, *Hypoth.* 8.7.2; Josephus, *c. Ap.* 2.215; Pseudo-Phocylides 225–226.
[37] Philo, *Hypoth.* 8.7.2; Josephus, *c. Ap.* 2.216; Pseudo-Phocylides 6.
[38] Philo, *Hypoth.* 8.7.2; Josephus, *c. Ap.* 2.217.
[39] Philo, *Hypoth.* 8.7.3; Josephus, *c. Ap.* 2.201.

children relationships,⁴⁰ and the honored place of elders.⁴¹ Although there are variations in the details, all three insist on ranking the honor of parents immediately after the honor of God.⁴² The fourth cluster presents laws that prohibit the mistreatment of others: do not take up what you have not deposited⁴³ and do not steal.⁴⁴ The fifth extends the fourth by including positive exhortations: do not deny fire and water,⁴⁵ but give food to those in need.⁴⁶ The sixth deals with burial customs: do not deny burial⁴⁷ and do not disturb a grave.⁴⁸ The fifth and sixth clusters combine three of the four concerns of Buzyges, the Athenian hero who pronounced curses on those who refused to provide fire, water, proper directions, or burial to the dead.⁴⁹ The seventh addresses issues relating to human reproduction: sterilization of males,⁵⁰ abortion,⁵¹ infanticide,⁵² and sexual intercourse with pregnant wives.⁵³ The eighth covers matters of economic honesty: unjust scales and standards of measurement.⁵⁴ The ninth expands the scope to include the humane treatment of animals in an argument *a minore ad majus*, i.e., if we treat animals with kindness, we will certainly treat humans well.⁵⁵ The specific laws include the prohibitions against emptying a nest⁵⁶ and

---

[40] Philo, *Hypoth.* 8.7.3; Josephus, *c. Ap.* 2.206; Pseudo-Phocylides 207–09, 8.
[41] Josephus, *c. Ap.* 2.206; Pseudo-Phocylides 220–22. This is an extension of the honor of parents.
[42] Philo, *Hypoth.* 8.7.2; Josephus, *c. Ap.* 2.206; Pseudo-Phocylides 8.
[43] Philo, *Hypoth.* 8.7.6; Josephus, *c. Ap.* 2.208,; cf. also 216.
[44] Philo, *Hypoth.* 8.7.6; Josephus, *c. Ap.* 2.208 (cf. also 216); Pseudo-Phocylides 18.
[45] Philo, *Hypoth.* 8.7.6; Josephus, *c. Ap.A* 2.211.
[46] Philo, *Hypoth.* 8.7.6; Josephus, *c. Ap.* 2.211; Pseudo-Phocylides 22–30, 109.
[47] Philo, *Hypoth.* 8.7.7; Josephus, *c. Ap.* 2.211; Pseudo-Phocylides 99.
[48] Philo, *Hypoth.* 8.7.7; Pseudo-Phocylides 100–01.
[49] Philo, *Hypoth.* 8.7.8, mentions Buzyges. For details see J. Bernays, 'Philon's Hypothetika und die Verwunschungen des Buzyges in Athen', *Monatsberichte des Kgl. Akademie der Wissenschaften zu Berlin* (1876) 589–609; reprinted in H. Usener (ed.), *Gesammelte Abhandlungen* (Berlin 1885) 1:262–82, esp. 277–82.
[50] Philo, *Hypoth.* 8.7.7; Pseudo-Phocylides 187.
[51] Philo, *Hypoth.* 8.7.7; Josephus, *c. Ap.* 2.202; Pseudo-Phocylides 184.
[52] Josephus, *c. Ap.* 2.202; Pseudo-Phocylides 185.
[53] Josephus, *c. Ap.* 2.202; Pseudo-Phocylides 186 (?). Philo and Josephus both mention the mistreatment of animals as well, although the specifics of their reference are opaque (Philo, *Hypoth.* 8.7.7; Josephus, c. *Ap.* 2.216).
[54] The three authors use different terms: Philo, *Hypoth.* 8.7.8, ζυγόν, χοῖνιξ, νόμισμα; Josephus, *c. Ap.* 2.216, μέτρον, σταθμός,; Pseudo-Phocylides 14–15, σταθμός, μέτρον. Philo and Josephus both have warnings against disclosing a friend's secrets, but this is in a different place in Josephus. I have noted it in the chart, but omitted it here.
[55] A. Terian, 'Some Stock Arguments for the Magnanimity of the Law in Hellenistic Jewish Apologetics', in B. S. Jackson (ed.). *Jewish Law Association Studies 1: The Touro Conference Volume* (Chico, California 1985) 141–49, demonstrates the function of the argument.
[56] Philo, *Hypoth.* 8.7.9; Josephus, *c. Ap.* 2.213; Pseudo-Phocylides 84–85.

rejecting the pleas of an animal.⁵⁷ We can summarize the clusters in the following chart:

Concept	*Hypothetica*	*Contra Apionem* 2	Pseudo-Phocylides
Sexual Offenses	1	215	3
Violations of Others	2	215–17	
Household Code	2–3	217	175–227
Mistreatment of Others	6	216	
Care for Others	6	211	
Burial Customs	7		99–101
Human Reproduction	7	202	184–87
Economic Honesty	8	216	14–15
Treatment of Animals	9	213	84–85

How should we explain these clusters? In some cases the grouping is due to the proximity of the laws within the Pentateuch;⁵⁸ however, in other cases this can not be true.⁵⁹ In some instances, the common element has nothing to do with the biblical text. For example, a household code and the Athenian traditions about Buzyges shaped some clusters. Thus the biblical text is a source for all three but is not a sufficient cause to explain the clusters as they have come down to us. Another possibility is that there was some literary relationship among the texts. Did Josephus use Philo here as he did elsewhere?⁶⁰ This has a degree of plausibility since the two have a significant amount of agreement. There are, however, two serious difficulties with this explanation: it does not explain the significant differences between the two and, more importantly, fails to account for the presence of a great deal of the same material in Pseudo-Phocylides. Perhaps all three drew from a common source. This might have been written⁶¹ or oral?⁶² While a written source is possible, the disparities among the texts

---

⁵⁷ Philo, *Hypoth.* 8.7.9; Josephus, *c. Ap.* 2.213.
⁵⁸ E.g., Unjust scales and weights in Lev 19:36, 35 and Deut 25:13–14.
⁵⁹ E.g., the laws of kindness, some of which have no basis in Torah. This is probably also true for the sexual laws which draw on different texts.
⁶⁰ This was primarily the view of an earlier generation of scholars, e.g., P. Wendland, *Die Therapeuten und die philonische Schrift vom beschaulichen Leben*, Neue Jahrbuch für classische Philologie Supplementband 22 (Leipzig 1896) 709–13, who thought that Josephus knew both Philo and another source; B. Motzo, 'Le Ὑποθετικά de Filone', *Reale academia delle scienze di Torino* 47 (1911–12) 562; S. Belkin, 'The Alexandrian Source for *Contra Apionem* II', *JQR* 27 (1936–37) 23–31; and idem, *The Alexandrian Halakhah in Apologetic Literature of the First Century C. E.* (Philadelphia, n.d.) 29–37.
⁶¹ Important representatives of this position are I. Lévy, *Recherches Esséniennes et Pythagoriciennes*, Hautes études du monde gréco-romain 1 (Genéve/Paris 1965) 51–56 and Küchler, *Frühjüdische Weisheitstraditionen*, 221–23.
⁶² Important advocates of this view are Niebuhr, *Gesetz und Paränese*, 43 and G. P.

are difficult to explain on this basis. I am inclined therefore to think that all three knew common oral traditions. In particular, I think that all three drew from (a) common tradition(s) of ethical instruction. We can identify the broad outline of this instruction through the clusters that we have noted. The nine clusters that we have identified represent standards themes of ethical instruction in Second Temple Judaism. I do not want to suggest that these would exhaust ethical instruction; rather, I propose that these were common ethical topoi held in common by many Jews in the Diaspora.

The *Sitz im Leben* for this instruction is more difficult to define. Some have thought that it was catechetical.[63] Others have thought that we should associate it with synagogue instruction.[64] The latter is the most likely since both Philo and Josephus associate this material with their observations on the Sabbath which they present as an occasion for instruction in the law.[65] If these observations are correct, we have evidence for a common body of ethical instruction in Alexandria and Rome. It would be possible to extend the geographical spread by comparing some of this material with other Diaspora texts.[66]

Natural Law and Mosaic Ethics

We are now in a position to explore the concerns that determined the development of this ethical instruction. I am convinced that there were several. In a related article I have suggested that there are several biblical texts that served as the central bases for ethical instruction in these texts and in the *halakhot* at Qumran, in particular, Leviticus 19, 20, and Deuteronomy 22.[67] As important as these texts were for ethical instruction, they were by no means the only controlling factor. Did the concept of natural law as it is attested among later Stoic authors exert any influence? At first glance, this seems improbable; however, there are several areas where the Stoic understanding of the universal law may have influenced the way in which Jews attempted to present their ethical codes. We will examine three possibilities.

Carras, 'Dependence or Common Tradition in Philo *Hypothetica* VIII.6.10–7.20 and Josephus *Contra Apionem* 2.190–219', *SPhA* 5 (1993) 24–47, esp. 47.
[63] G. Klein, *Der älteste Katechismus und die jüdische Propaganda-Literatur* (Berlin 1909).
[64] Niebuhr, *Gesetz und Paränese*, 65–66 and Collins, *Between Athens and Jerusalem*, 170–71.
[65] Philo, *Hypoth.* 8.7.10–20; Josephus, *c. Ap.* 2.171–78.
[66] Collins, *Between Athens and Jerusalem*, 155–85, compares *Sib Or* 3, 5, 4; Ps.-Phocylides; and *T. 12 Patr.*
[67] G. E. Sterling, 'Was there a Common Ethic in Second Temple Judaism?' *Sapiential Literature at Qumran, Orion Center Conference* (provisional title) (Leiden, forthcoming).

Ideal Codes. The Stoics thought that there were two communities. Seneca put it this way: 'Let us grasp in our minds that there are two communities: the one great and truly common in which gods and humans are included, where we neither look to this corner nor that but measure the limits of our state by the sun; the other to which the accident of our birth has assigned us.'[68] Corresponding to these two communities are two laws: a universal law and specific civil codes. Cicero stated the limitations of civil codes at the outset of his *Laws*: 'we must grasp in this investigation the full basis of universal justice and law in such a way that this civil (code), as we call it, will be limited to a small and narrow place.'[69] The law of the larger community is 'highest reason planted in nature which commands those things which should be done and forbids the opposites. This reason, when it is fixed and established in the human mind, is law.'[70] Since humans and gods have reason in common, they also have law in common. Reason is 'the first common property (*societas*) of humanity with god. Among those in whom there is reason, among these right reason is common. Since it is law, we must consider that humans have law in common with the gods.'[71] The Stoics thought that the gap which existed between reason and specific legislative codes of ethnic or political groups was unbridgeable. The Stoic ideal was to live on the basis of the universal law. Plutarch thought that this was the goal of Zeno's *Republic*: 'We should not live on the basis of cities and demes, each set off by its own system of justice, but we should consider all people to be demesmen and fellow citizens. There should be one lifestyle and structure like a herd grazing together and nourished by a universal law (νόμος κοινός).'[72] In this way the Stoics — or the Stoic sages — lived in harmony with nature.[73]

---

[68] Seneca, *De otio* 4.1. Cf. also Arius Didymus in Eusebius, *Praep. ev.* 15.15.3–5 (*SVF* 2.528 and *HP* 67C): 'The world is called the residence of the gods and humans ... and the composite of the things created for them. For just as polis has a double meaning, one as residence and the other as the composite of those who live there with the citizens, so this world is like a city consisting of gods and humans — the gods exercise leadership and humans are subjects. There is a partnership with each other because they participate in reason which is natural law (φύσει νόμος). Everything else is created for these.' Cf. also Aristo in Plutarch, *Exil.* 600E (*SVF* 2.472; *HP* 67H). Some Epicureans held similar views, e.g., Diogenes of Oenoanda 25.2.3–11 (*HP* 22P). *HP*=A. A. Long and D. N. Sedley, *The Hellenistic Philosophers*, 2 vols. (Cambridge 1987).
[69] Cicero, *Leg.* 1.17. Cf. also 1.19.
[70] Cicero, *Leg.* 1.18. Cf. also *Resp.* 3.33.
[71] Cicero, *Leg.* 1.23.
[72] Plutarch, *Alex. fort.* 329A–B (*SVF* 1.262; *HP* 67A). On Zeno's *Republic* see P. A. Vander Waerdt, 'Zeno's *Republic* and the Origins of Natural Law', P. A. Vander Waerdt (ed.), *The Socratic Movement* (Ithaca 1994) 272–308, esp. 290, where he summarizes his understanding of Zeno's *Republic* as an attempt to depict the life of Stoic sages.
[73] For a collection of the various Stoic articulations of the telos see Arius Didymus 6a

Some of these concepts were enticing to Jews who believed that their legislation was the law of God and immutable.[74] At the conclusion of his epitome of the Jewish law, Josephus contrasted the Jewish code with Greek attempts to write ideal codes. 'Suppose that our nation were not known to all humanity and our voluntary obedience to the laws were not an obvious reality.' He continues: 'Suppose that someone read (a lecture) to the Greeks claiming that he had invented or that outside the known world he had met people who held such a lofty view of God and who had reliably followed such laws for a great period of time. I think that all would be amazed because of the continual changes among themselves.' The vicissitudes of life and legislation became the basis for widespread critique of those who had tried to write such accounts: 'In fact, they accuse those who have attempted to write something similar in its constitution and laws as having invented the amazing, stating that they are operating on impossible premises.' The 'impossible premises' may be an allusion to Plato's recognition that the pattern of the ideal city is laid up in heaven and may never be realized on earth.[75] Whether Josephus knew the famous 'city in speech' allusion or a subsequent version of the same position, he went on to offer Plato's *Republic* as his parade example of a failed attempt to depict the ideal law.[76] It is clear that Josephus would like for us to believe that although the *Republics* of Plato, Zeno, Chrysippus, and Cicero had failed to bring the 'pattern laid up in heaven' down to earth, Moses had. Since we do not have similar statements from Philo or Pseudo-Phocylides in connection with this code, we can not claim that Josephus' statement is part of the tradition. It demonstrates how the Jewish historian appropriated the tradition. Did he do this on the basis of concerns *external* to the common ethical material or were there elements *internal* to the common ethical code that suggested this to him?

Severe Penalties. We can answer this only by examining some specific cases. As we noted above, both Philo and Josephus emphasized the severity of the penalties for violating the Jewish code. Philo opened his account with a comparative statement: 'Do we find any of these things or something similar to them among the former (i.e., the Jews), anything that seems to be soft or lenient, that leads to trials, pleas, delays, assessments (rather than capital punishments), or plea-bargains?' He answers; 'None at

---

(Stobaeus 2.7.6a). I have used the edition of A. J. Pomeroy, *Arius Didymus, Epitome of Stoic Ethics*, SBLTT 44/SBLGR 14 (Atlanta 1999).
[74] On this see M. Limbeck, *Die Ordnung des Heils: Zum Gesetzesverständnis des Frühjudentums* (Düsseldorf 1971).
[75] Plato, *Resp.* 592B.
[76] Josephus, *c. Ap.* 2.220–24.

all. Everything is clear and simple.'[77] The question presumes another body of legal material to which Philo contrasts Jewish legislation. The context of the *Hypothetica* suggests that the other legislation consists of Greek codes. His point is that Moses did not permit the circumvention of justice through judicial procedures; he set out clear and severe penalties. Philo demonstrated this by grouping capital offenses in the first two of his five subunits and mentioning the capital penalty again in the course of the third subunit. He concluded his epitome with a similar statement: 'Perhaps you would say that these matters (i.e., the laws relating to animals in the fifth subunit) are inconsequential; however, the law that governs them is great and demands complete attention. The proclamations and the curses that threaten annihilation are great. God is himself the guardian of such matters and the omnipresent avenger.'[78] The emphasis on the severity of the penalties is not unique to Philo. Josephus shared the same perspective; only he put it tersely and bluntly: 'Death is the penalty for most transgressions.'[79]

I find these statements curious. A number of the laws are capital offenses in the biblical text; however, some are not.[80] Further, the same authors do not present these as capital offenses in the other texts where they address them. For example, Philo does not think that theft is a capital offense in *De specialibus legibus* unless it is kidnapping.[81] Why is he so stringent here? The best explanation is that he is following a tradition.[82] This, however, only backs the question up one step: why is the tradition more severe than the biblical text?

Several answers have been offered. Isaak Heinemann thought that this was an extrapolation of the death penalty that Philo attached to violations of the first five laws of the Decalogue.[83] The difficulty with this position is that the laws in the code cover more than the first five laws, even if we

---

[77] Philo in Eusebius, *Praep. ev.* 8.7.1.
[78] Philo, *Hypoth.* 8.7.9.
[79] Josephus, *c. Ap.* 2.215.
[80] If we examine the biblical bases for the laws in the first two clusters where Philo assigns the death penalty, we find that only half of the laws mandate a capital punishment. The other half either offer various penalties or do not envision the death penalty: Deut 22:22-29, stipulates the death penalty for most rapists, but not for all (vv. 28-29); Exod 21:20-27, offers various penalties for the abuse of a slave but rarely envisions a capital offense; Exod 20:15//Deut 5:19; Lev 19:11, 13, do not require the death penalty for theft.
[81] Philo, *Spec.* 4.1-40. For kidnapping see §§ 13-19.
[82] L. Cohn wondered whether this might argue for the inauthenticity of the treatise. See I. Heinemann, *Philons griechische und jüdische Bildung: Kulturvergleichende Untersuchungen zu Philons Darstellung der jüdischen Gesetze* (Hildesheim 1962) 353.
[83] Philo, *Spec.* 2.242-56, esp. 242-43. See Heinemann, *Philons Griechische und jüdische Bildung*, 353-58.

view the five as headings. Arthur Darby Nock made a more helpful suggestion: the severity is a Jewish attempt to make the penalties as stringent as those of the Stoics.[84] I would like to expand his suggestion by considering two possibilities. First, the Stoics insisted on justice. Arius Didymus summarized their perspective: 'They say that the good person is not lenient (ἐπιεικής). For the lenient can be persuaded to back off from a just penalty. It is the quality of such a person to be lenient and to suppose that the penalties stipulated by the law for the unjust are too severe and to think that the legislator has distributed penalties that are not proportionate.'[85] It could be that the Jewish moralists imitated this severity. There is, however, a second possibility. Since natural law was innate, it was essential to humanity. The penalties are therefore severe and inexorable. Cicero explained: 'The one who will not submit, will flee himself. Having rejected human nature, he will pay the greatest penalties, even if he escapes other punishments which are assessed.'[86] Thus, even if someone is able to escape human justice, he or she can not avoid the divine justice which is associated with the law of nature. Which of the two served as a background for the claims in Philo and Josephus? The lacunose nature of the epitomes makes certainty impossible. Since the former dealt with civil penalties and the Jewish law does as well, we might be inclined to think that it constitutes the intellectual framework: there is no equivocation of justice. This does not, however, explain the severity of the punishments. One can refuse to equivocate without requiring a death penalty: justice requires a sense of proportion between crime and penalty, not a severe penalty. For this reason I am inclined to think that the severity of the penalties was in some way due to a violation of immutable divine law. Philo hints at this in his final comment: 'God is himself the guardian of such matters and the omnipresent avenger.'[87] Violation of Mosaic legislation is not the mere misstep of a civil code, but a violation of the divine code. It is not necessary to equate divine law with natural law to reach this conclusion; Jewish authors might have made this point independent of dependence on natural law based on their own belief in the sovereignty of God. However, the similarity in reasoning between the statements in Philo and Cicero suggests that Jewish authors made their point — at least Philo — under the influence of natural law.

---

[84] A. D. Nock, 'Philo and Hellenistic Philosophy: Review of Colson, *Philo IX*', *CR* 57 (1943) 77-81; reprinted in Z. Stewart (ed.), *Arthur Darby Nock: Essays on Religion and the Ancient World*, 2 vols. (Cambridge, Massachusetts 1972) 2:559-65, esp. 563. Nock cited Horace, *Sat*. 1.3, as an example of the critique of Stoic severity.
[85] Arius Didymus 2.7.11d (*SVF* 3.640).
[86] Cicero, *Resp*. 3.33 (*SVF* 3.314; *HP* 67S).
[87] Philo, *Hypoth*. 8.7.9.

Homosexuality. There is at least one case where the connection with natural law is explicit. Pseudo-Phocylides recast the prohibition of homosexual relations into the following dactylic hexameters: 'Do not transgress the natural limits of sexuality for unlawful Cypris./ For sex between male and male does not please even animals./ And do not let women imitate the sexual role of the male.'[88] Here there can be little doubt that the pseudonymous Jewish poet has used natural law to explain a biblical prohibition, even if his zoology is deficient. While there are some similar critiques in the philosophical tradition[89] and among Roman authors,[90] it is a commonplace among Second Temple Jewish authors: *The Testaments of the Twelve Patriarchs*,[91] the *Sibylline Oracles*,[92] and Paul all make the same connection.[93] Philo also condemned homosexuality on the basis of natural law, but not in the *Hypothetica*. He described the actions of the residents of Sodom in these words: 'Unable to endure the satiety of such (good things), they became unruly like cattle and shook off the law of nature (τὸν τῆς φύσεως νόμον) from their necks, pursuing large quantities of unmixed drinks, dainty foods, and unlawful intercourse.' He then explains the last of these: 'For not only do they destroy the marriages of others in their mad lust for women, but even though they are men they mount males with no respect for the common nature, (joining) active partners with passive partners.'[94] This widespread attestation suggests that popular Jewish ethical instruction did make some use of natural law.

Conclusion

We may now return to our initial question: Did Second Temple Jews use natural law in popular ethical instruction? The evidence that we have collected makes our answer ambiguous. On the one hand, it is clear that Jewish authors such as Philo, Josephus, and Pseudo-Phocylides all made connections between ethical instruction and natural law. On the other hand, the evidence that we have examined reflects the views of each author on a

---

[88] Pseudo-Phocylides 190–92.
[89] Plato, *Leg.* 636C; Musonius Rufus 12; Plutarch, *Brut. an.* 990E–F. On homosexuality in the Greek world see K. J. Dover, *Greek Homosexuality* (Cambridge, Massachusetts 1978).
[90] Nepos, *Alcibiades* 2.2–3 and Tacitus, *Ann.* 14.20. Cf. also Livy 34.4.1–4.
[91] *T. Naph.* 3.4.
[92] *Sib. Or.* 5.430.
[93] Rom 1:26–27. On Paul see the analysis and bibliography in W. R. Schoedel, 'Same-Sex Eros: Paul and the Greco-Roman Tradition', D. Balch (ed.), *Homosexuality, Science, and the 'Plain Sense' of Scripture* (Grand Rapids 2000) 43–72.
[94] Philo, *Abr.* 135. See also *Spec.* 2.50.

separate occasion rather than a collective view that was common to all three or even to two of them. The exception to this statement is the presence of severe penalties in Philo and Josephus. This piece of evidence is not, however, solid enough to lean upon heavily. Natural law may lie behind this position, but the rationale is not offered and we are left only to speculate on the basis of the rough analogy between Philo and Cicero.

Does this mean that we have reached a negative conclusion? Not entirely. There are two pieces of evidence that still require consideration. First, the fact that all three authors made connections between ethical instruction and natural law is noteworthy, even if we were unable to show that they did so jointly in connection the nine clusters of material they share in common. It is clear that Second Temple Jews knew how to make the hermeneutical move that identified the law of Moses with the law of nature. Second, the widespread presence of natural law in discussions of homosexuality indicates that this connection was not limited to a handful of Jewish intellectuals, but was known more broadly.

These two observations make it possible to speculate that the equation of Mosaic legislation and natural law took place on a routine or semi-routine basis in Second Temple Jewish circles. The limited hints that we have explored suggest that the equation was made on an ad hoc basis, i.e., Jewish moralists used it when they thought appropriate but did not work out a full-scale or systematic analysis. This coheres with the popular level on which most of this teaching took place. It is doubtful that most Jewish instructors would have had adequate philosophical training to develop the material on a sustained basis. Further, it is unlikely that their audiences would have appreciated extended and nuanced treatments on a technical level. On the other hand, it must have seemed natural to equate the law of God with the law of nature: both were immutable. It gave a patina of intellectualism to specific positions where the equation worked most easily. Further, this would have given Jews the opportunity to counter the charges of misanthropy and particularism leveled against them by their elitist opponents. They did not practice 'ridiculous and vulgar customs', but the law of God. While few Jews could have expressed themselves as carefully as Philo, he spoke for many when he explained why the account of the law began with creation: 'it consists of an account of creation since the world is in harmony with the law and the law with the world and since the lawful person is at the same time a citizen of the world directing his actions according to the will of nature by which the entire world is administered.'[95] It was in such articulations — some careful and some

---

[95] Philo, *Opif*. 3. This statement does not equate the law of Moses with natural law, it does argue for their harmony. For a detailed exposition of the text with bibliography

careless — that Second Temple Jews attempted to universalize their particular moral code.⁹⁶

University of Notre Dame

---

see D. T. Runia, *Philo of Alexandria,* On the Creation of the Cosmos according to Moses, Philo of Alexandria Commentary Series 1 (Leiden 2001) 105–06. Josephus, *AJ* 1.21–24, esp. 24, expresses the same thought, but is probably dependent on Philo in this instance. Cf. also the later rabbinic statement in *Gen. Rab.* 1.2.

[96] I want to thank Thomas Tobin, S. J., of the Loyola University of Chicago for his careful response to an earlier draft of this paper at the conference which forms the basis for this collection.

The Studia Philonica Annual XV (2003) 81–99

NATURAL LAW IN SENECA

Brad Inwood

The theme of natural law has often been controversial in the study of ancient philosophy, in part because its later history is intricately entangled with Christian theology and with seventeenth-century notions of natural law, but also because of an occasional failure to define with sufficient clarity what is meant by the term. It was Plato who first juxtaposed 'law' and 'nature' in the famous speech of Callicles[1] in the *Gorgias*; since then the coupling of terms which had previously and almost inevitably been seen as polar opposites has raised a wide range of problems and puzzles. Many of these involve the fragmentary remains of early Stoicism, and I have made some effort to sort out a few of these issues in a discussion of moral rules and practical reasoning in Stoic thought.[2] Cicero's philosophical works have also provoked interest, especially the *De re publica* and the *De legibus*. But no matter how much sympathy Cicero had for Stoicism and despite his use of characters whose persona is Stoic, he is himself an Academic by inclination as well as by choice, and the synthesizing tendencies of Antiochus of Ascalon left their mark on him. In these two works there is an unmistakable Stoic influence; this extends even to the inclusion of the famous proem of Chrysippus' *On Law* (*De legibus* 1.18), though it is highly significant that throughout this work Stoic ideas are attributed not to the school nor even to philosophers, but to 'learned men'. Where Stoics are mentioned, it is in a discussion of the demarcation disputes between various Socratic schools and the importance of focusing on their common ground (*De legibus* 1.53–56). Overall, the flavour of the books is heavily Platonic and for whatever reason Cicero has chosen to conceal the level of Stoic influence.[3] Hence it is

---

* Earlier versions of this paper were read at a number of universities: Boston College and UC Berkeley in the fall of 1998, the Universities of Cincinnati and New Brunswick and Dartmouth College in the spring of 1999 and the University of British Columbia in March of 2001. I am grateful for comment and criticism to audiences at all of these institutions, to the company assembled at Notre Dame in the fall of 2001, and especially to Malcolm Schofield for his detailed written comments on the 1999 version. Since this paper was conceived initially as an oral presentation I have not attempted to change its basic character.
[1] *Gorg.* 483e3, and see Dodds ad loc.
[2] 'Rules and Reasoning in Stoic Ethics' in K. Ierodiakonou (ed.), *Topics in Stoic Philosophy* (Oxford 1999).
[3] See my review of J. Zetzel *Cicero On the Commonwealth and On the Laws* in *BMCR* 00.04.20.

difficult to distinguish with confidence the Ciceronian themes we can claim for the Stoics and those which we cannot.[4]

For now, then, this is as far as I want to go with Cicero's notion of natural law as evidence for Stoic ideas, and so if we want to deepen our understanding of the notion of natural law in ancient Stoicism, another recourse is to turn to Seneca the Younger, the earliest Stoic author from whose pen complete works survive in significant volume.[5] And in Seneca's prose corpus we certainly find an abundant use of the idea of natural law, variously expressed.[6] But perhaps I should say, 'the ideas of natural law', for there is a considerable range of uses of this idea detectable behind Seneca's various wordings, most of which go well beyond Chrysippean usage. And these different applications of the idea of natural law give us an insight into several important aspects of ancient Stoicism in general and, of course, Seneca in particular. In this article I give a rapid, perhaps even crude sketch of the range of these senses of natural law and their connections to each other. I then focus on the kind of 'law of nature' which seems most distinctive of Seneca, the law governing human mortality; having done so I want to connect it to a significant Socratic antecedent and to show how careful consideration of this sense of law can help us to resolve a philosophical worry about law-based moral theories, including Stoicism.

'Natural law' and 'law of nature' are now such familiar phrases that their oddity can sometimes escape our notice. Yet when Plato first juxtaposed them the peculiarity of the coupling was the whole point of the exercise. We should keep in mind that 'law' is properly speaking a creation of human social and intellectual activity, so that when we speak of laws of 'nature' we are inevitably transferring some, perhaps not all, of the associations of the term from their proper sphere to a novel environment.

---

[4] For a fuller discussion of Cicero's views on natural law, see my chapter in F. Miller (ed.), *The Philosophy of Law in Antiquity* (forthcoming Kluwer).

[5] It is likely enough that the *Hymn to Zeus* by Cleanthes is a complete work, and it does juxtapose the ideas of nature, logos and universal law in its praise of Zeus; but there is not enough context to determine what he means very exactly. Aratus, the author of the *Phainomena*, was a Stoic, but the amount of usable Stoic doctrine we can detach from the astronomical poem is slight.

[6] Yet he has been oddly neglected in discussions of natural law. Gerard Watson, for example, virtually ignores him (*Problems in Stoicism*, ch. 10, London 1971). Similarly, in the most recent treatment of Seneca's political thought (Miriam Griffin in ch. 26 of C.J. Rowe and M. Schofield (edd.), *The Cambridge History of Greek and Roman Political Thought* (Cambridge 2000), the idea of natural law is not discussed. The themes I deal with in this essay do not, of course, exhaust Seneca's interest in the philosophical applications of the idea of law; he has a particular interest in the conceptual work which can be done with the legal notion of judgement, a theme which I discuss in 'Moral Judgement in Seneca' forthcoming in *Stoicism: traditions and transformations* (edd. Zupko and Strange, Cambridge University Press).

Natural law, then, is in its origins a metaphorical concept. We should ask what it is about nature that makes it seem law-like, and what aspects of law are being projected onto nature when the phrase is used. We will find, as we consider Seneca's conceptions of natural law, that there is some variation in this regard, that natural law in Seneca's works invokes a variety of different associations. And the only way to sort through this variety is to get down to particular applications as directly as possible.

An obvious starting point would be the many cases where Seneca talks about real laws, the ordinances and legal conventions of his own society. In the *De ira*, for example, Seneca presents the law as a sober and unemotional force, able to punish where need be but without the loss of control and partiality characteristic of an angry man (1.16.5–6). This is an unremarkable connotation for 'law'. Also familiar is the idea that laws are inflexible and often fall short of the subtlety needed to guide moral deliberations and evaluation (an unremarkable point made by both Plato and Aristotle). Hence throughout the *De beneficiis*, especially in book 3, Seneca argues that the morally significant relationship between willing donor and grateful recipient should not be legislated: too much would be lost. And, again in the *De ira* (2.28.2), Seneca emphasizes how narrow the focus of the law can be:

> Who is there who can claim that he is innocent under all the laws? And suppose that he can: what a narrow form of innocence it is to be 'good' for legal purposes alone! The guidelines for appropriate action extend so much wider than those of the law. Piety, decency, generosity, justice, and honor demand so much, all of which lies beyond the scope of publicly promulgated law (*publicae tabulae*).

In Letter 94, on the vexed problem of the utility of moral precepts (*praecepta*), Seneca defends the claim that there is some moral utility in laws, as in precepts (94.37–39), but even in such a context he does not go so far as to claim that laws can capture the content of morality. For it is only if they are framed in such a way as to teach rather than merely command that they can perform a positive function (rather than the merely negative function of dissuading from wrong behavior by threats). Seneca's final rhetorical flourish (*quid autem? Philosophia non vitae lex est?* 94.39) obviously does not use the term 'law' in its literal sense and so does not actually contribute to Seneca's immediate issue (which concerns whether real laws contribute to moral development).

Nevertheless, the claim that philosophy is a kind of 'law for life' is clearly pertinent to our investigation into natural law, and gives us our first ethically important sense of 'natural law'. For it calls to mind the traditional definition of philosophy as an 'art of life' (*technê tou biou*). Like the skill of a craftsman, law is organized, directive, and (at least as regards the proper function of the art) impersonal. If philosophy is a law for life, it is because it guides us about what to do in an orderly and coherent way. So it is not surprising to find that Seneca very often employs such language in his description of moral principles, though it is just as important to note how general these principles are. For example, in the final book of the *De beneficiis* (7.2.2) Seneca is outlining the great invariant moral principles which the *proficientes* must cling to and use as a reference point in all of their practical decisions:[7]

> Let him know there nothing is bad except what is shameful and that nothing is good except what is honourable. Let him allot the duties of life by reference to this standard; let him undertake and complete all his duties in accordance with this law,[8] and let him judge to be the most wretched of mortals those who, no matter how great and splendid their wealth may be, are devoted to greed and lust and whose minds lie around in sluggish inactivity.

This is the kind of 'conviction bearing on life as a whole' which Seneca labels a *decretum* (*Ep*. 95.43–4; cf. 95.54 where the values of glory, wealth, etc. are instances of *decreta* which we need in order to interpret *praecepta*). These 'moral laws' determine the basic values of things, and so make up the set of *leges totius vitae* (*Ep*. 95.57)[9] and *vivendi iura* (*Ep*. 119.15). This kind

---

[7] But it is important to remember that such laws are general, and that they do not dictate to the sage what he ought to do in specific cases. Consider *Ben*. 2.18.4 (compare *De brevitate Vitae* 15.5): 'Let me remind you repeatedly that I am not talking about sages, who take pleasure in whatever they ought to do and who have control over their own minds and who declare for themselves any law that they want and obey the law they declare....' The self-imposed law of sages will, clearly, be in accord with the law of nature. But they do not experience it as an imposition from outside, dictated by a theory they happen to subscribe to. Rather, the law just is their own decision about what to do in the case at hand — in this passage Seneca is considering choices about who to receive a favour from, an example of the kind of particular moral decision which people must make on a daily basis. But despite the fact that the law is a self-imposed decision, it is no doubt just as deeply rooted in the natural principles which underlie all of the passages we have considered so far. So too in Letter 70: 'A wise man, then, lives as long as he ought to, not as long as he can', and the factors which go into deciding how long one ought to live are the kinds of situational particulars with which we are familiar from Aristotle's account of morally sensitive deliberation in the *Nicomachean Ethics*: *videbit ubi victurus sit, cum quibus, quomodo, quid acturus. Cogitat semper qualis vita sit, non quanta sit*. (70.4–5). Sometimes circumstances indicate a rapid acquiescence to threatening circumstances (70.5–7), sometimes a delay (70.8–10). There is a particularistic variability in how this kind of situation should be approached. Hence Seneca generalizes: *non possis itaque de re in universum pronuntiare, cum mortem vis externa denuntiat, occupanda sit an expectanda; multa enim sunt quae in utramque partem trahere possunt* (70.11).

[8] *Hac regula vitae opera distribuat; ad hanc legem et agat cuncta et exigat....*

[9] This may be the use of 'law' which we see at *Nat*. 3 Pref. 16: *haec res efficit non e iure Quiritum liberum sed e iure naturae*. Cf. *Ep*. 65.20–22 on the freedom which we have

of 'law' can be used to guide character development (*ut aliquam legem vitae accipiant qua mores suos exigant, Ep.* 108.6). It also serves to set a limit on the role which wealth and pleasure play in our lives, even on Epicurean principles (see *Ep.* 4.10, 25.4, 27.9, where *lex naturae* is used to refer to the limits imposed by nature in Epicurean ethics). In a similar sense Nature is portrayed as our teacher, one whose *leges* we refer to in shaping our lives (*Ep.* 45.9).

In this first application of the idea of law 'laws of nature' are basic principles of Stoic ethics, principles which apply with great uniformity and therefore great generality; they always stand in need of interpretation, and they work, as the passage from the *De beneficiis* just cited says, as a standard to which we refer when making choices.[10] Such laws are, of course, natural because they are rooted in nature. This is what Seneca says at *Ep.* 90.34:

> You ask what the sage inquired into and what he brought to light? First of all, the truth about nature,[11] which he followed in a manner unlike that of other animals, who use their eyes (which are slow when it comes to the divine). And next, the law of life, which he extended to everything and taught us not just to know the gods but to follow them and to accept the events which occur as commands. He forbade us to obey false opinions and determined the worth of each thing by its true valuation...

Here the content of the 'law of life' is clearly similar basic moral doctrines, but the unmistakable suggestion of the passage is that the investigation of nature which precedes provides a basis for it.

The foundation of moral principles on an understanding of nature also turns up in another important application. As we saw, in *Ep.* 95 Seneca outlines key *decreta* which are used to ground decisions about what to do in life. One of these (95.51–53) asserts the fundamental community of all human beings.[12] It is nature, he says, who has made us all *cognati* and instilled in us a love for our fellow humans. Hence, the basic moral principle which asserts our fundamental social bond to our fellow man is also a law of nature. This particular moral principle is regularly referred to with the language of the law. Let us quickly survey some examples of this usage of the notion of a law founded on nature.

---

under the law of nature. In both these cases it is our ability to see the minimal value of life and so to part with it readily which constitutes our freedom under natural law. But this assessment of the value of life is precisely one of the basic axiological claims of Stoic ethics. Similarly at *Ep.* 70.14–15: the eternal law makes it easy for us to die, a fact emphasized in its relation to human autonomy at *Ben.* 6.3.1 (*ius mortis*).
[10] Law as a *kanôn* (or standard to refer to) appears in the proem to Chrysippus' *On Law* (SVF 3.314).
[11] *verum naturamque*, which I take as a hendiadys.
[12] Cf. Cicero *Off.* 3.20–22.

At *De beneficiis* 3.18.2 the *ius humanum* is an assertion of the common humanity of all, slave and free alike. And in book 7 (7.19.8–9) Seneca invokes the *societas iuris humani* which is broken by the actions of the bloodthirsty tyrant;[13] the same kind of basic bond is referred to as a *lex naturae* at *Ben.* 4.17.3: 'no one has so thoroughly abandoned the law of nature and shed his humanity as to be wicked just for the fun of it' (*animi causa*). In the *De clementia* the *commune ius animantium* is invoked (1.18.2), presumably an even wider law, while a bit later at 1.19.1–2, Seneca the adviser to young Nero urges that it is a law of nature which dictates that a king should never harm his subjects. (And this is a natural law in a wider sense too, since Seneca supports it by invoking the behavior of king bees.) More typical is the notion of the *ius generis humani* which Seneca invokes in *Ep.* 48.2–3:[14]

> Am I speaking like Epicurus again? Truly, my advantage *is* the same as yours. Otherwise I am not a friend unless whatever is done which matters to you is also mine. Friendship creates between us a shared interest in all things; neither good nor bad fortune applies to us separately; we live for the common interest. Nor can anyone live life happily who looks only to himself and turns everything to his own advantage. One ought to live for the other if one wants to live for oneself. This bond, carefully and piously observed, which unites us humans with each other and maintains that there is a common law of humanity, makes a big contribution to that closer bond of friendship I was talking about. For he who shares a great deal with another human being will share everything with his friend.

This law of nature is a law both descriptively and prescriptively; it is the result of nature's arrangements and describes a fact about all human beings, a fact from which general prescription for our behavior follow.

In twentieth-century usage the notion of a natural law most often designates a description of a uniform natural process or the principles which determine it. The underlying notions are fixity and non-arbitrariness, and therefore reliability. Seneca often uses the notion of law in just this way, which gives us our third application of the notion. For example, in the *De ira* (2.27.2) he is emphasizing the irrationality of projecting onto the gods and the natural world the kind of vengeful mentality humans are capable of.

> And so it is madmen and those who are ignorant of the truth who blame the gods for the sea's cruelty, for torrential rains, and for a stubbornly prolonged winter, while all the time none of the things which harm or help us are directed specifically at us. For *we* are not the motivation for the cosmos to bring back summer or winter; they have

---

[13] This is again comparable to the view Cicero takes of Caesar's tyranny in *De officiis*.
[14] The rhetorical strategy of the *De clementia* is importantly different from that of other works; hence the invocation of nature here has a generic character not necessarily typical of Stoic doctrine.

their own laws, laws by which divine matters are worked out (*divina exercentur*). We think too highly of ourselves if we think that we are worthy objects of such great activities. Therefore none of these things is done to hurt us, rather they are done to help us.

Such 'laws' are echoed in the introductory paragraphs of the *De providentia*. There, at 1.2, Seneca is stressing that the orderly movements of the world are under divine supervision rather than being matters of mere chance. But his reference is to the normally impersonal divinity of Stoic physics and theology: reason, nature, and god rolled into one. And this is a regular, law-like process: the movements of the heavenly bodies occur *aeternae legis imperio*. Law, not chance, underlies Stoic cosmology. There is a similar use at *Ep*. 65.19 when Seneca asks, 'Shall I not investigate who is the craftsman of this world and by what means (*qua ratione*) such a huge object was brought to regularity and order (*in legem et ordinem venerit*)?' At *Ep*. 117.19 very similar thoughts are expressed:

> Let us investigate the nature of the gods, the nourishment of the heavenly bodies, and these quite complicated orbits of the stars — do our affairs respond to their motions? do the bodies and souls of all things derive their action from them? are even those things which we call fortuitous bound by a fixed law (*certa lege*), with nothing in this world developing in a sudden or disorderly fashion?

In the *Natural Questions* Seneca inevitably makes frequent reference to such laws: there are beneath the earth *iura naturae* less known to us but no less fixed (3.16.4); various forms of liquid are produced in accordance with a natural law (3.15.3); regular biological phenomena are said to follow a law (3.29.3); nature's laws determine that earthquakes can occur anywhere (6.1.12). Only at the unparalleled moment of cosmic cataclysm are the tides 'released from the laws' which normally govern them (3.29.7). In book 7 laws again are invoked to describe the fixity and predictability of the heavenly bodies. There is a *lex celeritatis* (7.12.4) for stars. Later Seneca observes that people do not notice regular phenomena so much as they do aberrant ones, those which are not *ex consuetudine et lege*; comets provoke wonder because they are not bound by fixed laws (7.25.3). By contrast, any heavenly apparition which is to function as a sign must be *comprehensa legibus mundi* (7.28.2).

Seneca also refers, hypothetically, to special laws of nature which *might* override the regular processes we count on — a curious kind of non-occurrent law which underscores by its absence the normal sort. Thus at *De otio* 5.5 he wonders whether 'some loftier power could impose a law on individual objects overriding the weight and momentum of their bodies.' If Seneca really does think that this sort of special 'law' can occur in nature, it would point to a greater emphasis in some contexts on the imperatival nature of a law than on its uniformity.[15] But most often Seneca emphasizes the uniformity of natural processes, as at *Ben.* 4.28.3: something put in place for humanity as a whole must inevitably affect even the wicked. Rainfall, for example, is uniform and law-like and good for human beings; *nec poterat lex casuris imbribus dici ne in malorum improborumque rura defluerent.*

Seneca does not restrict the language of law to individual phenomena which occur in an orderly, predictable and stable way. In fact, he more often uses the language of law to refer to larger and more comprehensive patterns of events in the cosmos, often making it explicit that this is the same as fate — a generalization of the third sense which might as well be flagged as a fourth distinct sense. This sense is clear in the *De providentia* (5.6–7):

> I am not compelled and I suffer nothing against my will. It is not that I am a slave to god; I give him my assent, all the more so because I know that everything proceeds in accordance with a law which is certain and proclaimed for all eternity (*omnia certa et in aeternum dicta lege decurrere*). The fates lead us and the first hour of our birth determines how much time remains for each person.

This law-like stability and predictability can also be expressed as a feature of the gods' rational determination. In the *Natural Questions* (1 Pref. 3) Seneca enumerates the important questions one can ask in physics, and these include: 'is god permitted to make decisions even today and to alter in some respect the law of fate?' The answer is given in another work, in the context of his consideration of whether we humans need to feel gratitude to Nature and the gods for the benefits given by providence. (We do owe them gratitude, as it turns out.) At the relevant point he says, 'consider too that external pressures do not compel the gods. Rather, their own will is an eternal law for them' (*Ben.* 6.23.1). In making a law for themselves by their rational decision the gods provide us humans with the most reliable framework for our own lives, since they cannot deviate from what is already determined to be the best possible arrangement (*nec imbecillitate permanent, sed quia non libet ab optimis aberrare et sic ire decretum est* 6.23.2). This law-like decree of the gods has built into it a consideration of the best interests of mankind.

The law-like character of fate is also at issue in book 2 of the *Natural Questions*, in the discussion of portents and divination and how they might

---

[15] Malcolm Schofield, to whom I am grateful for challenging written comments on an earlier draft of this paper, would put more emphasis on the commanding quality of Seneca's laws and less on their uniformity and predictability. Obviously both aspects will be present in most applications of the idea of law. The reason for my greater interest in the fact that law provides a reliable set of expectations, rather than in its capacity to compel us, will become clear towards the end of the paper.

affect our lives. The Stoics are criticized for making human endeavor useless, since they hold that the fates are unalterable (2.35–38.), which they emphasize by the use of the language of law (*ius suum peragunt* 2.35.2; *nihil voluntati nostrae relictum, et omne ius faciendi <fato> traditum* 2.38.3). Seneca here defends his own school (*rigidam sectam* 2.35.1), which he does not always undertake to do, going out of his way to align himself with the difficult views of the school on the matter of human responsibility and choice in the face of fate. (The Stoics regard the expiatory hopes of humanity as the *aegrae mentis solacia*, 2.35.1.) Humans, on the Stoic doctrine, are left with all the choice they need, since (in accordance with the familiar doctrine of *confatalia*) their actions are part of the pattern of fate laid up from all eternity. 'But now I have explained what is at issue, viz. how, if the ordering of fate is certain (*si fati certus est ordo*), the expiations and procedures which deal with portents avert dangers: for they do not conflict with fate but are themselves subsumed in the law of fate' (*sed et ipsae in lege fati sunt*, 2.38.3). Fate, the law of the gods, i.e., nature, is stable and reliable because it is already by definition comprehensive. Neither the gods nor the sage who so emulates the gods should be expected to change (2.36). What matters to us, Seneca thinks, is that we should *know* that the fated sequence of events can be counted on to be consistent and impersonal (*sic ordinem fati rerum aeterna series rotat, cuius haec prima lex est, stare decreto*, 2.35.2). Fate is to this extent like the gods of Epicurus, immune to irrational and emotional influences such as prayer, pity and favor (*prece, misericordia, gratia* 2.35.2), but not because the gods neither notice nor care for us; but rather because fate and the Stoic gods are endowed with the detached *apatheia* which is characteristic of normal human laws (see above on *De ira* 1.16.5–6).[16] One result of this unemotionality is that the events governed by law are predictable by a rational agent.

Of course, it is one thing to know that the events of fate are governed by a law-like rationality and quite another to know the details of what is to come. We turn to *Letter* 101.5:

> Believe me, all things are uncertain even to the blessed. Each person ought to promise himself nothing about the future. Even what he has in hand slips away and chance cuts short the very moment we are bearing down on. To be sure, time does proceed by a fixed law (*rata lege*), but amidst obscurity. However, what is it to me if nature is certain about what I am uncertain about?

Seneca goes on to argue that it is in fact useful to know *that* whatever happens proceeds from a fixed law; and because it is a divine law he elsewhere maintains that this knowledge is a crucial component of piety

---

[16] Good human laws are also uniformly applied to all: see *Ep.* 30.11 and below p. 92.

towards the gods (*Ep.* 76.23: *lege divina qua universa procedunt*). Not to see and accept that such unpleasant eventualities as our own death are governed by this law (stable, predictable, part of a benevolent plan) is ultimate folly (*Ep.* 101.7). Daily uncertainty about such prospects is a source of the wretchedness which comes from *timor... et cupiditas futuri exedens animum* (101.8); the rational solution is to live each day as though it were our last (101.7).

In *Letter* 107 (esp. 107.6–12) the law-like regularity and impartiality of events in the world is again invoked to motivate rational adaptation to the inevitable (note *ius* at 107.6, *legem* at 107.9 and compare *ordine mundi* at 107.12). Reflection on the fact that natural inevitabilities flow from a divine law grounds the ready acceptance of fated events characteristic of a Cato (*magnus animus deo pareat et quidquid lex universi iubet sine cunctatione patiatur*), a great man who faced death with a genuinely Socratic confidence (*Ep.* 71.16). At *Ep.* 76.23–24, though, the implications of knowing that there is a natural law are, if anything, more profound. Piety is based on such knowledge, and so is a Catonian tranquillity in the face of events. But Seneca goes on to claim that if the good man knows that things happen 'by the divine law in accordance with which all things occur' then it follows that for him 'the only good will be the honorable, since this is the foundation for obedience to the gods, for not flaring up at sudden events and not lamenting one's fate but rather accepting fate with patience and obeying its dictates.' This is a surprisingly strong claim about the relationship between two senses of the law of nature: fate and the basic Stoic doctrine about the good. But the connection is supplied. For if someone takes anything except the honorable to be good,[17] then he falls prey to *aviditas vitae*, a greedy clinging to life and to the things which adorn life. That kind of lust for instrumental 'goods' is open-ended and unsatisfiable. Hence only someone who recognizes such natural limits can accept that only the honorable is good.

This passage connects the natural law of human mortality (an objective and impersonal part of the grand plan of fate) with two less cosmic laws of nature we have already met — the Epicurean doctrine that there is a natural limit to desires and pleasures (which Epicurus did not describe as a law but Seneca did) and the claim that basic principles of Stoic axiology are laws of nature. In Seneca's mind, then, there is a tight connection between the rational commitment to truth about the world governed by Stoic physical principles (see 76.22) and the Stoic doctrine that virtue is the only genuinely

---

[17] *Si ullum aliud est bonum quam honestum*, 76.24; clearly this means, if the agent thinks that anything but the honorable is good. An ethic dative is to be supplied, parallel to *illi* in 76.23.

good thing. The connection as asserted here seems to be largely psychological, but it seems clear to me that the psychology of the passage is founded on what he takes to be a conceptual connection between physics and ethics.

Natural laws, for Seneca, include the rational regularities which anyone devoted to a frank assessment of the world unclouded by passionate emotion will come to see. Wisdom, then, depends on this kind of acceptance of the facts of nature: 'Meanwhile, as all the Stoics agree, I consent to the nature of things. Wisdom consists in not deviating from it and in being shaped in accordance with nature's law and example' (*Vit. beat.* 3.3). If one wonders why good people have to bear misfortune, we are reminded at *De providentia* 3.1 that such things are fated facts of life, and that bad things happen to the good by the same law (clearly fate) as governs their very goodness.

As Epicurus focussed heavily on the fear of death, so too Seneca concentrates heavily on the inevitability of the transitions and changes dictated by nature. His interest in this feature of the general laws of nature is so strong that it makes sense to mark it as a distinct application of the metaphor. We could label it the *lex mortalitatis*. Such emphasis is naturally prominent in consolatory contexts. In *ad Helviam matrem* 6.8 Seneca refers to the *lex et naturae necessitas* which governs people's comings and goings, and later in the same work (13.2) he explicitly claims that if we regard death not as a penalty but rather as a law of nature we will be able to conquer the fear of death. (As in Epicureanism, the thought that a negative event is being inflicted rather than happening by some impersonal necessity plays a major role in consolation.) In the *Consolatio ad Marciam* Seneca (section 10, esp. 10.3, 10.5) refers to the law governing human life. The *lex nascendi* is that we are mortal and transient beings; being born under the terms and conditions of this law we cannot reasonably complain about it when the inevitable occurs. This consolatory work will be central to the conclusions I want to draw at the end of my paper, so at this point I will pass on to other places where Seneca exploits this particular feature of natural law. In the *Consolatio ad Polybium* the law represents fixed and fair terms, as though in a commercial transaction,[18] not catering privately to individual preferences but to its own regularities (10.4–5).[19] Death will come — it is the *lex* or *ius mortalitatis* (11.4, 17.2) that it should come to each

---

[18] For the quasi-commercial sense of *lex* as the terms under which life is undertaken, cf. *Ben.* 7.8.3, 7.12.6. If the supplement <*leges*> is right at *Ep.* 48.9 this will be another instance of 'law' indicating the basic ground rules for life as a whole.

[19] When Seneca refers to things being mortal *incerta lege* at *Ep.* 63.15 he does not mean that their mortality is at all in doubt; he refers, rather, to the uncertainty we suffer about the exact timing, the fact that we can never know just when someone will die.

at its own time.[20] And to grieve irrationally can only be the result of ignorance of this law of nature or impious rebellion against it. At 11.4 Seneca says that he doesn't know which is more foolish, to be ignorant of this law of human mortality or to reject it brazenly. Even Scipio Africanus fell prey to such folly: his *pietas* was *impatiens iuris aequi* (14.4). But all such misfortunes are part of nature's law-governed plan, so that once we have taken on our assignment in this world our job includes bearing all the misfortunes sent our way. At *Vit. beat.* 15.5 this law of nature is compared to the duty of a soldier, and in the *De ira* (2.28.4) Seneca urges his audience to bear in mind that whatever unpleasantness occurs comes about by the 'law of mortality' not by the malevolence of the gods. Book 6 of the *Natural Questions* concludes with the ringing declaration that death is the 'law of nature, the duty and obligation of mortals' (6.32.12). The necessity of suffering death is also referred to as a 'law' at *Ep.* 94.7,[21] and at *Ep.* 123.16 death is called 'the just law for human kind' (*mors malum non est: quid <sit> quaeris? Sola ius aequum generis humani*).

In *Ep.* 77.12 Seneca emphasizes again features of the law of mortality into which we are all born: it is fixed and established, necessary, predictable and comprehensible, uniformly applicable to all. Death is a law for humans because it represents the impartial and fair terms under which we all live. Like any just legal regime in the human sphere, nature treats all its subjects alike (*Ep.* 30.11):

> Death brings a fair and inevitable necessity. Who can complain about being in the same condition that everyone is in? For the most important part of fairness is equality. But now it is unnecessary to plead Nature's cause. She didn't want our law to be any different from hers: whatever she put together she dissolves and whatever she dissolves she puts together again.

Again, Nature's law has the same features as a good human law, and it is for that reason that it commands our rational allegiance.

There are, then, five basic uses of the idea of natural or cosmic or divine law in Seneca's work (though the individuation of them is somewhat arbitrary). For the basic principles of Stoic ethics are 'natural' laws for life (1). And the fundamental sociability of human nature is a crucial special case of this (2), one rooted in our biological nature more obviously than are the principles of Stoic axiology. (3) The basic uniform operations of the physical world are also treated as 'laws'; and so too is the entire system of divinely ordained fate (4). But for Seneca, the key sense of natural law

---

[20] Though we may not know when to expect it, see *Ep.* 63.15 (*incerta lege*).
[21] Cf. *Ep.* 91.15–16: the *conditor iuris humani* is presumably the divine force which laid down the rules for human life, rules which include the uniform inevitability of death and our equality in death.

emerges as the natural and inevitable fact of human mortality (5), a sense of natural law which draws on all of the other senses of the term.

It has become clear that the various applications of the metaphor of cosmic or natural or divine law in Seneca's work have built in to them (a) the notions of impersonal detachment and uniformity of application which he recognizes in the literal law of his own culture (as we saw in the passage from *De ira* I above) as well as (b) the risk of an inflexibility inappropriate for moral contexts which is featured so prominently in the *De beneficiis*. Before going on to consider the 'law of mortality' and how Seneca puts it to work, I want to underline again some general features of Seneca's views on law and nature.

First, the uniform operations of nature and natural processes are frequently and significantly described as being law-like, and even when Seneca considers the possibility (whether counterfactual or not) of something happening which violates this law he stays within the framework of concepts derived from law. For such descriptive laws of nature are only violable by a direct authoritative edict — either another law (what we might think of as a *privilegium*) or a command overriding the law.[22]

Second, 'law of nature' often designates fundamental principles of Stoic ethics, such as the principle that nothing is good except the honorable and nothing bad except the shameful. In this sense there is a 'law of life' similar to the more generally Socratic 'art of life'. These law-like principles are general and the key to their usefulness is the flexibility with which they are applied to the specific cases which form the principal focus of most moral deliberation. Another of these laws is the statement of the basic notions of Stoic axiology, the realization that considerations external to virtue (such as pleasure and wealth) play a subordinate role in the good life — hence the application of the notion of natural law to the idea, shared with Epicurus, that there are natural limits to pleasure. Such laws are both descriptive and prescriptive: they describe what the world is like, just as much as the 'laws' governing the behaviour of the tides do, but they also establish guidelines for human behaviour. Another substantive application of natural law does the same: the basic bond of sociability and kinship among all humans is, in Stoic eyes, a basic biological fact, but the *ius humanum* which rests on it is the requirement that we behave accordingly.

Such features of nature are law-like in several regards: their uniformity of application, their impersonal application, and their authoritative relationship to human beings. The most important and certainly the most common single application of the notion of natural law in Seneca brings the various aspects of the idea together. The 'law of mortality', the inevitable fact of

---

[22] See above and *De otio* 5.5.

our precarious mortality — something which had been as central to human nature as rationality itself, since the time of Homer — is a natural law. According to this law, we all must die but cannot know when. This is one of those brute facts which apply to all and none can avoid. It is not at all a feature of Stoic physics in particular or any specifically Stoic doctrine. Lucretius and other Epicureans and indeed the entire sub-philosophical consolatory tradition rest heavily on this idea. But for Seneca the idea is expressed as a law of nature in a specifically Stoic way.

For Seneca, this law of precarious human mortality is a basic principle for ethics, comparable to the axiological principles already mentioned and used similarly as a guideline in the practical tasks of moral life: deliberation, deciding and advising. And although we may suspect that Seneca must have acted in the light of this law of nature when he faced his own suicide, we mostly see him in the role of advising. This arises in an important letter, number 70.

In this letter, the first of book 8 of the collection, Seneca opens with reflections on the swift passage of life. Life, he reminds Lucilius, is not always worth hanging on to, since (following the basic Stoic axiology) it is not a good — that is reserved for living well (70.4). This basic principle is not, in fact, called a 'law' here, as it is elsewhere, but the discussion which follows does provide a clear illustration of how such moral laws of nature are to be followed.

There is one small detail in this section of *Letter* 70 which is particularly important. In 70.9 Seneca is looking at cases where delaying in life is appropriate even when a certain death is imminent. Socrates is his first example:

> Socrates could have ended his life by starving himself and could have died by lack of food rather than by poison. Nevertheless he passed thirty days in jail, waiting for death, not in the belief that 'anything could happen and that such a long time gave grounds for many hopes'. Rather, [he stayed] in order to submit to the laws [*ut praeberet se legibus*] and to make available to his friends Socrates in his final days.

The context here is unmistakably the *Crito* and *Phaedo* of Plato. The benevolent desire to make himself available for continuing conversations with his friends is a clear reflection of the opening pages of the *Phaedo*, indeed, of the entire ambiance of that dialogue with its moving emphasis on the warm personal and philosophical bonds between Socrates and various members of his school. But the desire to submit to (more literally, 'make himself available to') the laws — or perhaps to the Laws — is more significant for us. For in the *Crito* Socrates engages in direct conversation with the Laws of Athens, which make the case for submission to the law of the city. Socrates is there urged not to escape prison, and it is clear that Seneca has applied this to a rather different form of escape, since it is the prospect of suicide before the execution which he has in view. But in Seneca's application and in Plato's dialogue, the issue is the relationship between Socrates and the laws, and in both contexts Socrates honors his obligation to the laws.

What does this have to do with natural law? Are the laws of the *Crito* not civic laws personified rather than laws founded on Stoic cosmic rationality? They are, but at the same time they stand for something considerably more important than the contingent laws of the city of Athens. For the determinative feature of their exhortation to Socrates is not their ability to compel him (their power in that regard is clear enough) but their appeal to his sense of reasonableness and fairness. In a nutshell, they remind Socrates that basic principles of fairness and rationality govern all of his behaviour. He has entered into a bargain by living in Athens, an agreement to abide by the laws in return for enjoying the benefits of Athenian law and culture. And he is deemed by the Laws to have undertaken this agreement in a willing and informed spirit. Hence if he were to fail to obey the Laws he would be acting in a manner which is either unjust or foolish: unjust if he abandons the agreement to his own benefit and to the detriment of the other party (hence the importance of the claim that flouting the Law counts as destroying it in so far as it is in his power)[23] or foolish if he does not appreciate the nature of the agreement he has undertaken.

Hence when Seneca gives as one of Socrates' motivations for passing the thirty days before execution in prison his desire *praebere se legibus* he is reminding us of Socrates' commitment to follow wherever the *logos* may lead and to stand by his agreements. I suggest that Seneca sees our relationship to the law of nature, in particular the law of mortality, on this model. Nature can be portrayed as another person (as in the wonderful passage from book 3 of Lucretius[24]), one with whom agreements can be made and with whom understandings can be reached. And if that is the case, then our obligation to follow the law of nature (which, we should remember, is intimately dependent on the full apparatus of Stoic cosmological theory) will be grounded in our commitment to rationality and fairness. This moral commitment to a law dependent on the outdated cosmology of ancient Stoicism will not be heteronomous, as critics of law-based theories of morality often fear. If I am right, a good Stoic follows cosmic nature because he is rational enough to understand the agreement he has undertaken and fair-minded enough to respect it. It is a further consideration that he is rational enough to understand that resistance to the law of

---

[23] It is the fact that harm would be done to the Laws which also brings the situation under the injunction against returning harm for harm.
[24] *De rerum natura* 3.931–965.

nature is futile. But this further consideration leaves the misleading impression that in following nature we are yielding to the brute force of the natural world, something which one might well do but would hardly help us to rebut the charge that Stoicism is heteronomous.

But at least with regard to human mortality that is not how Seneca thinks that things work. There are laws of nature which govern our mortality, laws in terms of which we must decide how to handle the particular situations of life. But our acquiescence in those laws is not motivated by a sense of capitulation to the brute force of overmastering fate. We follow nature (or follow the facts, as Lawrence Becker puts it[25]) for the same reasons that Socrates put himself at the disposal of the laws: their claim on us is reasonable and fair. To the extent that the choice to acquiesce is our own and is based on our sense of justice and rationality, there is no threat of heteronomy.

The best illustration of this is, as I hinted earlier, found in the consolations, though I think it is also present elsewhere. In section 17 of the *ad Marciam* Seneca portrays the terms of the law of human mortality as being fair and open (*neminem decipio*) so that complaint against it would be unreasonable: *post has leges propositas si liberos tollis, omni deos invidia liberas, qui tibi nihil certi spoponderunt.* He offers a comparison for human life in 18. Marcia is to imagine being born as rather like going to visit a tourist destination (Syracuse, in this case); as you debate whether to go, a well-informed adviser explains both its attractive and its irritating features. Now suppose that the advice is being given to someone about to be born. The advisor begins: 'You are about to enter a city shared by gods and men, all-embracing, bound by definite and eternal laws...' (18.2). The laws, then, represent the terms and conditions of human life. They are prior to any particular person, fair, impersonal, and fixed. In being born we choose to be bound by such laws, and to rebel against them at the moment of death is irrational.

Let us look more closely at sections 17 and 18 of the *Consolation to Marcia*. First, 17.6–7:

> Nature says to us all: 'I deceive no one. If you raise sons, you could have good-looking or ugly ones. Maybe you will have many sons: one of them could just as well save his country as betray it. You have no reason to abandon the hope that they will be so worthy that no one would dare to blame you on their account; still, imagine that they will be so shameful that they will themselves be a curse to you. Nothing stops them from performing your funeral rites and nothing stops you from being eulogized by your

---

[25] In *A New Stoicism* (Princeton 1998) Becker himself sometimes seems to think that our motivation to capitulate is based upon mere realistic capitulation to the brute force of natural limitations.

own children, but prepare yourself for the task of having to cremate one of them as a young boy, a youth, or an old man — for the age doesn't matter, since any funeral attended by a parent is painful.' If you raise children after these laws have been promulgated, you are freeing the gods from any trace of resentment, for they haven't promised you anything reliable.

It is striking here that the seemingly harsh facts of life, elsewhere called the law of mortality, are presented to us by nature in a speech which is honest and frank. There are facts of nature which we all know — or are deemed to know — and these are public and impersonal, like laws posted on public display. Anything we undertake in light of these laws is done on one's own responsibility. It is either unfair or irrational to complain about the application of laws to which one has willingly bound oneself. The parallel with the *Crito* is close.

But if the fragility of human life is just part of the deal for us, it is one thing to apply it to choices like having children. But what of the very choice to live oneself — for that would be the better parallel to Socrates' choice to live in Athens. He, after all, didn't choose to be born there any more than anyone chooses be born into the wide world. So one might think that the voluntary nature of the bargain is compromised. It was not in fact compromised for Socrates, because he chose freely to stay in Athens and enjoy the benefits of life there. So too for a Stoic. We choose to stay in life and enjoy its benefits. There is, we might say, a constructive choice to live if we agree to stay in life to enjoy its benefits and if it is the case that *if* we had had the choice to be born or not we would have chosen to do so voluntarily.[26] The need for this choice to be truly voluntary is certainly one of the reasons why Seneca emphasizes so frequently that one can always commit suicide when one doesn't like the bargain of life.[27] In a similar vein, at Letter 91.15, Seneca considers our proper reaction to the often unpredictable power of *fortuna*:

> None of this is grounds for outrage. We have come into a world where life is governed by these laws. If it suits you, obey. If not, leave however you like. Be outraged if any unfair conditions have been set down for you in particular; but if the same necessity binds the mighty and humble, then be reconciled with fate, by which all things are settled.

---

[26] Compare Rawls' use of the fiction of the original position to bring out the underlying nature of our commitment to just social institutions. It is as though we made an agreement based on certain facts. There are analogous features in most uses of social contract theory to justify political institutions. What Seneca is doing here is applying this kind of reasoning to human life as a whole.

[27] See also *Ep.* 70.15: *Bono loco res humanae sunt, quod nemo nisi vitio suo miser est. Placet? Vive. Non placet? Licet eo reverti unde venisti.*' No one, then, has any right to complain about the quality of his or her life.

In Seneca's view, remaining alive is part of the bargain, proof that we adhere to the contract voluntarily.

Seneca, however, does not just assert this; he argues for it, in his own rhetorical way. In sections 18 ff. of the *Consolation to Marcia* Seneca considers life as a whole and the terms on which it might be lived:

> Come then, compare the entry into life as a whole to this image. You were debating whether to visit Syracuse, and I explained to you all its potential pleasures and it potential annoyances. Suppose that I am similarly advising you as you are about to be born. 'You are about to enter a city shared by gods and men, all-embracing, bound by definite and eternal laws, revolving with the tireless duties of the heavenly bodies. There you will see stars without number shining, you will see everything filled with the light of a single star, the sun which marks with its daily course the intervals of day and night and divides more evenly with its annual course summers and winters. You will see the nightly progress of the moon, borrowing from meetings with her brother a gentle and diminished light, alternately hidden and visible all around the world, changing as it waxes and wanes, constantly unlike its most recent self.

Seneca extends his somewhat florid recital of the wonders of nature in what follows, but then balances it with an honest disclosure of the contrasting drawbacks.

> You will see five stars pursuing different paths and moving in opposition to the headlong motion of the cosmos. The fortunes of entire peoples depend on the smallest of their movements and the most important and most trivial events are shaped by whether a favorable or unfavorable star advances. You will marvel at masses of clouds and falling waters and twisted lightning bolts and the fracture of the heavens. When you have had your fill of the spectacle of the heavenly bodies and turn your eyes down to the earth, another category of things awaits you, amazing in its own way: on one hand the broad expanse of fields stretching off without limit, on another the lofty peaks of mountains rising in huge snow-capped ranges; waterfalls and rivers spreading from a single source to east and west and groves nodding with their lofty treetops and so many forests with all their animals and the contrasting harmonies of birds; varied urban locales and tribes remote and difficult of access, some holed up on high mountains and others cut off by rivers and lakes; cultivated fields and wild orchards; and the gentle outflow of streams among the meadows and pleasant bays and shores leading into a harbour; so many islands scattered across the deep, separating the seas from each other by their presence. What of the shining gemstones and gold washed in the sands of rapid streams and fiery torches in the midst of the land and even in the middle of the sea, and the ocean which binds the lands together, dividing the continuity of peoples with its three bights and surging with boundless licence? Here you will see animals far larger than land animals swimming among the troubled waters which billow even without a wind, some heavy and moving themselves with an awkward governance, some rapid and more swift than speedy oars, some ingesting the waves and spouting them forth with great danger to those who sail by; here you will see ships seeking unknown lands. You will see nothing untried by human courage and you will yourself be both spectator and a significant part of the

endeavour: you will learn and teach the arts, some of which provide for life, others of which adorn it, others of which govern it.

But there will also be a thousand plagues for body and soul: wars, pillaging, poison, shipwrecks, bad weather, and the bitter longing for one's loved ones — and their deaths, perhaps easy deaths and perhaps bound up with pain and suffering. Think about it and ponder what you want: to get to your goal this is the path you must depart on.

What will the prospective visitor to the shores of human life decide when faced with this depiction of the terms and conditions?

> You will answer that you want to live. Of course you will. In fact, in my opinion, you will not go after anything that you would grieve about if part of it were taken away. So, live in accordance with the agreement [*vive ergo ut convenit*]. You say, 'nobody asked my opinion'. Well, our parents gave their opinion for us when, after learning the conditions of life, accepted us into life.

Life, as Seneca portrays it, is so wonderful that anyone would choose to live on the terms offered. It may have been our parents who made the proxy choice for us by deciding to let us live, but (and this is common to many contract models of justice) the contractual obligation is, in fact, our own. If, *per impossibile*, we had been able to choose to live on those terms or not at all, anyone would so choose — a not surprising view for a Stoic to hold. So, we are, like Socrates with regard to the laws of Athens, parties to a bargain which it would be as unjust as it would be inconsistent to repudiate. Hence when the law of mortality comes into our deliberations, as it certainly must, we embrace the law not because it is the brute force of nature; we embrace it because we are by nature rational beings, committed by nature to rational consistency and the kind of detached, impartial fairness characteristic of the law. Seneca is not the first philosopher to exploit the appeal of something like contract law in unfolding a model of practical rationality, nor is he the last. But he is without a doubt committed to this conceptual strategy in a manner completely coherent with the rest of what we know about Stoic natural law. To the extent that our implicit choice is a voluntary adherence to a bargain, like that made by Socrates in the *Crito*, the Stoic attitude to the inevitabilities of fate and natural law, deprecated so often for bad faith or heteronomy, proves to be as 'autonomous' as any reasonable critic would want a moral choice to be.

University of Toronto

REVIEW ARTICLE

The Ancient Synagogue

Tessa Rajak

The ancient synagogue has been studied with remarkable intensity in recent years, absorbing archaeologists and theologians, art historians and philologists, New Testament scholars and students of Judaism alike.[1] Lee Levine's is not only the largest book, but, in many important ways, the summation.[2] In terms of breadth of conception, and the ability to draw on

---

[*] Lee I. Levine, *The Ancient Synagogue*. New Haven: Yale University Press, 2000. xvi + 748 pages. ISBN 0-30-007475-0. Price $75.

[1] These brief comments on a book which constitutes a major step forward in our understanding of the synagogues of the Greco-Roman world, and of its context in recent debate, are a somewhat expanded but otherwise unaltered version of a panel presentation given at the Annual Meeting of the SBL in 2001, under the chairmanship of Gregory E. Sterling.

[2] I would mention in particular the large studies by R. Hachlili, *Ancient Jewish Art and Archaeology in the Diaspora*, Handbuch der Orientalisk I.35 (Leiden 1998), as well as S. Fine, *Sacred Realm: The Emergence of the Synagogue in the Ancient World* (New York 1996) and *This Holy Place: on the Sanctity of the Synagogue during the Greco-Roman Period*, Christianity and Judaism in Antiquity 11 (Notre Dame, Indiana 1998); D. Binder, *Into the Temple Courts: The Place of the Synagogues in the Second Temple Period*, SBL Dissertation Series (Atlanta 1999); the collections of papers by J. Guttman, ed., *The Synagogue: Studies in Origins, Archaeology, and Architecture* (New York 1975), Kasher et al., (in Hebrew) *Synagogues in Antiquity* (Jerusalem 1987), L. Levine, ed., *The Synagogue in Late Antiquity* (Philadelphia 1987), D. Urman and P. Flesher, edd., *Ancient Synagogues: Historical Analysis and Archaeological Discovery*, Studia Post Biblica 47 (Leiden 1995), S. Fine, *Jews, Christians, and Polytheists in the Ancient Synagogue* (New York 1999), and H. Kee and L. Cohick, edd., *Evolution of the Synagogue: Problems and Progress* (Harrisburg, Pa. 1999). There is also the important series of articles by A. Kraabel, 'Unity and Diversity among Diaspora Synagogues', in J. Overman and R. McLennan edd., *Diaspora Jews and Judaism: Essays in Honour of and in Dialogue with A. Thomas Kraabel*, South Florida Studies in the History of Judaism 41 (Atlanta 1992) 21–33, as well as new editions of Jewish inscriptions and a number of significant individual papers, such as M. Hengel, 'Proseuche und Synagoge: jüdische Gemeinde, Gotteshaus und Gottesdienst in der Diaspora und in Palästina', in G. Jeremias, H. Stegeman., edd., *Tradition und Glaube. Das frühe Christentum in seiner Umwelt. Festgabe für Karl Georg Kuhn zum 65 Geburtstag* (Gottingen 1971), M.H. Williams, 'The Structure of Roman Jewry Reconsidered: Were the Synagogues of Rome Entirely Homogeneous?', ZPE 104 (1994) 129–141 and M. Goodman, 'Sacred Space in Diaspora Judaism', B. Isaac and A. Oppenheimer, edd., *Studies on the Jewish Diaspora in the Hellenistic and Roman Periods*, Te'uda 12 (1996) 1–16. Earlier trailblazers were J. Gutmann, ed., *The Synagogue: Studies in Origins, Archaeology and Architecture* (New York 1975) and L.M. White, *Building God's House in*

all types of evidence, his *The Ancient Synagogue: The First Thousand Years* is in the line of a distinguished antecedent, Samuel Krauss's acute and learned survey of 1922. But of course Krauss made his compilation when both the archaeology and the methodology of synagogue research were still in their infancy.

Throughout the period between then and now, the question of synagogue origins has been a preoccupation and Levine not only provides an excellent résumé, but also offers some new ideas on the subject. The beginnings continue to be debated: pre-exilic, Babylonian, post-exilic, Egyptian Hellenistic, all these contexts have been earnestly advocated. It is perhaps unsurprising that this, like so many questions about the genesis of time-honoured institutions, is not susceptible to resolution. I do not propose to adjudicate between interpretations of how and why synagogues emerged, in Palestine or in the Diaspora, or how the characteristic architectural forms evolved. Certainly, Levine's own suggestion, of an antecedent in the institution of the city gate in first temple and post-exilic Palestine will deserve discussion in another framework.

Again, known synagogues have been conscientiously catalogued; various of their functions have been studied many times now, and nowhere better than in Levine's book. My considerations however centre rather around one major historical question which underlies so many of these studies, including Levine's, and that concerns our evidence for the character of the synagogue, especially its functioning in the life of the diaspora Jews who inhabited a (broadly-speaking) Greco-Roman environment. The synagogue has almost universally been declared the centre point of Jewish existence in late antiquity. Levine writes (p. 124), 'by the first century C.E., the synagogue was playing a pivotal institutional role within the Jewish communities of Judaea and the diaspora. This centrality is particularly evident in the wide range of activities which took place there' (cf. p. 271, for some discussion of this range of activities).

An array of different scenarios might in fact be encompassed by such a statement, a range broadened by the very nature of the Greek word 'synagogue' with its various senses — a building, an assembly or an association. Thus, for some scholars the main point has appeared to be that the principal public activities of Jewish communities in the diaspora were carried out in buildings described often as 'synagogues', places which operated, it is held, as particularly effective and highly developed community centres. This seems to be Levine's main point. Others will foreground the religious life of the Jews — reading of Torah and prophets, prayer, the singing of

---

the Roman World: Architectural Adaptation among Pagans, Jews and Christians (Baltimore 1990).

psalms — in essence suggesting that it was the evolution of these practices which defined the post-biblical Jewish world. Thus too the leading role played by Torah (or in Greek terms *nomos*) in Jewish existence may be automatically transferred by historians to the synagogue as the place where the scrolls of the Law were housed. On the other hand, some commentators might be considering rather the commitment of the individual Jew, in the belief that the major part of this individual's life in society will have been mediated through the synagogue — or at the very least his life as a Jew. Yet again, the synagogue might leap to the fore when it is a case of identifying the administrative structures of the Jews, and especially for those who bear in mind that, where a Jewish population was not large, synagogue officials clearly served as the community's leaders.

By contrast, the centrality claim might concern essentially the synagogue, and especially the post-destruction synagogue itself rather than its members; this might then amount to identifying the institution as the prime religious innovation of the day; or even, to going further — as certain scholars have done — and highlighting the synagogue as a distinctive and unique Jewish creation. Often enough, such a strong claim seems intended, involving several of the above points, including the last. In other words, it is widely believed that, precisely in the Greco-Roman diaspora, the synagogue as an institution became — and indeed stayed — the focus of both individual and collective commitment for Jews, a primary affiliation and a basis for a definition of identity. A common pattern is thought to have existed, in which communities established unified locations for their political, social and cultic activities together.

Proponents of the latter view (implicit or explicit) might be described as synagogue maximalizers. Of these there are two kinds. One kind is that which emphasizes Jewish particularity. For a recent instance of such a totalizing description, we may turn to Burtchaell, who speaks of the 'synagogal way of life' as something 'so integrated, so omnicompetent, so communitarian that our distinctions between public and private, or between sacred and secular, or between the person and the community ... are largely inapplicable.' Synagogal structure, according to Burtchaell, is not Greek but 'inveterately Jewish.'[3]

The other kind of maximalizer will embrace the synagogue as prime vehicle for and manifestation of the increasing acculturation of Jews of this period — first in the diaspora and later in Palestine — to their non-Jewish environments. They will draw on common architectural language, on Greek terminology, on institutional parallels as David Noy and I did in our

---

[3] J.T. Burtchaell, *From Synagogue to Church: Public Services and Offices in the Earliest Christian Communities* (Cambridge 1992) 205, 208.

1993 study of the *archisynagogoi*.[4] Even a possibility of two-way traffic has been in the air. Thus one recent author finds himself able to say that 'the synagogue was among the most notable institutions that helped shape the face of the ancient city.'[5]

Where then does Levine stand? I suppose he must be a synagogue maximalizer, given the size of his book. However, he is a cautious, empirical scholar, often choosing the middle way. So he observes much regional diversity among synagogue structures, along with some Jewish particularity, expressed in common features. He is an archaeologist, so he is sensitive to local differences and intrigued by them. And when there is a major issue to be probed, he is admirably ready to break down the institutional generalities. This appears to very good effect in the attempt to push to some sort of conclusion the conflicting evidence on women's participation in the social world of the synagogue. Analysis suggests that we must admit real differences over time and also that the world of Asia Minor has its own distinct patterns of high level female involvement, at any rate in office holding and benefaction, patterns not found in Palestine or in Rome or in Syria (pp. 483–7). Although the picture is somewhat complicated by the need to include Crete with Asia Minor, Levine is probably right to identify a regional feature relating to the latter area. And yet the explanation of pagan influence from the surrounding ambience ('Hellenization'?) only takes us so far, for Levine hears no echo in the synagogue of the religious voice of the distinctive pagan priestesses of Asia Minor, and he does not ascribe major liturgical functions to the Jewish participants, as Brooten (1982) did.[6] On this view, then, there is both acculturation and difference in this sphere, and Levine is sensitive to both.

Archaeology is now perhaps the major contributor to our conception of the synagogue, and this is visible in the balance of Levine's book. Levine reveals that the remains of some fifteen excavated buildings or building complexes from Italy and around the Roman empire may be identified with varying degrees of certainty as synagogues, along with the traces of over a score more. These are certainly our most vivid and evocative evidence for the life of dimly understood communities, from the third century C.E. onwards. The number of known synagogue-related inscriptions has been estimated as above three hundred (p. 233), while it is epigraphic evidence alone (this too produced by the spade, of course) that reveals to

---

[4] T. Rajak and D. Noy, '*Archisynagogoi*: Office, Title and Social Status in the Greco-Jewish Synagogue', *JRS* 83 (1993) 75–93.
[5] L. Rutgers, *The Hidden Heritage of Diaspora Judaism*, Contributions to Biblical Exegesis and Theology 20 (Leuven 1998) 118.
[6] B. J. Brooten, *Women Leaders in the Ancient Synagogue* (Chico, California 1982).

us the existence of eleven apparent synagogues in the city of Rome during late antiquity, interestingly named after individuals, districts, groups or trades. Elsewhere, the archaeological remains attest to units of some scale, and in the case of the best known of them, Sardis, of rather grand proportions. The edifices had sizeable main halls, as well as, often, surrounding rooms which must have served various functions, including (in at least two known cases) the preparation of food. Taking archaeological and literary evidence together, attestation for over one hundred diaspora synagogues has been found by one reckoning.[7]

The sites may seem to support the assimilationists, if I may so describe them, since architecture is perhaps the most permeable of cultural phenomena to the reception of influence. Various scholars have commented upon the architectural diversity and regional variation of these synagogues, notable among them being Kraabel.[8] Levine too is ready to identify a ubiquitous responsiveness to the local idiom with the phenomenon of 'Hellenization'. It is possible also, however, to make something of a case for a 'common architectural language' of the Jews, that is to say a distinctive collection of features which made up what was appropriate to a synagogue, even if not all were present. This suggestion has recently been promoted by Rutgers,[9] who at the same time does not forget the intimate connection of Jewish art and of the Jews for whom it was created with their Greco-Roman environment. Rutgers can perhaps produce one telling feature that seems to be specifically Jewish: the main halls of the complexes are characterized by the presence of an apse, alcove or niche of some sort, evidently designed to house scrolls.[10] Levine, in fact, does not deny that this is a distinctive phenomenon (p. 283) and at one point he offers the interesting observation that, if the remains of what appears to be a first-century synagogue on Delos are to be connected with the two inscriptions of the Samaritan Israelite community found nearby, then the absence in this divergent group of the key Torah shrine element may be seen to reinforce the role of the shrine as a marker for Jewish communities (in the narrow sense).[11] Among other archaeological features commonly found in Greco-

---

[7] Rutgers, *op. cit.* 127.
[8] Kraabel, 'Unity and Diversity' 21–33.
[9] Rutgers, *op. cit.* 104–13.
[10] See Hachlili, *op. cit.* 68–79 and E. Meyers who puts the emergence of the 'Torah shrine' not before the mid-second century c.e. The presence at Sardis of not one but two Torah shrines (if that is indeed what they were) is perhaps a difficulty for Rutgers' view.
[11] It is preferable to associate texts with building rather than to take the synagogue as Jewish and the texts as lacking any context: discussion in Levine pp. 100–5, with citation of earlier literature.

Roman synagogue sites were mosaic floors (in ten known cases), which may be described as a Jewish appropriation from the environment, often depicting a *menorah* with perhaps other Jewish symbols. Additional Jewish elements are the reading platform (*bimah*); and the very much rarer Seat of Moses. Some synagogues also had courtyards containing a fountain or a cistern, not in conception Jewish, yet perhaps indispensable for the assurance of ritual purity, in the absence of a neighbouring seashore or spring, such as the sites at Aegina, Hammam Lif, Delos and Ostia possessed.[12]

Nor is the difficulty in interpreting these buildings simply a question of how we build history out of what is on the ground. It may be more fundamental, for what is on the ground is itself often in doubt and there is a possible damaging circularity in some of the archaeological labours on which all rely and which Levine is bound to report. The problem is simply this: what we expect in a synagogue, that is what we reconstruct. Levine is commendably alert to this problem in relation to the question of women's accommodation, where he states that only the preconceptions of certain excavators led to the identification of such a room or space (p. 475). In his view, there has been a reluctance to admit what the archaeology was indicating, quite simply that in antiquity seating for women, in significant contrast to practice in pagan temples, must have been always mixed.

It is also necessary to appreciate that the prevailing interpretative strategies are themselves problematic. The various dichotomies identified by scholars in their attempts to understand synagogue buildings and synagogal communities in relation to their environments tend to get conflated. Three related yet not identical polarities may be singled out:

— Jewish v. Greco-Roman (or sometimes 'Hellenized') characteristics.
— Imported influence v. appropriation from the immediate environment.
— Features common to or specific to synagogues v. unique features of one locale.

To unpack and refine these distinctions would take us too far from our subject. But I hope I have said enough to suggest that there is a cluster of separate issues inside these seemingly similar pairings which must be clearly distinguished. We are not dealing with just one simple polarity. Levine has not fully succeeded in keeping the strands apart. But his summary of our ultimate uncertainty is judicious (p. 287):

> We are left with the puzzling phenomenon of a diaspora as united as it was diverse, utilizing symbols and reflecting values that were common to most synagogues

---

[12] Hachlili, *op. cit.* 89; M. Pucci ben Zeev, *Jewish Rights in the Roman World: The Greek and Roman Documents Quoted by Josephus Flavius*, TSAJ 74 (Tübingen 1998) 215–6 and n. 22.

throughout antiquity...there may indeed be enough evidence to justify the assumption of a common shared tradition which affected and influenced Jews everywhere, a heritage which found expression in similar communal and religious frameworks, despite differences of language, culture and immediate social and political contexts.

Fuller publication and new exploration would no doubt make significant additions to our dossier. How far would it resolve any of the difficult issues? Even the acquisition, in many cases relatively recent, of the great treasures described by Levine should not shield us from the harsh realities, and of two in particular:

— The archaeology is often so inconclusive that the architecture remains in some cases critically uncertain. The Ostia synagogue is such a case. Squarciapino's[13] reconstruction of the building history has been improved upon by White's reassessment of the stratification,[14] but revisiting the site recently left me still with many anxieties. Levine, to his credit, makes the problems of this site particularly plain, reminding us (pp. 255–7) that the original state of the finds is disputable, that the second to third century dating of Mindis Faustus' famous dedication of the *kibotos* (ark) is reliant only on palaeography and that the inscription itself was found relocated from its original position and in secondary usage in a later synagogue vestibule.[15] The great synagogue of Sardis, on which so many historical reconstructions have been built, evokes some of the same concerns, especially because of the rather rapid immediate preservation and restoration of the site (a consequence of successful fundraising), together with the absence, to this very day, of full excavation reports.[16]

— As much as the architecture, the actual functioning of the Greco-Roman synagogue remains desperately elusive.

So does Levine make due allowance for what we do not know? Or has he tricked us by spinning a sort of seamless web? The problems, I have suggested, are evidential, interpretative and methodological. These problems may be illustrated by putting under the microscope a couple of paragraphs of Levine's text, with the aim not of criticism but simply of illustration. The starting point is the quotation cited earlier, where 'centrality' is said to be evident in the wide range of activities undertaken by synagogues (p. 124).

---

[13] M. F. Squarciapino, *Leptis Magna* (Basel 1966).
[14] L. M. White, 'Synagogue and Society in Imperial Ostia: Archaeological and Epigraphic Evidence', *HThR* 90.1 (1997) 23–58.
[15] At the time of this lecture, I had not yet had the opportunity to read the book length study edited by B. Olsson *et al*, *The Synagogue of Ancient Rome: Interdisciplinary Studies* (London and New York 2001).
[16] T. Rajak, *The Jewish Dialogue with Greece and Rome: Studies in Cultural and Social Interaction* (Leiden 2001).

For these activities in the first century C.E., the evidence cited is the pre-70 inscription from the synagogue of Theodotus in Jerusalem, unique and surprising as that text is,[17] together with 'a number of documents cited by Josephus', even though some of these, when we look at them, speak solely about *synagogai* as communities, or not about synagogues at all. Then comes an allusion to rabbinic tradition, with the disclaimer that this is of later date, yet still relevant. After this we get to the specific issue of honorific inscriptions for prominent synagogue members, but here the evidence is once again a single item, and a very unusual one, the honours for a Roman citizen in the first century town of Berenice in Cyrenaica. Finally, on p. 125, we meet the following argument:

> Moreover, the fact that these various activities are documented for synagogues and *proseuchai* throughout the empire argues for a basic similarity in the role of both institutions at this time. If these institutions served first and foremost the needs of a community, then it is most likely that such needs — be they of an economic, social, political or religious nature — did not differ significantly from Judaea to the diaspora, nor among the communities in Egypt, Asia Minor or Rome.

I should add that the arguments of few modern historians could stand such relentless scrutiny: it is simply the inadequacy of the evidence that I have sought to expose.

If then the Greco-Roman synagogue over this period was not quite as important as Levine hopes, how important was it? I would suggest a developmental model. Through the early centuries C.E., we observe the progress of institutionalization of the synagogue. This runs in tandem with a process of 'monumentalization', with the acquisition or construction of buildings and the visibility of common features. Such developments required both changes in Judaism and changes in the relationship between Jews and their neighbours. In concrete terms, they necessitated, on the one hand, the means and legal possibility of acquiring or leasing land, that is to say, civic standing. And equally, as far as the communities themselves went, the developments could not have occurred without the Jews having a certain sense of being at home in a place and being accepted, at least to a degree, together with a general intention on their part of staying put. Naturally, these processes were not unidirectional: many diaspora communities simply disappeared. But others in this way became rooted. Many endured. During the centuries of the Greco-Roman diaspora, we can begin to trace the evolution of patterns which would be consolidated in Jewry in subsequent periods. There would indeed come a time when, within a world

---

[17] For a full reassessment, see J. Kloppenborg, 'Dating Theodotus (*CIJ* II 1404)', *JJS* 51.2 (2000) 243–80.

of Christians and Muslims, the ubiquity of the synagogue would mark Jewish communities out worldwide as sharing a common affiliation, and when, moreover, the synagogue might rightly be judged the prime contributor to the self-identity of individual Jews, and even to the survival of Judaism. But that is to look far ahead, to the second thousand years.

University of Reading

The Studia Philonica Annual XV (2003) 109-137

BIBLIOGRAPHY SECTION

PHILO OF ALEXANDRIA
AN ANNOTATED BIBLIOGRAPHY 2000

D. T. RUNIA, E. BIRNBAUM, K. A. FOX, A. C. GELJON, H. M. KEIZER,
J. P. MARTÍN, R. RADICE, J. RIAUD, D. SATRAN, T. SELAND, D. ZELLER

2000*

R. A. ARGALL, 'A Hellenistic-Jewish Source on the Essenes in Philo, *Every Good Man is Free* 75–91, and Josephus, *Antiquities* 18.18–22,' in R. A. ARGALL, B. A. BOW, and R. A. WERLINE (edd.), *For a Later Generation: The Transformation of Tradition in Israel, Early Judaism, and Early Christianity* (Harrisburg PA 2000) 13–24.

Argall pursues the suggestion of Morton Smith that a common Hellenistic Jewish source about the Essenes underlies *Prob.* 75–91 and *Ant.* 18.18–22 rather than that Josephus drew upon Philo. He also posits that this source and Pliny may both make use of a core of older material found in the work of Marcus Agrippa. Although R. Bergmeier had proposed an outline of such a source based upon additional passages from Philo and Josephus, Argall suggests that the focus should be limited to the two passages mentioned

---

* This bibliography has been prepared by the members of the International Philo Bibliography Project, under the leadership of D. T. Runia (Melbourne). The principles on which the annotated bibliography is based have been outlined in *SPhA* 2 (1990) 141–142, and are largely based on those used to compile the 'mother works', R-R and RRS. The division of the work this year has been as follows: material in English (and Dutch) by D. T. Runia (DTR), E. Birnbaum (EB), K. A. Fox (KAF), A. C. Geljon (ACG) and H. M. Keizer (HMK); in French by J. Riaud (JR); in Italian by R. Radice (RR); in German by D. Zeller (DZ); in Spanish and Portugese by J. P. Martín (JPM); in Hebrew (and by Israeli scholars) by D. Satran (DS); in Scandinavian languages (and by Scandinavian scholars) by T. Seland (TS). Once again this year there has been close co-operation with L. Perrone (Bologna/Pisa), indefatigable editor of *Adamantius* (Origen studies). I am also grateful to colleagues who have drawn my attention to bibliographical material which I missed or who have helped me locate obscure items. They include this year A. Pawlaczyk (Poznan), M. Stol (Leiden), S. Torallas Tovar (Madrid), S.-K. Wan (Boston). I am once again extremely grateful to my former Leiden colleague M. R. J. Hofstede for efficiently performing diverse electronic searches. The bibliography is inevitably incomplete, because much work on Philo is tucked away in monographs and articles, the titles of which do not mention his name. Scholars are encouraged to get in touch with members of the team if they spot omissions (addresses below in 'Notes on Contributors').

in the title of his article. This allows him to argue that the Hellenistic source encompassed the additional topic of sacrifice, which Philo and Josephus each mention and address in their own ways. Argall provides a list of *topoi* covered in the hypothetical common source, including the older material used also by Pliny. He notes that Philo and Josephus discuss these *topoi* in the same order; that their common source had inserted a moralizing commentary, e.g., about the injustice of slavery; and that this list of topics is shorter than Bergmeier's because Argall includes only those topics mentioned in both *Prob.* and *Ant.* (EB)

G.-H. BAUDRY, *Le péché dit original*, Théologie historique 113 (Paris 2000), esp. 115–135.

This work, which undertakes to reexamine the problem of original sin with reference to the history of ideas, represents a complete and very well documented study. It contains a chapter devoted to Philonic views on the subject, a first version of which appeared earlier in 1993 (see *SPhA* 8 (1996) 124, RRS 9308, p. 183). Philo's views depend on the manner in which he understands the revealed doctrine of the creation of the world and of humankind. In first presenting these themes, the author highlights the dualistic emphasis of Philo's anthropology. This dualism, even though it is mitigated by a monotheistic faith in creation, nevertheless does remains a dualism, situating the origin of evil in the sensible, corporeal and terrestrial world. A pessimistic view of humankind is the result. Human beings are born marked by a 'congenital stain'. They are driven to wickedness by a dominant evil tendency within their make-up. (JR)

P. J. BEKKEN, 'Abraham og Ånden. Paulus' anvendelse av Genesis 15:6 i Galaterbrevet 3:6 belyst ut fra jødisk materiale' (Abraham and the Spirit. Paul's application of Genesis 15:6 in Galatians 3:6 in light of Jewish material), *Tidsskrift for Teologi og Kirke* 71 (2000) 265–276.

The author discusses the usage of Gen 15:3 within the literary context of Gal 3:5–6 against the background of Jewish material. In particular he points to the lack of parallels in the Hebrew Scriptures with regard to Abraham receiving the spirit. However, authors like Paul did not only draw upon the texts of the Hebrew Scriptures, but on traditions of exegesis of these Scriptures. Hence the author further argues that Paul probably had access to traditions that associated Abraham and the spirit. He briefly discusses Philo's *Virt.* 212–219, Pseudo-Philo *De Sampsone* 25 and Mekhilta De-Rabi Ishmael *Beshallah* 7:134–140, arguing that these provide interesting parallels to the emphasis on the spirit in Gal 3:5–6. (TS)

P. J. BEKKEN, 'Misjon og eskatologi: Noen observasjoner til Paulus' misjonsteologi på bakgrunn av eskatologiske forventninger i tidlig jødedom' (Mission and Eschatology. Some observations on Paul's theology of mission against the background of eschatological expectations within early Judaism), *Norsk Tidsskrift for Misjon* 54 (2000) 85–104.

This study seeks to locate some aspects of Paul's mission and theology within the framework of expectations related to Israel and the nations in Early Judaism. In this endeavour Philo of Alexandria plays a major role in the Jewish texts the author draws upon. Central topics in his presentation are: the universal Reign of the Messiah; the eschatological role of the Law; the blessings of Israel as shared with the Gentiles in the end-time; the conversion of the Gentiles; and the restoration of Israel. On this basis the author suggests it is possible to see Paul's view on the relationship between Israel and the nations as a redefinition of Jewish hopes, and Paul as Israel's eschatological apostle. (TS)

R. M. BERCHMAN, 'Philo and Philosophy', in A. J. AVERY-PECK and J. NEUSNER (edd.), *Judaism in Late Antiquity: vol. 4 Where We Stand: Issues and Debates in Ancient Judaism*, Handbuch der Oreintalistik 1.53.3 (Leiden etc. 2000) 49–70.

Berchman deals with the issue of Philo and philosophy. Many modern scholars—for example Nikiprowtzky, Winston, Runia, Radice—consider Philo to be not a philosopher but an exegete. Berchman opposes this view, arguing that philosophy can be found in Philo's connection of allegory and rhetoric. Furthermore, it is Philo's aim to connect Jewish and Greek wisdom. Berchman sums up Philo's philosophy in three words: (1) atomism, (2) fundamentalism, (3) criticism. (1) Philo employs philosophical ideas, but never wrote a philosophical commentary. (2) His borrowings of philosophical ideas are stripped of their technical philosophical value. (3) His criticism does not consist in evaluating ideas, but he considers their meaning only within the exegetical context. (ACG)

E. BIRNBAUM, 'Philo of Alexandria', in M. TERRY (ed.), *Reader's Guide to Judaism* (Chicago 2000) 474–477.

This is a short bibliographic essay covering works in English on Philo. Resources described include the translations published by the Loeb Classical Library and by Hendrickson, the Radice-Runia bibliography (1992, 2nd ed.), and *The Studia Philonica Annual*. Also discussed are works by E. R. Goodenough, S. Sandmel, J. Morris, H. A. Wolfson, D. Winston, D. T. Runia, T. H. Tobin, P. Borgen, A. Mendelson, S. Belkin, N. G. Cohen, and E. Birnbaum. (EG)

P. BORGEN, 'Philo's *Against Flaccus* as Interpreted History', in K.-J. ILLMAN, T. AHLBÄCK, S.-O. BACK and R. NURMELA (edd.), *A Bouquet of Wisdom: Essays in Honour of Karl-Gustav Sandelin*, Religionsvetenshapliga Skrifter 48 (Åbo 2000) 41–57.

In recent years increasing attention has been paid to the interpretive activity in Philo's work *Against Flaccus*. The present study reviews the studies of M.A. Kraus, M. Meiser, and R. Alston , focusing on how they may contribute to a holistic perspective on this work and on the relationship between Philo's interpretations and historical events. In the final part the author elaborates on his own view of Jewish laws and customs in community conflict as interpreted by Philo, and at the end offers some observations on comparative material, briefly focusing on 2 Maccabees, Revelation 18 and Acts 12:1–24. According to Borgen points of similarity between *Against Flaccus* and other writings of Philo support the view that Philo applied Pentateuchal principles, as understood and formulated by him, to his interpretation of historical events. (TS)

P. BORGEN, K. FUGLSETH and R. SKARSTEN, *The Philo Index: A Complete Greek Word Index to the Writings of Philo of Alexandria* (Grand Rapids–Leiden 2000, 2nd edition).

Beautifully produced commercial edition of the Index first provisionally published in 1997. See the summary at *SPhA* 12 (2000) 151. The main innovation of this edition, aside from the more elegant presentation, is the addition of the Greek fragments of *QG* 2.1–7 published by J. Paramelle. The Greek text of *QE* 2.62–68 is still not included (for these see the Instrumenta section in this volume). For further details see the review at *SPhA* 12 (2000) 205–206. (DTR)

A. P. Bos, 'De wijsgerige theologie van Philo van Alexandrië als wegbereidster van gnostische theologieën' (The philosophical theology of Philo of Alexandria as trailblazer for Gnostic theologies), *Kerk en Theologie* 51 (2000) 52–63.

In *Opif.* 7–9 Philo rejects the view, attributed to the Chaldeans, that the universe itself is divine. Bos calls this view 'cosmic theology'. Philo, by way of contrast, does not regard God as part of the cosmos but as a transcendent, meta-cosmic principle. Important in Philo's theology is the difference between God himself on the one hand and God's Logos and his powers on the other. God himself is the creator of the universe but he uses his powers as an instrument to create and to rule his creation. In *Abr.* Philo narrates that Abraham is aroused from the Chaldean mentality and discovers the existence of a transcendent God. The image of the awakening is borrowed from Aristotle. Bos argues that Philo is not a true Platonist, but a rather a Platonist in the image of Aristotle. Philo's theology is inspired by the Aristotelian treatise *De Mundo* (which Bos regards as authentic). Finally, it is argued that Philo's meta-cosmic theology is a source of inspiration for Gnostic ideas. (ACG)

A. P. Bos, 'Philo van Alexandrië: Joodse spiritualiteit in Griekse geest' (Philo of Alexandria: Jewish spirituality in a Greek spirit), in G. GROENEWOUD (ed.), *Tussen de regels van de filosofie: spiritualiteit bij grote filosofen* (Zoetermeer 2000) 14–32.

In his treatment of Philo's philosophical spirituality, Bos discusses three texts: *Opif.* 7–9, *Abr.* 60–70 and *Congr.* 1, 6–11, 79. In *Opif.* Philo, rejecting the cosmic theology of the Chaldeans, opts for a meta-cosmic theology: God is not part of the universe, but is transcendent. In *Abr.* Philo narrates that Abraham awakes from the Chaldean state of mind and gains the insight that there exists a transcendent God. In the last text Philo interprets the allegory of Hagar and Sarah in terms of preparatory general education and virtue. Explaining this interpretation, Bos affirms that Philo brings a Greek philosophical message and fails to do justice to the biblical text. Finally, some remarks are presented on Philo's dualistic anthropology, based on Gen. 2:7. (ACG)

F. CALABI, 'Galeno e Mosè', *Rivista di storia della filosofia* 4 (2000) 535–546.

The article takes its origin from the passage in Galen (*De usu partium* 11.14, 3.905–906 Kühn) in which he criticizes Moses and Epicurus with regard to their views on providence. Whereas Epicurus denies that there is a providential order in nature, Moses does admit its existence, but also retains the possibility that God can intervene at any moment to modify that order by acting in a manner that is arbitrary and lacking regularity. The author seeks to determine what Galen is referring to when he speaks about Moses: does he have a particular author in mind, e.g. Philo, when he recalls the Bible here, or does he cite an opinion which was widely held about Jewish thought. Referring to the interpretation put forward by R. Radice, she notes that certain aspects of Galen's statement could make one think of Philo, e.g. the principle of the divine word, the absoluteness of God, divine omnipotence, the simultaneous nature of creation. If, however, in the Galenic passage certain aspects appear to be reducible to Philo, others seems to recall the biblical text of Genesis more directly. Calabi's hypothesis is that Galen, when speaking about Moses, does not distinguish precisely between the views of Jews and Christians, but on the contrary tends to assimilate them. Invoking other authors, in particular Celsus and Irenaeus, she puts forward the view that Galen's reference is composite, consisting of Genesis, Philo and Christian authors, all seen in a unitarian manner as presenting 'the view of Moses'. (RR)

B. CENTRONE, 'Platonism and Pythagoreanism in the Early Empire', in C. J. ROWE and M. SCHOFIELD (edd.), *The Cambridge History of Greek and Roman Political Thought* (Cambridge 2000) 559–584, esp. 561–567 (on Philo).

As a historiographical category Middle Platonism is somewhat problematic. The authors of most interest during this period in the area of political thought are Philo and Plutarch. Both had active involvement in politics but their theoretical reflections are of limited importance for their thought. This is because the programmatic and utopian aspects of Plato's political legacy could not be influential in the differing political circumstances of their time. A brief account of Philo and his political ideas follows. The paradigms of kingship for him are the biblical figures of Joseph and Moses. The principal themes of Philo's teaching on politics, rule and kingship, are rooted in Greek traditions, but for realization of his ideal he looks to Judaism, inspired by what he read in its scriptures. (DTR)

N. L. COLLINS, *The Library in Alexandria and the Bible in Greek*, Supplements to Vetus Testamentum 82 (Leiden etc. 2000), esp. 144–56, 165–72.

In this study it is argued that the reliability of the *Letter of Aristeas* regarding the history of the Greek translation of the Pentateuch has since the 17th century been discredited for no good reason. The author establishes the date of the translation as 281 B.C.E., deducing this date from the evidence found in the Fathers of the Church who preserved eleven relevant dates. Analysis of the accounts of the translation in Philo (*Mos.* 2.25–44) and Josephus (notably *Ant.* 12.107–109) leads to the conclusion that both 'are based on Aristeas, and that changes made by each author to Aristeas are a reflection of their opinion on the divinity of the text' (p. 169). Philo, in his overriding desire to convince his reader of the sanctity of the text, minimises the role of the Greeks and in so doing completely distorts the account of the translation (p. 156). We can probably learn next to nothing from Philo and Josephus about the factual history of the translation (p. 169), but the accounts of both authors 'suggest that they are part of a persistent debate within Hellenistic Judaism concerning the question of the sanctity of the Pentateuch in Greek, of which Philo provides the earliest proof' (p. 171). (HMK)

N. L. COLLINS, 'Who Wanted a Translation of the Pentateuch into Greek?' in G. J. BROOKE (ed.), *Jewish Ways of Reading the Bible* (Oxford 2000) 20–57.

Collins defends the basic premise of the Letter of Aristeas that the Greek translation of the Pentateuch was initiated by Demetrius of Phalerum, librarian to Ptolemy II Philadelphus, for acquisition in the royal library. While acknowledging that not all aspects of the Letter are true, she selects details of the Letter which, she claims, challenge the current scholarly consensus—held for only two hundred years—that the Jews themselves initiated this translation because they no longer knew Hebrew. Although Aristeas relied upon an earlier source, which contained hints of Jewish opposition to the translation, by his time the translation was viewed as divinely inspired, and he adapted the earlier source to conform to the later view. Philo 'continue[d] the fight to prove the divine origins of the translation' (p. 39), consistent with his purpose to spread knowledge of Judaism among the Greeks, and he omitted any account of Jewish opposition to the translation. Josephus, who did not believe in the divine inspiration of the translation, follows the account of Aristeas in large part. Later Jewish sources expressed very negative attitudes toward the Greek translation, presumably because it was used against them. (EB)

E. DASSMANN et al., *Reallexikon für Antike und Christentum*, Lieferung 151 (Stuttgart 2000).

S. Schrek, art. 'Kain und Abel', 943–972, esp. 950–951.

D. DAWSON, 'Plato's Soul and the Body of the Text in Philo and Origen', in J. WHITMAN (ed.), *Interpretation and Allegory: Antiquity to the Modern Period,* Brill's Studies in Intellectual History 101 (Leiden etc. 2000) 89–107.

Beginning with a bibliographic overview, this essay explores how the allegorical readers Philo and Origen used the metaphor of body and soul in relation to text and meaning. Because both writers were so strongly influenced by Plato, it is ironic that Plato himself rejected 'as philosophically pointless' the practice of reading poetic narratives allegorically (p. 96). Dawson adduces three Philonic examples that show how Philo highlights 'the positive and productive interaction of mind and body' (p. 98). One example (*QG* 4.117) emphasizes the epistemological importance of sense-perception and likewise of the narrative aspect, or body, of the text. Another example (*Migr*. 89–93) presents the text as 'recorded law,' whose meaning is discerned through physical performance. The third example (*Contempl*. 78) underscores that one arrives at the inner meaning, or soul, of Scripture only through its outward, literal text, or body. Origen, who opposed excessive literalism, posited three levels of meaning of the text, using the metaphor of body, soul, and spirit. As one progresses in understanding, 'the body becomes more and more spiritualized, but it is never simply left behind' (p. 105). (EB)

G. DELLING, *Studien zum Frühjudentum. Gesammelte Aufsätze 1971–1987,* edited by C. BREYTENBACH and K. W. NIEBUHR, Göttingen 2000.

This is another collection (the first one appeared in 1970) of previously published essays by the well known specialist who died in 1986. The studies giving an overall view of Hellenistic Judaism and concerning Philo are already registered in R-R 7214, 7411, 8420 and RRS 8728f. The rest deals with *LAB* (cf. R-R 7105), Joseph and Aseneth, Josephus and the Alexander novel. The three contributions collected under 'Varia' might be relevant for Philo research as well: 'Biblisch-jüdische Namen im hellenistisch-römischen Ägypten' (392–422, though relying mainly on *CPJ* and *CIJ*), 'Die Bezeichnung 'Söhne Gottes' in der jüdischen Literatur der hellenistisch-römischen Zeit' (423–434, summarized in R-R 7712, and finally a survey on the influence of Jewish thought on the Greek Christian Fathers of the Church (435–460). On p. 438 the monographs on Philo in the series TU are enumerated, on p. 442 Clement of Alexandria's use of Philo is mentioned, on p. 450 his etymologies of Jewish names. (DZ)

R. ERVINE, 'Antecedents and Parallels to Some Questions and Answers on Genesis in Vanaken Vardapet's *Book of Questions*', *Muséon* 13 (2000) 417–428.

In the *Book of Questions*, the 13th century Armenian writer Vanakan Vardapet gives citations from several church fathers, among which Efrem, Gregory of Nazianzen and Epiphanius of Cyprus. He also offers four citations from Philo, of which three are derived from *Questions in Genesis* (1.27, 1.86, 4.56). (ACG)

S. ETIENNE, 'Réflexion sur l'apostasie de Tibérius Julius Alexander', *SPhA* 12 (2000) 122–142.

The exceptional *cursus honorum* of Philo's nephew, the Roman knight Tiberius Julius Alexander, has been the object of numerous investigations and studies. Yet historians have often failed to reflect on the validity of the accusation of apostasy with which he has been carelessly charged. Further, the majority of modern authors rely on the *testimonium* of Flavius Josephus (*AJ* 20.100) without expressing the least suspicion in respect to it. The personality of Tiberius Julius Alexander and the events of his prestigious career agree with this statement of the case since, at first glance, everything leads us to think that he had to renounce his ancestral religion. The innovative aspect of the analysis given in this article lies in the fact that an investigation of all the elements of the life of Tiberius Julius Alexander—not just the statement of Josephus—leads us to think that he had to apostatize or stand in opposition to the Jewish law. It is, however, imperative to determine which elements actually merit consideration and to justify their selection. The essay does this by setting out the concept of apostasy, the evidence of the two Philonic treatises that involve Tiberius Julius Alexander, the evidence of his career, and finally how all of this evidence affects our understanding of Josephus' statement. (KAF, based on the author's English abstract)

L. H. FELDMAN, *Flavius Josephus Translation and Commentary: vol. 3 Judean Antiquities Books 1–4*, (Leiden etc. 2000).

This is the first volume to be published in the Brill Josephus project under the general editorship of Steve Mason. It consists of a fairly literal translation together with copious annotations linked to the translation. Philo is used extensively for comparative purposes; see the index at p. 522–524, with a special concentration on *Mos.* and *Spec.* For a more detailed account see the review by D. T. Runia in *SPhA* 14 (2002) 219–223. (DTR)

N. FÖRSTER, 'The Exegesis of Homer and Numerology as a Method for Interpreting the Bible in the Writings of Philo of Alexandria', in G. J. BROOKE (ed.), *Jewish Ways of Reading the Bible* (Oxford 2000) 91–98.

Greek interpreters preserved the central role of Homer in their educational system by interpreting his work allegorically to bring his message up to date. Some interpreters also applied different kinds of Pythagorean arithmological exegesis. We have evidence of this kind of exegesis from various writings, including those of Nicomachus of Gerasa and Anatolius, Pseudo-Plutarch and excerpts in Stobaeus, and various Scholia on Homer. Philo occasionally quotes lines of the *Iliad* in providing arithmological interpretations of the Bible as well as in other contexts. Although the *results* of his exegesis differ from those of other known arithmological interpreters of Homer, his exegetical *method* is similar to theirs, and it is likely that he was familiar with the traditions upon which they drew. (EB)

D. H. FRANK, O. LEAMAN and C. H. MANEKIN (edd.), *The Jewish Philosophy Reader* (London–New York 2000) esp. 11–23.

This book claims to be 'the first comprehensive anthology of classic writings on Jewish philosophy form the Bible to postmodernism. Part I is entitled Foundations and First Principles. Its first four chapters fall under the heading The Bible and Philosophical Exegesis. Philo is included in chapter 1, Creation: Divine Power and Human Freedom. It contains first Genesis 1–3 in the modern Jewish version Tanakh, followed by extracts from Philo's *De opificio mundi*, i.e. 1–36, 69–90, 151–172, in Whitaker's Loeb translation (the use of the old chapter numbers in Roman numerals will be confusing). The text is presented without any form of annotation. It is followed by passages from Maimonides' *Guide of the Perplexed* and David Hartman's *A Living Covenant* (1985). (DTR)

E. FRÜCHTEL, 'Das Problem des 'peccatum originale': Zu Herkunft und Wirkung der augustinischen Erbsundenlehre', *Perspectiven der Philosophie* 26 (2000) 357–383, esp. 363–366.

The radical opposition in Augustine between love of god and self-love is traced back to Plato and Aristotle. In his exegesis of Ex 12:23 (*QE* 1.23ff.) Philo underlines the necessity of divine grace to overcome the destructive forces in the soul. In *Sacr.* 55–59 he shows how victory over self-love is possible. This vice is inherited and corresponds in that respect to original sin. More directly, however, Augustine depends on Plotinus. To declare the abuse of human freedom the cause of all evil does not resolve the problem of theodicy. (DZ)

J. DE GARAY, 'Bárbaros e infieles en el pensamiento de Filón de Alejandría', in J. CHOZA and W. WOLNY (edd.), *Infieles y bárbaros en las tres culturas* (Sevilla 2000) 41–67.

The author shows that according to Philo, virtue and faithfulness are not bound to an ethnic conception, but opened to the universal call of Jewish law. All humankind can belong to the nation of priests by virtue, and only by virtue. In this sense, the concepts of foreigner and unfaithful correspond. (JPM)

J. DE GARAY, 'La extrañeza de la inteligencia en Filón de Alejandría', *Anuario Filosófico* 33 (2000) 203–216.

The author emphasizes the novelty of Philo's thought with respect to the theory of knowledge. Going beyond the idea of an appropriation on the part of a subject that reaches the identity with the object, Philo proposes a concept of knowledge which extends towards hearing and hoping, i.e. not far from the modern proposal of Lévinas. Understanding occurs in intellectual attention, but also in the presence of otherness. It reaches a higher degree in the recognition of the difference between being and not being. (JPM)

A. C. GELJON, *Moses as Example: the Philonic Background of Gregory of Nyssa's De vita Moysis* (diss. Leiden 2000).

In the first part of this study, the author argues that Philo's *Mos.* does not belong to the so-called Exposition of the Law, as has been generally assumed. It has points of similarity with the genre of introductory *bioi* of philosophers. Examples of such *bioi* are the Lives of Democritus and Plato, written by Thrasyllus, and Porphyry's *Vita Plotini*. A *bios*, describing the most important facts from the philosopher's life—his descent, birth, death—and discussing his treatises, has an introductory function. In the same way, Philo's *Mos.* introduces readers without any knowledge of the Pentateuch to Mosaic philosophy, as more elaborately explained in the allegorical writings. Part II analyses the Philonic background of Gregory of Nyssa's *De vita Moysis*. In his analysis the author makes a distinction between Philonic phraseology on the one hand and exegesis derived from Philo on the other. It appears that on the level of phraseology Gregory offers more than 25 borrowings from Philo, the greatest part of which is derived from *Mos.* The most important exegetical theme in which Gregory uses Philo's exegesis is the interpretation of Egypt, Pharaoh, and the Exodus from Egypt. Like Philo, Gregory interprets Egypt as the land of the passions, Pharaoh as lover of the passions and the Exodus as the liberation of the passions. It is remarkable that Origen does not offer this interpretation of Egypt. Other important exegetical themes, showing Philo's influence, are the necessity of education, the interpretation of the serpent as a symbol of pleasure, and the exegesis of the Royal highway. In all these themes Gregory does not rely on Philo's *Mos.* but on the treatises belonging to the Allegorical Commentary. Gregory does derive two interpretations specifically from Philo's *Mos.*: the dark blue of the High priest's robe referring to the air and the interpretation of the hardness of the nut of Aaron's staff as a symbol of the austerity of the virtuous life. Part III investigates Gregory's use of Philo's philosophy and theology on the basis of two important themes, namely God's infinity and his unknowability. The author concludes that Gregory is not the first to attribute infinity to God, as Mühlenberg claimed. Aspects of divine infinity are already found in Philo and occur also in other church fathers like Gregory of Nazianzus and Basil of Caesarea. Regarding the notion of God's unknowability, there is a great similarity between Philo and Gregory, who both use Ex. 20:21 as a scriptural basis. In the Epilogue the author remarks that Gregory is by no means a slavish imitator of Philo, but an original and creative thinker and exegete. (ACG)

L. GRABBE, 'Eschatology in Philo and Josephus', in A. J. AVERY-PECK and J. NEUSNER (edd.), *Judaism in Late Antiquity: vol. 4 Death, Life-after-Death, Resurrection and the World-to-come in the Judaisms of Antiquity*, Handbuch der Orientalistik 1.53.4 (Leiden etc. 2000) 163–185.

Philo's eschatology is discussed under three headings: (1) individual eschatology; (2) national eschatology; (3) cosmic eschatology. (1) Important in Philo is the distinction between the rational and the irrational soul. Whereas the rational soul is immortal, the irrational soul, from which the passions originate, is mortal and corruptible. At death the rational soul can escape from the body. (2) According to P. Borgen, Philo claims a national role for the Jews: they have the cosmic divine law which will establish universal peace. Grabbe is not convinced by Borgen's interpretation. (3) Philo's description of a paradise in *Praem.* 87–126 has been interpreted as referring to the age to come. Grabbe rejects this view, arguing that Philo is basically following the text of Lev. 26 and Deut. 28. (ACG)

L. GRABBE, *Judaic Religion in the Second Temple Period: Belief and Practice from the Exile to Yavneh* (London–New York 2000), esp. 89–92 and *passim.*

This book is meant to be 'a synthetic history of religion among the Jewish people' during the Second Temple period (p. 1) and a companion to the author's earlier history book, *Judaism from Cyrus to Hadrian.* Part I is a chronological survey of major sources during several different periods: Persian, early Greek, later Greek (including Hasmonean), Roman, and Yavneh. Here Philo is discussed briefly (pp. 89–92) in the chapter 'Under Roman rule (63 B.C.E.–70 C.E.)'. Part II covers special topics, including temple and priesthood; Scripture, prayer, and synagogue; sects and movements; concepts of the Deity and spirit world; prophecy, apocalypticism, the esoteric arts, and predicting the future; eschatologies and ideas of salvation; messiahs; and Jews and Judaism in the Hellenistic world. Philo is mentioned here in scattered places, but especially in the chapters on concepts of the Deity and on messiahs. Part III by way of conclusion provides a holistic perspective on Judaism in the Second Temple period. Bibliographies are provided throughout. (EB)

V. GUIGNARD, 'Le rapport d'Israel à l'histoire dans l'œuvre de Philon d'Alexandrie', in L. J. BORD and D. HAMIDOVIC (edd.), *De Jérusalem à Rome: Mélanges offerts à Jean Riaudpar ses amis, ses collègues et ses anciens élèves* (Paris 2000) 175–194.

Philo's view of history is fundamentally sceptical. This is the reason that messianism represents no more than a marginal part of his preoccupations. Apart from Divine providence, to which he attaches great importance, he looks above all to Rome when evoking the security and earthly prosperity of the Jews. The particular concern that Providence shows towards Israel testifies to her election. A sign of this election is the observance of the Law. This gives Israel a separate state in history, because she is not subject to its 'cyclical revolutions'. (JR)

G. HATA, *Filon Furakusu he no Hanron + Gaiusu he no Shisetsub* (Japanese: Philo *Against Flaccus* and *Embassy to Gaius*) (Kyoto 2000).

This volume represents the first translation of some of Philo's works into Japanese. It purpose is introductory, and the author hopes that younger scholars will continue his work. It consists of annotated translations of the two writings in question, together with the translation of six documents which illuminate their contents and a final introductory discussion on Philo's life and the contents of the two works. For a more detailed table of contents see the Note at *SPhA* 13 (2001) 291–292. (DTR)

C. T. R. HAYWARD, 'Philo, the Septuagint of Genesis 32:24–32 and the Name 'Israel': Fighting the Passions, Inspiration and the Vision of God', *Journal of Jewish Studies* 51 (2000) 209–226.

Philo's understanding of the etymology of Israel as '[the] one who sees God' occurs frequently throughout his work and appears to derive from an earlier tradition. Because the Septuagint is central to Philo's exegesis, Hayward explores how Philo uses the LXX in relation to his discussions of Israel. Although Philo does not use the LXX to explain the link between Israel and 'seeing God,' he draws from the LXX several other themes, which he develops in connection with Israel. These themes include the portrayal of Jacob as a wrestler and athlete; Israel's name change as 'a blessing uttered in prophecy' (215); and, especially, Israel's role as a 'boundary figure' between heavenly and earthly things—a role similar to that played by the Logos, the high priest, and the first man. In addition, Philo uses the episode at Bethel (Genesis 28) rather than the one at Penuel (Genesis 32) to illustrate the experience of Israel as 'the one who sees God.' Underlying these various complex associations may be an understanding of divine inspiration, which Philo himself may have experienced. In turn, this experience may account for his 'evident fascination' with Israel and the vision of God and 'his expressed wish that others, too, might share such a privilege' (226). (EB)

R. HENKE, *Basilius und Ambrosius über das Sechstagewerk. Eine vergleichende Studie*, Chrêsis 7 (Basel 2000), esp. 22 ff., 106–109.

In his Homilies on Genesis 1 Ambrose relies less on Philo than in other works. But in his interpretation of heaven and earth in Gen 1:1 as the two principles of form and matter he follows—deviating from Basil—the exegetical line of Philo and other Jewish sages. (DZ)

A. VAN DEN HOEK, 'Endowed with Reasons or Glued to the Senses: Philo's Thoughts on Adam and Eve', in G. P. LUTTIKHUIZEN (ed.), *The Creation of Man and Woman: Interpretations of the Biblical Narratives in Jewish and Christian Traditions*, Themes in Biblical Narrative: Jewish and Christian Traditions 3 (Leiden etc. 2000) 63–75.

Philo's interpretations of the creation of man and woman, which rely upon two contradictory biblical accounts, are themselves complex and inconsistent. In one set of interpretations—classified here as '*anthropos* undivided and divided'—Philo first posits creation of an exemplary human being, modeled upon the noetic world. Changing the biblical wording of Gen. 1:27, he declares this *anthropos* to be neither male nor female, i.e. undivided. In another interpretation, based upon Gen. 2:7, Philo sees the creation of a human who could be male or female. Elsewhere, Philo modifies these interpretations in ways that produce various inconsistencies. In another set of interpretations of passages which come after the creation story—classified here as '*anthropos* divided: man and woman'—Philo moves away from the cosmological to the anthropological realm. Here he leaves his 'generic, non-gendered concept of *anthropos*' and uses allegorical interpretation to present man as mind and woman as sense-perception becoming entangled with sensual pleasure. Both in his allegorical interpretations and elsewhere in his works, Philo speaks of women in very negative terms, preferring male-oriented language to discuss the general human condition. (EB)

A. VAN DEN HOEK, 'Philo and Origen: a Descriptive Catalogue of their Relationship', *The Studia Philonica Annual* 12 (2000) 44–121.

This catalogue of no less than 414 items is meant to serve as the foundation for a comprehensive assessment of the extent and nature of Philo's role in Origen's work. Every passage in Origen where there is a potential parallel in Philo is briefly analyzed and the degree of dependency on Philo assessed on a sliding scale of A (certain dependency) to D (no evidence of relationship). The rigorous criteria for making the evaluations, which err on the side of caution, are explained. At the end of the catalogue a reverse catalogue appears, in which Philo's works come first and Origen is in the second position. (KAF)

P. W. VAN DER HORST, *Mozes, Plato, Jezus: Studies over de wereld van het vroege christendom* [Moses, Plato, Jesus: Studies on the World of Early Christianity] (Amsterdam 2000).

The 1993 study on Philo's conception of divine anger is reprinted here (cf. RRS 9344), and also Dutch translations of the study on silent prayer (cf. RRS 9432) and on the Synagogue before 70 C.E. (cf. *SPhA* 14 (2002) 150). Note too the study on the *ekpyrosis* which briefly discusses Philo on p. 168. (DTR)

M. HOSE, 'Philo und die hellenistische Philosophie', in W. STEGMAIER (ed.), *Die philosophische Aktualität der jüdischen Tradition*, Suhrkamp Taschenbuch Wissenschaft 1499 (Frankfurt am Main 2000) 113–132.

The subject of divine providence is selected to illustrate Philo's attitude to Hellenistic philosophy. First, the author gives an outline of the Stoic and the Peripatetic views on this subject. He then analyzes Philo's treatise on providence (*Prov.*). It is not a shaky early writing, but consciously plays one philosophical school off against the other to establish a Jewish view which takes a middle position between determinism and complete freedom. (DZ)

K.-J. ILLMAN, T. AHLBÄCK, S.-O. BACK and R. NURMELA, *A Bouquet of Wisdom: Essays in Honour of Karl-Gustav Sandelin*, Religionsvetenshapliga Skrifter 48 (Åbo 2000).

Festschrift in honour of the 60th birthday of the Finnish scholar who was a member of the International Philo Bibliography Project from 1994 to 2000 (see *SPhA* volumes 6 to 12). A list of his publications is given at the end of the volume. Only one article, by P. Borgen (see above), specifically deals with Philo. For further details see the review by D. T. Runia in *SPhA* 14 (2002) 238–239. (DTR)

J. C. INOSTROZA, *Moisés e Israel en el desierto. El midrás paulino de 1Cor 10, 1–13* (Salamanca 2000), esp. 101–111.

Studies the history of Israel according to *1 Cor.* 10: 1–13 with its double character: on the one hand God unfolds a plan to rescues his people and lead them through the desert; on the other a part of the people does not accept the divine gift and loses God's favour. In order to illustrate this complex idea, the author extensively analyzes its antecedents in Palestinian, Qumranic and Hellenistic Judaism. In this context he incorporates a careful study on Philo, focusing especially on *Mos.* 1.163–211. (JPM)

T. H. JANSSEN, *Heel de wereld beschreven. Lucretius, Philo en anderen over kosmos, aarde en mens* [The whole world described: Lucretius, Philo and others on cosmos, earth and humanity] (Amsterdam 2000), *passim*.

This anthology contains translations from fragments of texts dating from 100 BC until 100 AD. They are arranged according to several themes, such as cosmos, cosmology, and man. The following fragments of Philo are included: *Opif.* 1–17, 53–56, 62–70, 87–89, 103–104, 117–119, 136, 139–142, 148–163, 165–167, *Leg.* 2.49–50, 74, *Aet.* 4, 7–9, 145–149. (ACG)

H. JUNGBAUER, *Ehre Vater und Mutter*, Wissenschaftliche Untersuchungen zum Neuen Testament 2.146 (Tübingen 2000), esp. 217–230.

This dissertation describes the story of the fourth (or fifth) commandment not only in the Old and the New Testament, but also in the Jewish tradition in between. Philo in *Decal.* 106–120 reflects on its close connection with the duties towards God and subsumes under it several social laws (*Decal.* 165–167; *Spec.* 2.224–248; 261f.). In a second step, Philo's interpretation of laws outside of the Decalogue establishing the rights of the parents is considered. Other passages also illustrate the relation between parents and children. There, the care about the aging parents is marginal; more important is the education of the subsequent generation and the safeguard of the patriarchal order. (DZ)

H. M. KEIZER, "'Eternity' Revisited: a Study of the Greek Word 'Aiôn''', *Philosophia Reformata* 65 (2000) 53–71.

A succinct presentation of the author's 1999 dissertation on the meaning of the word *aiôn* in Greek literature, philosophy, the Septuagint and Philo. It is concluded that in whatever way Philo uses the words *aiôn* or *aiônios* himself (whether or not philosophically) or in whatever way he interprets them (when he finds them in the LXX), the words refer to what belongs to the created realm. In the philosophical discourse of *Deus* 32, *aiôn* is not the life of God, as a double text emendation of this passage has led scholars to believe. And Philo's exegesis of Ex. 3:14–15 in *Mut.* 12 as well as his comment on Prov. 8:22–23 in *Ebr.* 31 show that for Philo 'the *aiôn*' in the LXX correlates with the created world. (HMK)

J. KÜGLER, 'Spuren ägyptisch-hellenistischer Königstheologie bei Philo von Alexandria', in M. GÖRG and G. HÖLBL (edd.), *Ägypten und der östliche Mittelmeerraum im 1. Jahrtausend v. Chr.* (Wiesbaden 2000) 231–249.

Kügler here elaborates a chapter from his *Habilitationsschrift* (see *SPhA* 12 (2000) 161). Philo in *Mos.* 1.149–162 ascribes to Moses qualities well known from the Hellenistic royal ideology; the messianic-eschatological concept does not matter for him. In allegorizing the conception of the mothers of the patriarchs (*Cher.* 40–50) Philo is far away from the Egyptian-Hellenistic idea of a royal Son of God. He sees in God, however, the true king who delegates his authority to the Logos, his firstborn Son. People who follow his direction and do what is good can be called Sons of God too (*Spec.*

1.318). In *Conf.* 145–149 this sonship is mediated by the Logos as Image of God; he thus fulfills a similar soteriological function as the Egyptian king. In Philo's image of the shadow (here, *Her.* 53 must be erroneous; for the Logos cf. *Leg.* 3.96) Egyptian traces are also detected. On the whole, political ideas are spiritualized; this however has political consequences in the critique of contemporaneous aspirations of emperors. See further the critique of D. Zeller in A. von Dobbeler *et al.* (edd.), *Religionsgeschichte des Neuen Testaments: FS Berger* (Tübingen-Basel 2000) 541–552, esp. 547–550. (DZ)

A. KUSHNIR-STEIN, 'On the Visit of Agrippa I to Alexandria in A.D. 38', *Journal of Jewish Studies* 51 (2000) 227–242.

Although scholars generally recognize that Philo's so-called historical treatises, *In Flaccum* and the *Legatio*, contain many questionable details, one detail that has generally gone unquestioned is Philo's claim that Gaius advised Agrippa to sail to Syria via Alexandria. Evidence suggests, however, that the northern Mediterranean route was shorter, safer, and more comfortable than the way via Alexandria. It is also fairly well accepted that Agrippa left Italy in July and arrived in Alexandria in early August, but this dating does not accord with other events linked to the death of Gaius' sister Drusilla in June. It is more likely that Agrippa set sail for Alexandria earlier in the spring, specifically to help the Jews in their struggle with the Greeks. His purpose would have been to obtain and convey to Gaius a letter from the Jews expressing their congratulations upon his accession and presenting their complaints against the Greeks. Because the Greeks feared the potential success of Agrippa's intervention, his visit sparked their violence against the Jews. Philo's explanation that Agrippa stopped in Alexandria because of Gaius's advice was therefore provided to cover up the real intent behind his visit. (EB)

A. LEBEDEV, 'Xenophanes on the Immutability of God: a Neglected Fragment in Philo Alexandrinus', *Hermes* 128 (2000) 385–391.

It is argued that the anonymous couplet of archaic verses at Philo *Aet.* 41 should be attributed to Xenophanes. The main argument is the parallel at Ps.Arist. *De Melisso Xenophane Gorgia* 3, 977a14 (= Xenophanes 21A28 DK). The comparison with children on the sea shore, drawn from Homer, may also go back to Xenophanes. Both arguments can be well fitted into an understanding of Xenophanes' theological argument. (DTR)

L. I. LEVINE, *The Ancient Synagogue: The First Thousand Years* (New Haven 2000).

This is a magisterial volume about the synagogue from its origins through to the early seventh century C.E., presented from diachronic and synchronic perspectives. Part I covers the historical development of the synagogue and includes chapters on origins, pre-70 Judaea, pre-70 Diaspora, role and functions of the Second Temple synagogue, later Roman Palestine, Byzantine Palestine, and Diaspora synagogues. Part II, entitled 'The Synagogue as an Institution,' covers such topics as the building, the communal dimension, leadership, the Patriarch (Nasi), sages, women, priests, liturgy, and iconography. Although Philo's works pertain to just a brief segment of these 'first thousand years,' his writings are deemed to be 'of inestimable importance as a source for Alexandrian Jewry generally and for the synagogue in particular' (p. 82). His works are used here especially to shed light upon sermons, Torah reading, and women in the synagogue. See further the review by T. Rajak in this volume. (EB)

C. LÉVY, 'Philon aus Alexandria: Glaube und Philosophie', in M. ERLER and A. GRAESER (edd.), *Philosophen des Altertums: vom Hellenismus bis zur Spätantike. Eine Einführung* (Darmstadt 2000) 70–90.

In this second volume of introductory portraits of ancient philosophers, Philo ranges between Cicero and Seneca. First his works are presented (*Mos.* is missing). Then his attitude to philosophy is discussed. A conflict between his identity as Jew and as philosopher cannot be denied. Through use of the allegorical method he wants to avoid contradictions in the revealed text. As for his philosophical presuppositions, Lévy points out that in Philo's time the borders between the Platonists and the Stoics have become fluid, and that Eudorus established the absolute transcendency of the highest principle. In Philo, however, this transcendency is that of a person, not of an abstraction. His doctrine of the Logos allows Philo to maintain a God who is immanent to the world without being inconsistent regarding his transcendence. Finally, Philo's ambivalent attitude towards scepticism and education as well as towards the passions is outlined. (DZ)

C. LÉVY, 'Philon d'Alexandrie et l'épicurisme', in M. ERLER (ed.), *Epikureismus in der späten Republik und der Kaiserzeit*, Philosophie der Antike 11 (Stuttgart 2000) 122–136.

Although the presence of Epicureanism in Philo's *œuvre* is much less marked than that of Stoicism and Platonism, it is still a subject well worth studying. The author first discusses those passages, in *Prov.* 1.50, *Post.* 2 and *Aet.* 8 where Epicurus and his school are mentioned explicitly. The main questions on which Philo strongly disagrees are those of divine providence in creation and the role of pleasure. Lévy is inclined to downplay the specific role of Epicurean themes in Alexander's arguments in Book 2 of *Prov.* It would be a mistake to think that Philo's references to the Epicurean doctrine of pleasure were wholly superficial. An analysis is given of the defence of pleasure that Philo places in the mouth of the serpent in *Opif.* 160–161. This text puts forward the Epicurean theory of *oikeiôsis*. The only other text with the same argument is found at Sextus Empiricus *Adv. Eth.* 96, but Philo's presentation is in actual fact more precise and informative. Other texts in the Allegorical Commentary confirm that his knowledge of Epicurean doctrines is far from superficial. It would be a mistake, however, to conclude that there is not a single point of confluence between Epicurus and Philo. Surprisingly his use of the theme of 'cataleptic sensation' is closer to the Garden than the Porch. He is prepared to accord an important role to sensation, but obviously cannot regard it as the supreme good. The author ends his article with three conclusions. (1) Philo's philosophical knowledge is much more precise and deep than often thought. (2) In relation to Hellenistic philosophies Philo has a double mission, to refute them when they deny transcendence, but at the same time use their views to bolster it. (3) Epicureanism paradoxically tries to unite all systems of dispersion in one thought. It thus symbolizes the very antithesis of monotheism. But it is possible that Philo did appreciate its quest for unity. (DTR)

J. P. MARTÍN, 'Las *Quaestiones* del Pseudo Justino: un lector cristiano de Aristóteles en tiempos de Proclo', *Tópicos* 18 (2000) 115–141.

In an attempt to determine the historical place of *Quaestiones christianorum ad gentiles* attributed to Justin the Apologist, the author compares this treatise with the *Commentary on the Timaeus* by the Neoplatonist Proclus. In this context the author cites

Philo in connection with two topics: (1) the *paradeigmatikê aitía*, cf. *QG* 2.34; (2) the perichoretical function of Divinity, cf. *QE* 1.1. (JPM)

M. J. MARTIN, 'Philo's Interest in the Synagogue', *Ancient Near Eastern Studies* 37 (2000) 215–223.

The article poses the question: why does Philo refer so seldom to the synagogue? In fact almost all of his references to this institution occur in the two so-called historical treatises. Martin argues that the lack of references should not be taken to indicate a lack of interest. It may well be a consequence of the genre of most of Philo's extant writings, as well as the fact that he just takes the synagogue for granted as a central institution of Alexandrian Jewish life. Although he expresses distaste for the common masses, Philo is nevertheless devoted to the maintenance of Jewish praxis, which includes the study and interpretation of scripture in a synagogue setting. The most powerful evidence for the importance of the synagogue for Philo's Judaism is probably his description of the practices of the community of the Therapeutae. (DTR)

A. M. MAZZANTI, Art. 'Filone di Alessandria', in A. MONACI CASTAGNO (ed.), *Origene Dizionario* (Rome 2000) 168–171.

In the view of the author 'the methodological and conceptual influence which Philo exerted on Origen was noteworthy' and concerns above all the problem of the allegorical interpretation, especially the corporeal (i.e. literal or historical), the psychical (i.e. moral) and the spiritual (i.e. mystical) exegesis of the Bible (p. 168). Mazzanti recounts in brief terms the views held by scholars on this issue. Other points of contact between Philo and Origen are the dominance of Platonic themes and the figure of the Logos. Origen's anthropology also seems to be influenced by the Alexandrian, and especially the allegory of the human being created in the image and the human being formed from the earth. (RR)

H. NAJMAN, 'The Writings and Reception of Philo of Alexandria', in T. FRYMER-KENSKY *et al.* (edd.), *Christianity in Jewish Terms* (Boulder, Colorado 2000) 99–106.

As a Jew who wrote before Judaism and Christianity parted ways but whose writings were preserved by Christians, Philo offers a unique opportunity to study links between the two traditions. Influenced by the universalist concerns of Greek philosophy and aided by allegorical interpretation, Philo presented Biblical figures like Moses and Abraham as paradigms, and he explained the Mosaic laws as embodiments of the universal, unwritten law of nature. Philo upheld, however, both the particularity of the law for the Jews and the need for obedience to the law. After the decline of the Alexandrian Jewish community, his works were preserved by Clement and Origen in the 2nd century C.E., who applied Philo's universalizing interpretations to suit Alexandrian Christians. To maintain the distinctiveness of Judaism, the rabbis shunned the universalizing tendencies found in Philo, although shared exegetical traditions can be found in rabbinic and Philonic works. Some later Jewish philosophers addressed issues similar to those raised by Philo, but universalizing tendencies were often controversial also among later Jews. Study of Philo can help Christians appreciate particularistic aspects of Jewish law and interpretation and can help Jews appreciate the universality of the divine-human encounter emphasized by Christians. (EB)

S. T. NEWMYER, 'Philo on Animal Psychology: Sources and Moral Implications', in S. KOTTEK, M. HORSTMANSHOFF et al. (edd.), *From Athens to Jerusalem: Medicine in Hellenized Jewish Lore and in Early Christian Literature* (Rotterdam 2000) 143–155.

Published in a volume recording the partial proceedings of a Symposium held in Jerusalem, the article concentrates almost exclusively on Philo's treatise *De animalibus*. The disappearance of the original Greek text of the work is a great loss, since it makes it more difficult to determine Philo's sources, but nevertheless it deserves careful study for the insights it yields on his views in the area of psychology. The paper examines how Philo interprets classical animal psychology through his presentation of Alexander's case for animal rationality and his own rebuttal of that position. The question is not only important on theoretical grounds; it also has clear juridical implications, since Philo's position entails that animals do not fall under the purview of human justice. When Alexander argues that animals outstrip humans in some attainments, this recalls what G. Boas has called 'theriophily'. The author also notes that Philo, though plainly hostile to Alexander's case, does not try to answer all the points that he makes, but rather resorts to generalizations and rhetorical effects. At the end of the article the title page and first page of Aucher's *editio princeps* of the work is reproduced. (DTR)

C. NOACK, *Gottesbewußtsein. Exegetische Studien zur Soteriologie und Mystik bei Philo von Alexandrien*, Wissenschaftliche Untersuchungen zum Neuen Testament 2.116 (Tübingen 2000).

This dissertation is dedicated to the phenomenon of divine inspiration in Philo seen from a perspective of religious psychology ('mysticism'). Against H. Jonas, who generalizes the model of prophetic ecstasy, Noack wants to show that inspiration does not necessarily exclude human 'consciousness'. In introductory remarks Philo is situated sociologically, and his writings are differentiated form-critically into three categories: the missionary writings (the *Expositio legis* together with the philosophical and historico-political treatises), the *Quaestiones et solutiones*, and the Allegorical commentary. From each group Noack analyzes an exemplary text, enabling him to establish three types of 'Gottesbewußtsein'. (1) *Virt.* 211–219 is a kind of encomium presenting Abraham as a model for proselytes with features of a 'divine man'. Through inspiration he becomes a successful teacher of wisdom. He is also impressive in terms of bodily beauty. The contact with God has the effect of a holistic improvement which, however, does not persist. (2) In *QE* 2.29 the ascent of Moses is an allegory for the temporary ecstatic identity of the consciousness with God while the sensual world disappears. In contrast to Abraham's case this does have an external manifestation. (3) In *Her.* 63–74 inspiration functions only as analogy for the non-ecstatic, persisting change of consciousness, the decision for a view of reality where everything depends upon God. This is conceived in dualistic terms, but acquires a new relation to the sensual world. Noack also wants to read *Her.* 263–265 in the same vein. In prophetic ecstasy the mind is excluded only in so far it insists in its own absoluteness. In his final synthesis Noack tries to sharpen the soteriological profile of the three genres under consideration and even attempts to make some suggestions on their 'Sitz im Leben' and their chronological order. See further the review by D. Zeller in *SPhA* 12 (2000) 199–205. (DZ)

M. OLIVIERI, 'Influenze di lessici greci nelle traduzione armene di Filone', *Eikasmos* 11 (2000) 235–247.

The Armenian translation of *Prov.* (with particular reference to 2.15, 22, 26, 36, 95) and *QG* (with particular reference to 3.16) has been influenced by exegetical material which was not just in the form of marginal glosses or scholia to the Alexandrian's text, but also in the form of lexicographical repertoria independent of the author being translated. This is how glosses were included which do not regard Philo specifically but are 'traditional' (p. 245). In this respect one might think of the lexicon of Diogenianus or its Epitome. (RR)

K.-H. OSTMEYER, *Taufe und Typos*, Wissenschaftliche Untersuchungen zum Neuen Testament 2.118 (Tübingen 2000), esp. 18–26.

In his comprehensive survey on the semantics of τύπος the author wants to resolve the contradiction that the term can signify 'model' as well as 'image'. He therefore reduces its semantic content to 'that what makes visible an other thing or forms it'. Against the older work of L. Goppelt (1939) he insists that the term is used without connotations of time and value. It expresses a relation, not an entity. This is evident also in Philo, where the Logos can be conceived as model of the earthly man as well as as image of the Creator. In this flexibility the author sees a difference to the Platonic ideas. He challenges the view of Goppelt (relying among others on a false interpretation of *Mos.* 2.76), that τύπος in Philo usually means the minor image. Philo uses the concept in his cosmology, in his exposition of Scripture and in his doctrine of the soul. Here, the τύποι have an active character. In this connection, the 'third type' in *Her.* 231 is explained as model of the mind, not as imprint. Other passages which seem to contradict this view (the idols *Leg.* 2.255f; *Mos.* 1.119) are interpreted in this sense, too. In an appendix he shows that Philo uses ἀντίτυπος only in the classical sense of 'resistant'. (DZ)

K.-H. OSTMEYER, 'Typologie und Typos: Analyse eines schwierigen Verhältnisses', *New Testament Studies* 46 (2000) 112–131.

The article summarizes the main theses of the monograph reviewed in the previous item. (DTR)

A. PAWLACZYK, 'The Motif of Silence in Philo's of Alexandria Treatise 'Quis rerum divinarum heres sit'. Some Remarks', *Polish Journal of Biblical Research* (Kraków) 1 (2000) 125–130.

Although Philo is not the first author writing in Greek to place speech and silence on an equal footing—this honour must go to Plato—, he is certainly very aware of the role of silence in relation to speech and the various forms that such silence can take. The article briefly analyses the kinds of silence in relation to speech that occur in Philo's treatise *Her.* The author concludes that 'the process of speaking, creating and articulating logos becomes a complex one, where the very elocution of words and statements is preceded by 'quiet' mental activity, the soul's discourse with itself' (p. 131). (DTR)

F. PETIT, *La Chaîne sur l'Exode. II Collectio Coisliana. III Fonds caténique ancien (Exode 1,1–15,21)*, Traditio Exegetica Graeca 10 (Louvain 2000).

In this volume the author continues her edition of the ancient Catenae, now turning to the Catena on Exodus. She argues that the 26 texts of the Collectio Coisliana should first be separately treated, since they are not part of the original Catena. There are no

Philonic texts among these, although no. 23 from Clement's *Stromateis* is heavily dependent on Philo. For the Chain itself Petit follows the same method as in previous volumes, editing the excerpts, identifying the original source where possible and making brief comments. In the section up to Ex. 15:21, which is quite well preserved, there are five excerpts from Philo, all from the first book of *Mos.* For further details on the transmission of this complex exegetical work see the review elsewhere in this volume. (DTR)

A. PIÑERO (ed.), *Textos gnósticos. Biblioteca de Nag Hammadi III: Apocalipsis y otros escritos* (Madrid 2000), esp. 272–278.

In the last volume of the Nag Hammadi Library translated from Coptic to Spanish some passages of Philo are cited. Although few texts are given, this edition recognizes a relation of common patterns between *The teachings of Silvanus* and *Migr.* (p. 272). (JPM)

R. RADICE, *Allegoria e paradigmi etici in Filone di Alessandria. Commentario al «Legum allegoriae»*, Pubblicazioni del Centro di Ricerche di Metafysica. Collana Temi metafisici e problemi del pensiero antico. Studi e testi 79 (Milan 2000).

The work consists of two parts. The first has the character of a monograph (pp. 19–87) with the title 'Interpretative synthesis of the *Legum allegoriae*: the philosophical significance of the treatise'. The second part is analytical, with the title 'Analytical interpretation of the *Legum allegoriae*: sequential commentary on the treatise'. This latter part takes up the notes to the translation of the treatise by Radice in *La filosofia Mosaica* (cf. RRS 2405), expanding and correcting them where necessary. The first part is new and wishes to offer a synthesis of the chief philosophical terms that emerge in the treatise. The first chapter examines the problem of the knowability of God and the complex relation between faith and reason, in which neither is sacrificed to the other, because to the former is assigned the axiological superiority, to the latter the methodological superiority (p. 35). The second chapter interprets Philonic philosophy as a (rationalistic) hermeneutic of sacred scripture. On the basis of these assumptions Radice interprets in a comprehensive manner the contents of the three books of *Leg.*, developing the two lines presented above in the Philonic allegory. The double result, as the author observes on p. 85, is indicative of a double allegorical perspective, in terms of a moral meaning and a psychological meaning. But every allegorical linkage gives rise to a fundamental philosophical problem, which in this treatise would appear to be that of the freedom of the prototypical human being, or in biblical terms, of original sin. The deepest significance of this sin in Philo's view is the rejection of the creator in favour of created reality (p. 86). The book concludes with an extensive bibliography and copious indices which take up more than 120 pages. (RR)

V. REBRIK, 'Hermetik und jüdische Überlieferung', in J. U. KALMS (ed.), *Internationales Josephus-Kolloquium Aarhus 1999*, Münsteraner Judaistische Studien 6 (Münster 2000) 298–301.

The *Poimandres* betrays not only the influence of the LXX known to the author perhaps through synagogue-worship, but also of Philo. Numerous agreements in ideas and terms (e.g. the Logos as son of God, the primordial man, the concept of the divine forces, the double nature of man) foster the hypothesis that the author knew the works of Philo at least in excerpts or compilations. (DZ)

R. ROUKEMA, 'Studies about the Alexandrian Tradition in the Dutch Language', *Adamantius* 6 (2000) 98–108, esp. 99–100.

The article surveys publications in the Dutch language (including Flemish) which have been devoted to the Alexandrian tradition (Jewish, Patristic and Gnostic) during the last 25 years. Although most scholars in the Low countries publish their research in English and French, there remains a lively tradition of publication of studies written in Dutch. Scholars mentioned in connection with Philonic studies are R. A. Bitter, D. T. Runia and A. P. Bos. (DTR)

J. R. ROYSE, 'The Text of Philo's *Legum Allegoriae*', *SPhA* 12 (2000) 1–28.

The author summarizes the transmission of the text of Philo's works and of the *Legum allegoriae* in particular. He indicates the uneven attestation of the *Legum allegoriae* and affirms that the two well-known third-century papyri from Coptos and Oxyrhynchus should not be seen as deriving from the exemplars of Euzoius. A collation of Oxyrhynchus Papyrus fragments containing small portions of the text of *Leg*. 1 and *Leg*. 2 that differ from the *editio critica* of Cohn-Wendland is provided. Because differences are slight, Royse infers the essential integrity of the medieval textual tradition but warns about the possibility that genuine readings have disappeared. Next, a preliminary report of the planned new edition of Philo's works by Peter Katz, which was left unfinished at his death in 1962, is given together with a list of alterations to the PCW edition from *Leg*. 1–3 which he proposed. Detailed analysis of several of Philo's scriptural quotations (*Leg*. 1.52, 3.161, 1.31, *Cher*. 74) supports Katz's argument for the secondary character of the 'aberrant text'. The article concludes with a list of textual variations where the German (Heinemann), English (Whitaker), and French (Mondésert) translations differ from the text of Cohn-Wendland. (KAF)

D. T. RUNIA, 'Alexandria and Cambridge: James Kugel's *Traditions of the Bible*', *SPhA* 12 (2000) 143–147.

This review article, a contribution to a panel discussion at the Society of Biblical Literature's Annual meeting (Boston 1999), light-heartedly compares James Kugel (*Traditions of the Bible: A Guide to the Bible as it was at the Start of the Common Era*, Harvard 1999) and Philo of Alexandria as interpreters of Scripture, presenting first similarities and then differences. Among other things, in their profound concern for biblical interpretation, Kugel and Philo love to pose questions at the biblical text and then see what answers they can come up with. Further, they emphasize the centrality of exegetical traditions and thus are pluralist and inclusivist in their approaches. For both, 'there is no single interpretation that represents the truth' (p. 145). (KAF)

D. T. RUNIA, 'Art. Philo the Theologian', in T. A. HART (ed.), *The Dictionary of Historical Theology* (Carlisle-Grand Rapids 2000) 424–426.

Brief general presentation of Philo's thought with an emphasis on his theological ideas, ending with a brief bibliography. (DTR)

D. T. RUNIA, 'The Idea and the Reality of the City in the Thought of Philo of Alexandria', *Journal of the History of Ideas* 61 (2000) 361–379.

The theme of the paper is the conception of the city as a social and cultural phenomenon in Philo's thought. As an inhabitant of Alexandria Philo was thoroughly immersed in urban life. But what were the views that he held on the nature of the city itself? Firstly Philo's views on Alexandria itself are noted. He was clearly proud to be a citizen of this great metropolis, even though during his lifetime life became increasingly precarious for the Jewish community. Next the city is treated as a potent symbol of order. This is best illustrated by the beautiful image used at *Opif.* 17–18 to illustrate the process of creation. Further material on the city is found in Philo's vast exegetical output, e.g. the allegorization of the passage in Genesis when Cain builds a city. The theme of the city is used to illustrate the inner workings of the human soul. Just as there are two kinds of city, so there are two kinds of soul, one marked by order and virtue, the other by disorder and vice. In certain passages Philo also criticizes the city and praises solitude. This theme is also relevant to his idealized descriptions of two extra-urban communities, the Essenes and the Therapeutae. Finally the article briefly touches on the theme of Jerusalem as the idealized city. Philo is a distant ancestor of Augustine's famous contrast between the city of God and the city of human beings. The articles ends with some conclusions. Philo is seen as ambivalent towards the city. He habitually makes three contrasts: between the ideal and the reality of the city, between the good and the bad city, and between city life and solitude. His thought represents a mixture of both classical and Judaic views. From a historical point of view his conception looks both backwards to the ideal of the classical polis and forwards to Christian views when the desert was to become like the city. (DTR)

D. T. RUNIA, *Philo of Alexandria: An Annotated Bibliography 1987–1996*, Vigiliae Christianae Supplements 57 (Leiden etc. 2000).

Continuation of the Annotated Bibliography prepared by R. Radice and D. T. Runia for the years 1937–1986, using the same method for the years 1987–1996. The work was prepared with the assistance of H. M. Keizer and the collaboration of a team of 13 scholars, most of whom are or have been associated with the International Philo Bibliography Project. Preliminary versions of the bibliography were published in this Annual in the years 1990 to 1999. A brief Introduction outlines the basic method of the work. A major difference with its predecessor is that now all linguistic restrictions have been dropped, although it is recognized that coverage of many language areas will be very incomplete. It is also noted that the entire volume contains 953 items for the period of 10 years. It would appear that scholarship on Philo is stabilizing at about 100 items per year. Part One contains bibliographies, critical editions, translations, anthologies, commentaries, indices, journal and interest sites for the relevant years. Part Two, which is by far the longest section, gives annotated listings of all the criticial studies published during this period. In Part Three additional items are given for 1937–1986, as well as some corrigenda for the previous volumes. Seven indices round off the work, including a very extensive subject index (pp. 376–408). For further details see the review by J. R. Royse at *SPhA* 12 (2000) 193–200. (DTR)

D. T. RUNIA, 'Philo's Longest Arithmological Passage: *De opificio mundi* 89–128', in L. J. BORD and D. HAMIDOVIC (edd.), *De Jérusalem à Rome: mélanges offerts à Jean Riaud* (Paris 2000) 155–174.

The article serves as a preliminary study for the author's commentary on *De opificio mundi* to be published in the Philo of Alexandria Commentary Series. The placement of such a long excursus on the hebdomad in Philo's commentary on the Genesis creation account is quite remarkable and gives rise to two questions which are examined in the article. Firstly, what is the principle of organization that Philo uses to structure the excursus? The author first examines two structural analyses made by K. Staehle and R. Radice and finds them both defective. A structural analysis of the entire passage is given. It can be divided into two main parts, §91–110 and §111–127. The chief difference between the two is that the former contains much arithmetical calculation involving the seven (e.g. four phases of the moon amounting to 7 x 4 = 28 days), whereas the latter only lists groups of seven things (e.g. seven planets, seven vowels). The latter part is well structured. The former part is much more difficult, with esp. the section §101–106 proving difficult to understand from a structural point of view. The author stresses the role that association plays in this section. It is possible to reconstruct Philo's mode of thought, but the result is far from satisfying. In order to understand it the methods of ancient authors, who make use of excerpted material, need to be taken into account. The second question to be discussed is why the long excursus is so little related to the rest of the treatise. Partly this is explained by the emphasis that scripture places on the hebdomad, which Philo wishes to explain in philosophical terms, i.e. by emphasizing the special features of the number, rather than exegetically. Another factor is that Philo did not wish to emphasize the role of the hebdomad as completing the other six days, as he did in *Spec.* 2.56–59. The article closes by looking at the relationship between Judaism and Hellenism in the excursus. Although Hellenism predominates, there are a number of hints that reveal that the writer is Jewish. In some respects the excursus is reminiscent of Philo's philosophical treatises. (DTR)

D. T. RUNIA, A. C. GELJON, H. M. KEIZER, J. P. MARTÍN, R. RADICE, J. RIAUD, K.-G. SANDELIN, D. SATRAN, and D. ZELLER, 'Philo of Alexandria: an Annotated Bibliography 1997', *The Studia Philonica Annual* 12 (2000) 148–191.

A further instalment of the yearly annotated bibliography of Philonic studies prepared by the International Philo Bibliography Project. This instalment primarily covers the year 1997 (91 items), with addenda for the years 1996 (13 items), and provisional lists for the years 1998–2000. (DTR)

D. L. SCHIFF, *Abortion in Judaism: The History of a Struggle to 'Choose Life'* (diss. Hebrew Union College–Jewish Institute of Religion 2000).

This dissertation presents a complete Jewish legal history of abortion from the earliest relevant biblical references to the present day. Three tasks are undertaken: to present the fullest picture of the unfolding Jewish legal response to abortion; to explain the relevant texts in detail; to derive some critical lessons about the functioning of Jewish law. The attitudes to abortion found in the works of Philo and Josephus form part of the survey of Jewish history, which is divided into five epochs. (DTR; based on DAI-A 61–02, p. 649)

K. SCHOLTISSEK, *In ihm sein und bleiben. Die Sprache der Immanenz in den johanneischen Schriften*, Herders Biblische Studien 21 (Freiburg etc. 2000), esp. 106–118.

In a preliminary section this *Habilitationsschrift* compares the Johannine reciprocal formulas μένειν and εἶναι ἐν with various materials of the history of ancient philosophy and religion. Philo uses μένειν to characterize the immutability of God. In particular he recognizes an indwelling of God, his Logos or his Pneuma in the human soul, although usually he cannot stay there for ever (*Gig.* 28). Reciprocity is never stated directly. The author wants to distinguish these statements from prophetic inspiration through *ekstasis* and substitution of the human mind. See further the review of G. Sellin in *SPhA* 14 (2002) 217–219. (DZ)

M. B. SCHWARTZ, 'Greek and Jew: Philo and the Alexandrian Riots of 38–41 CE', *Judaism* 49 (2000) 206–216.

Philo belonged to two worlds, the Jewish and the Greek, 'but he never felt quite at one with either' (p. 211). Although he believed that the highest truth could be found in Judaism alone, Philo remained outside the inner circle of rabbinic tradition and he wrote about Judaism 'almost as a foreigner' (p. 212). Well aware of tensions between Jews and Greeks in Alexandria, Philo defended the Jews in his writings and hoped for a time of harmony among different peoples. His essays *Against Flaccus* and *Embassy to Gaius on the Riots of 38–41*—summarized in detail in this article—are philosophical more than historical and are based upon the notion that God punishes the wicked and protects the Jews. (EB)

D. SLY, 'The Conflict over Isopoliteia: an Alexandrian Perspective', in T. L. DONALDSON (ed.), *Religious Rivalries and the Struggle for Success in Caesarea Maritima* (Waterloo 2000) 249–265.

In a volume that focuses upon religious rivalries in Caesarea Maritima, the author introduces the example of Alexandria as a useful comparison. She discusses the two cities in terms of location and population, arguing that the Alexandrian population of Hellenes, Egyptians, and Jews was more complex than the Casesarean population of Jews and non-Jews. She then summarizes details of the Alexandrian ethnic conflict of 38 C.E. and examines the complicated issue of *isopoliteia*, equality of civil rights. With very few exceptions, which included Philo and his brother Alexander, Jews were not citizens of Alexandria. They had a *politeuma*, whose authority is not clear, and discussions of *isopoliteia* may reflect Jewish membership in the *politeuma* rather than citizenship in Alexandria. As a source of information about Jewish-Gentile relations in Alexandria, Philo represents a narrow, elitist point of view. Philonic studies would thus do well to embrace social scientific approaches, which would provide a broader, more inclusive picture of all classes of society. (EB)

J. F. M. SMIT, '"You shall not Muzzle a Threshing Ox': Paul's Use of the Law of Moses in 1 Cor. 9, 8–12', *Estudios Biblicos* 58 (2000) 239–263, esp. 254–256, 262–3.

In this article it is argued that Paul appends to the saying 'You shall not muzzle a threshing ox' (Deut. 25:4), which he quotes in 1 Cor.9:9, an explanation in which he enlarges the scope of this rule in view of himself and Barnabas as founders of the Corinthian church. Philo (*Virt.* 145–46), Josephus and the Mishnah treat this biblical law in ways similar to Paul but, whereas their interpretation intends to enhance Jewish identity, Paul's interpretation exhibits a definitely ecclesiological character and ultimately intends to enhance the identity of the church in Corinth as the exclusive community of the one Lord. (HMK, based on the author's abstract)

H. G. SNYDER, *Teachers and Texts in the Ancient World: Philosophers, Jews and Christians* (London–New York 2000), esp. 123–136.

Snyder studies the function and use of texts in the following 'book-centered groups' in antiquity: Stoics, Epicureans, Aristotelians, Platonists, Philo (for lack of evidence, the author could not discuss Hellenistic Jews as a group), Qumran, Judaism in Palestine, and Christians. On the basis of an analysis of the formal characteristics of Philo's Allegorical Commentaries and *Quaestiones*, Snyder attempts to draw conclusions about their origin and use. Passages with an autobiographical tone like *Cher.* 49 and *Abr.* 23, contribute to the conclusion that 'by writing, Philo served his own devotional needs, in so far as reading and reflecting on scripture placed him at the feet of Moses and Jeremiah. No doubt he hoped that his own writings would do the same for others' (p. 136). Philo 'creates a 'virtual classroom' by means of written text' (p. 137). (HMK)

E. STAROBINSKI-SAFRAN, 'Philon von Alexandrien über Krieg und Frieden', in W. STEGMAIER (ed.), *Die philosophische Aktualität der jüdischen Tradition* (Frankfurt am Main 2000) 133–149.

The author quotes from various exegetical writings of Philo to show that God alone is true peace. Man can participate in peace by freeing himself from internal and external warfare and taking rest in God. Philo's historical and apologetic works depict the Hebrews and their Fathers as peaceful people, which does not exclude readiness for struggle, as the example of Phineas may illustrate. Finally, some hints as to the philosophical roots of Philo's conception are given, notably the theme of the cosmopolitan state of the wise. (DZ)

J. M. STARR, *Sharers in Divine Nature: 2 Peter 1:4 in its Hellenistic Context* (diss. Lund 2000).

Philo is part of the comparative material used to explain the unique expression in 2 Peter 1:4 that 'you may become partakers of the divine nature'. For the structural connection between divine virtue and divine incorruption, to which the believer can attain through Christ, interesting parallels are found in both Philo and Plutarch. (DTR; based on DAI 61–03C, p. 662)

C. TERMINI, *Le potenze di Dio: studio su dynamis in Filone di Alessandria*, Studia ephemeridis Augustinianum 71 (Rome 2000).

The critical debate on the doctrine of the Powers in Philo concentrates on two problems, one genetic, the other functional (p. 10). On the first problem it can be said that Philo inherits the concept of power from the Hellenistic-Jewish tradition which precedes him, which means that he inherits it in a theological, or rather a theophanic perspective, i.e. it is connected to the way that God reveals himself, either in revelation or in creation. At the same time Hellenistic Judaism, in developing the concept of divine *dunamis*, was influenced by the Hellenistic religious environment. The cultural polyvalence of the term finds its maximum extension in Philo. By speaking of powers in the plural (which represents a break with the Alexandrian Jewish tradition) and emphasizing a universalist and philosophical conception of God, Philo allows the transcendence of God to be preserved, though at the same time maintaining his direct concern with the world and the plurality of his manifestations in relation to humanity (p. 39ff.). The resultant osmosis between Judaism and Hellenism allows the problem of anthropomorphic expressions in the biblical text to be resolved at least to a certain degree. These in fact can be taken to be no more than symbols or descriptions of divine powers which allegory (esp. in the form of etymology or by means of division) succeeds in interpreting, in this way achieving a 'conception of God purified of anthropomorphic and anthropopathic elements' (p. 84ff.). With regard to the functional aspect of *dunamis*, it needs to be understood that Philo is not completely clear on the relationship between essence and power in God: there appears at times to be a partial overlap of the two, which does find a precise articulation because the powers too are rooted in the depths of the divine mystery. From the allegorical point of view, against the background of divine transcendence, the powers are channelled into the two major figures of *theos* and *kurios*, into the symbolism of the two cherubim (in various hierarchical schemes which are fully analysed), and in the allegory of the creation of the human being. Here the powers have above all the role of acting as a 'screen' for God, guaranteeing the extraneous nature of evil (cf. p. 187). On this basis it can be affirmed that 'in the creation of humanity no sin is introduced' and that 'evil depends wholly on the exercise of human freedom'. This means, according to the author, that the multiplicity of creators is only 'virtual' (p. 236) and that, when allegorical necessity does not impose, God remains the sole protagonist in creation, and that *dunamis* and *pneuma* have for Philo above all an instrumental value. The divine power has in Philo a cosmological and an anthropological role, which confers on creation its stability and gives the powers the function of bond (*desmos*). At this point, according to Termini, the distance between Philo and both the Platonic doctrine of the World-soul and the Stoic concept of the pneuma-logos becomes apparent, because the notion of *desmos* in no way implies that God is (only) immanently present in the cosmos. (RR).

C. TERMINI, 'Spirito e Scrittura in Filone di Alessandria', in E. Manicardi e A. Pitta (edd.), *Spirito di Dio e Sacre Scritture nell'autotestimonianza della Bibbia*. XXXV Settimana Biblica Nazionale (Roma, 7–11 Settembre 1998), Ricerche Storico Bibliche 1–2 (Bologna 2000) 157–187.

In Philo's thought the connection between spirit and scripture operates at three levels. The first corresponds to the actual process of formulating the sacred text and is reserved for Moses. The second is linked to the translation of the Bible into the Greek language in the Septuagint. The third involves the allegorizing exegete, and thus Philo himself, in the task of uncovering the hidden and fundamental contents of revelation. The author, after presenting this analytical analysis of the three relations with reference to numerous texts, points out that they are based on a particular concept of revelation as a non-conclusive process, which moves from inspiration to translation and then to reflection. In actual fact both translation and commentary have the task of 'unveiling the beauty of the Torah to the Greek-speaking world' (p. 187). (RR)

T. H. TOBIN, 'The Beginning of Philo's *Legum Allegoriae*', *SPhA* 12 (2000) 29–43.

The author explores the question whether Philo wrote a treatise interpreting Genesis 1:1–2:6 along the lines of *Legum Allegoriae* and the allegory of the soul. He says there is enough evidence to suggest that Philo wrote such a treatise. The fact that two of the four treatises of *Legum Allegoriae* have been lost makes it possible that a third treatise has been lost as well. The opening of *Leg.* 1 seems to refer to a previous interpretation of Genesis 1 (*Leg.* 1.1), one not found in *De Opificio Mundi*. Moreover *Leg.* 1.19, 21–30 and *Leg* 2.9–13 point retrospectively to an elaborate interpretation of Gen. 1:1–31 along the lines of the allegory of the soul. Tobin speculates that the treatise was intentionally suppressed by the Alexandrian Jewish community sometime between Philo's death and the Jewish revolt in Egypt in 115–117 C.E. (KAF)

G. ULUHOGIAN, 'Ricerche filologico-linguistiche su antiche traduzioni armene di testi greci: fra «archeologia» e attualità', *Lexis* 18 (2000) 181–192.

Observations on the interest that the Armenian translations have for the establishment of the original text of Greek works and on the necessity to understand these translations better. Among the examples given are Homeric citations found in Philo. (DTR; based on *APh* 71–08067)

R. WEBER, *Das Gesetz im hellenistischen Judentum: Studien zum Verständnis und zur Funktion der Thora von Demetrios bis Pseudo-Phokylides*, Arbeiten zur Religion und Geschichte des Urchristentums 10 (Frankfurt am Maim 2000).

This is the first part of a *Habilitationsschrift* (the second volume on Philo and Josephus appeared in 2001) which against the backdrop of the 'new perspective on Paul' tries to differentiate the Jewish understanding of the Law from the 3rd cent. B.C. until the first half of the first cent. C.E. For this eleven Greek speaking authors are selected, including Aristobulus, Ps.Aristeas and Sapientia Salomonis. Diaspora Judaism, confronted with the rationalizing tendency of Hellenism, tried to maintain its identity by means of the Torah. Hellenistic culture is related to the Law of a single people, and at the same time this particular Law gets an universal meaning. This implies an ethical interpretation of the entire Torah which is founded in the nature of the cosmos created by God. The appendix treats 10 special questions, mainly of a philosophical kind (nr. 4 about allegory) and mentions Philo on p. 333, p. 395 (the name(s) of God) and pp. 396–398 (Philo as founder of negative theology). (DZ)

H. WEDER, 'Abschied von der Welt und Ausdehnung des Ichs. Die Allegorese bei Philo von Alexandrien und die Schriftauslegung der Gnosis', in P. MICHEL and H. WEDER (edd.), *Sinnvermittlung. Studien zur Geschichte von Exegese und Hermeneutik I* (Zürich 2000) 93–113.

By means of two examples the author aims to demonstrate the interrelation between exegetical method and disclosure of the world. Through allegorical interpretation Philo can perceive the phenomena of the visible world as signs of an invisible One. In interpreting Abraham's way as farewell to the universe of the senses (*Abr.* 68–88), Philo at the same time justifies allegorical understanding as such. This shows the connection between cosmology, gnoseology and allegory. In the gnostic movement (e.g. the Naassenes Hippolytus, *Ref.* 5.7ff.) allegorical interpretation serves the emancipation of the true Self. Here, the sensual world no longer bears the traces of God as it does in Philo. (DZ)

J. Whitman, 'Present Perspectives: Antiquity to the Late Middle Ages', in J. Whitman (ed.), *Interpretation and Allegory: Antiquity to the Modern Period* (Leiden etc. 2000) 33–70.

The function of the essay is to introduce the section 'Antiquity to the Late Middle Ages.' The author aims to outline the variety of scholarly approaches to interpretation and allegory during the past three or four decades. For the period of antiquity he poses the question, 'What constitutes the 'unit' of writing that is to be analyzed?' He then reviews the status of this question in relation to ancient Homeric interpretation, Alexandrian allegorization of Jewish scripture, rabbinic interpretation in its midrashic forms, and early Christian typology. Philo, discussed on pp. 38–40, is said to have approached the spirit of Scripture through 'continual engagement with the 'letter' of the law'—i.e., in both its narrative and legal portions. The second part of the essay addresses the extent to which allegorical interpretation might have 'textures' of its own. Here the literature reviewed pertains to philosophic modes in medieval Islam, Jewish approaches to philosophic allegory, Christian allegorization of ancient philosophic writing, and philosophic attitudes toward signification in Christian Scripture. (EB)

W. Yange and V. A. Russell, 'Philo, *On the Embassy* 80: Caligula Dressing as Heroes?', *Journal of Ancient Civilizations (Changchun, China)* 15 (2000) 69–78.

Philo's treatise *Legatio ad Gaium* appears to be especially prone to textual problems and stylistic idiosyncracies. It is proposed that at *Legat.* 80 we read τὰς (τιμὰς) πάντων ἡρώων instead of τὰς (τιμὰς) πάντων ἀθρόων as conjectured by C-W (mss. ἄθροον). 'Heroes' is parallel to 'demi-gods', which Philo treats in §78–92. The suggestion of the emendation is preceded by an analysis of the use of ἄθροος in the treatise. (DTR)

Addenda for 1994–99

R. Radice, 'Modelli di creazione in Filone di Alessandria', in C. Moreschini and G. Menestrina (edd.), *Lingua e teologie nel cristianesimo greco: atti del convegno tenuto a Trento l'11–12 dicembre 1997* (Brescia 1999) 35–58.

In this article Radice makes clear the unity of method and content in *De opificio mundi* and *Legum Allegoriae*, locating both treatises in the development of the allegory of the creation in seven days. In his judgment the creation which is described in *Leg.* should be located on the seventh day and should rightly be regarded as the creation of values. The fact that God proceeds to this creative activity precisely on the day of his 'rest', is meant to indicate to human beings the superiority of contemplative activity in comparison with practical activity in accordance with a typical Greek attitude. From the theological point of view this unified interpretation of the two treatises would confirm the mixed nature of the divine action, which is *ex nihilo* for the conceptual aspect and demiurgic for the material aspect. In a previous work (RRS 8948) Radice has defined this creative activity as 'foundational', i.e. creation of the foundations of reality'. (RR)

G. Reale, 'La dottrina dell'origine del mondo in Platone con particolare reguardo al «Timeo» e l'idea cristiana della creazione', *Rivista di filosofia Neoscolastica* 88 (1996) 3–33.

The article corresponds to the paper presented and discussed by Reale at the conference on the *Timaeus* organized by the International Plato Society in Granada, Spain in September 1995. In the process of illustrating the Platonic creation account in the *Timaeus* and giving a precise philosophical and theological evaluation of it, Reale undertakes to speak about the Philonic conception of creation (28ff.), which constitutes 'the foundation that allows the birth of the complete construction of the theory of creation on which Christian thought is based'. Although Philo does make use of Platonic terms and formulas in this context, he nevertheless does advance well beyond Plato. Indeed Reale puts forward the hypothesis (based also on a valuable testimony of Seneca in *NQ* book 1 *pref.* 16) that the Alexandrian thinker, albeit with much wavering, did attribute the creation of matter itself to God. It is further recognized that the Philonic doctrine of the Ideas as thoughts of God is a fundamental presupposition of the Christian *creatio ex nihilo*. (RR)

G. Scarpat, 'Nota sulla λόγος αἰρῶν', *Paideia* 49 (1994) 17–20.

In determining the meaning of the phrase αἰρῶν λόγος, the evidence of Philo in *Cher.* 76, *Leg.* 3.156 and *Sacr.* 46 is highly valuable. The Alexandrian makes clear the Stoic overtones of the formula: it is concerned with reason 'which prescribes, chooses, dictates' (p. 19). (RR)

S. Wan, 'Commentary as Pedagogical Guide: Scripture and Commentary in the Thoughts of Philo Judaeus', *Journal of Humanities East/West (Taiwan)* 18 (1998) 65–98.

The article commences with reflections on the relation between scripture and education. They might seem to be natural allies, but in actual fact there is potentially a strong conflict between them. Scripture projects its authority through self-transcendence, but this can have the effect of making it remote. Education is meant to project its ideals on the community. One way of linking the two is through scriptural commentary as a pedagogical instrument to bridge the gap between scripture and educational ideals. In the remainder of the article the author pursues this subject with specific reference to Philo. He first explains how Plato and the Platonist tradition used allegory to make Homer morally and intellectually palatable. He then explains how the Torah or Law functioned in Hellenistic Judaism. It is clear that Torah-centred education was in competition with Greek liberal education. Philo accords the latter some value, but mainly because ultimately it will lead the soul to seek the higher reality of moral and spiritual values. In this process scriptural commentaries, especially in the allegorical mode, play a vital role. The remainder of the article sets out how Philo produced different kinds of commentaries to fulfil his aim of guiding the initiate into the deeper truth of the Torah, which leads the soul to a vision of God. It might seem, Wan concludes, that Philo's strategy was a failure, but in a different Christian setting it actually became 'wildly successful' (p. 87). It may be concluded that scripture and commentary can live in a hermeneutical symbiosis. It is in fact commentary that makes scripture finally acceptable to a community. Without a commentary tradition scripture would not survive. So educators have to be interpreters of their own traditions. At the end of the article there is a summary in Chinese. (DTR)

Lun chuangshiji: yuyi de jieshi (Chinese = *On Genesis: Allegorical Interpretation*), translated by WANG Xiaochao and DAI Weiqing, edited by SZE-KAR WAN (Hong Kong 1998).

This first translation of Philo into Chinese was produced by the Institute of Sino-Christian studies in Hong Kong. The works translated are *De opificio mundi* and *Legum Allegoriae*. The translation was mainly made on the basis of the Loeb Classical library version, with some further input from Sze-kar Wan as editor. There is a short introduction by Wang on pp. xi–xxii. He first gives some historical background, emphasizing how Hellenism became less rational and more religious as a result of contact with Eastern mysteries. There follow two paragraphs on the life of Philo, references to the Loeb and Yonge's English translations, and a list of Philo's works in Latin, English, and Chinese. Next Wang gives a general description of Philo's use of allegorical method to bridge Greek rational philosophy and Jewish revelation in Scripture. Some words are also devoted to Philo's *Nachleben* among early Christian writers, with a few examples from the New Testament (Hebrews & Paul) and from the church fathers (Clement & Origen). The introduction concludes with a comparison of Philo's development of Greek thought to modern development of Chinese theology. The volume also translates the Loeb introductions in vol. 1. (DTR; based on information supplied by the editor)

SUPPLEMENT

A Provisional Bibliography 2001–2003

The user of this supplementary bibliography of very recent articles on Philo is once again reminded that it will doubtless contain inaccuracies and red herrings, because it is not in all cases based on autopsy. It is merely meant as a service to the reader. Scholars who are unhappy with omissions or keen to have their own work on Philo listed are strongly encouraged to take up contact with the bibliography's compilers (addresses in the section Notes on contributors).

2001

S. P. AHEARNE-KROLL, '"Who are my mother and my brothers?" Family relations and family language in the Gospel of Mark', *Journal of Religion* 81 (2001) 1–25.

M. ALEXANDRE JR., 'Rhetorical Hermeneutics in Philo's Commentary of Scripture', *Revista de Retórica y Teoría de la Comunicación* 1 (2001) 29–41.

R. ALSTON, *The City in Roman and Byzantine Egypt* (London 2001).

C. BERMOND, *La danza negli scritti di Filone, Clemente Alessadrino e Origene: storia e simbologie* (Frankfurt am Maim 2001).

E. BIRNBAUM, 'Philo on the Greeks: A Jewish Perspective on Culture and Society in First-Century Alexandria', in D. T. RUNIA and G. E. STERLING (edd.), *In the Spirit of Faith: Studies in Philo and Early Christianity in Honor of David Hay [= The Studia Philonica Annual 13 (2001)]*, Brown Judaic Studies 332 (Providence RI 2001) 37–58.

P. BORGEN, 'Application of and Commitment to the Laws of Moses. Observations on Philo's Treatise *On the Embassy to Gaius*', in D. T. RUNIA and G. E. STERLING (edd.), *In the Spirit of Faith: Studies in Philo and Early Christianity in Honor of David Hay [= The Studia Philonica Annual 13 (2001)]*, Brown Judaic Studies 332 (Providence RI 2001) 86–101.

P. BORGEN, 'Greek Encyclical Education, Philosophy and the Synagogue. Observations from Philo of Alexandria's Writings', in O. MATSSON *et al.*, *Libens Merito. Festskrift till Stig Strömholm på sjuttioårsdagen 16 september 2001 (= FS Stig Strömholm)*, Acta Academiae Regiae Scientiarum Upsaliensis 21 (Uppsala 2001) 61–71.

D. BOYARIN, 'The Gospel of the Memra: Jewish Binitarians and the Prologue to John', *HThR* 94 (2001) 243–284, esp. 249–252.

G. R. BOYS-STONES, *Post-Hellenistic Philosophy: A Study of its Development from the Stoics to Origen* (Oxford 2001), esp. 90–95.

R. Cacitti, 'οἱ εἰς ἔτι νῦν καὶ εἰς ἡμᾶς κάνονες. I Terapeuti di Alessandria nella vita spirituale protocristiana', in L. F. Pizzolato and M. Rizzi (edd.), *Origene maestro di vita spirituale*, Studia Patristica Mediolanensia 22 (Milan 2001) 47–89.

F. Calabi, 'I sacrifici e la loro funzione conoscitiva in Filone di Alessandria', *Annali di Storia dell'Esegesi* 18 (2001) 101–127.

E. Carotenuto, *Tradizione e innovazione nella Historia Ecclesiastica di Eusebio di Cesarea*, esp. 134–142 (Bologna 2001).

A. Choufrine, *Gnosis, Theophany, Theosis: Studies in Clement of Alexandria's Appropriation of his Background* (diss. Princeton Theological Seminary 2001).

A. A. Das, *Paul, the Law and the Covenant* (Peabody Mass. 2001), esp. 23–31.

L. Díez Merino, 'El hombre: imagen y semejanza de Dios en la literatura judía antigua', *Ciencia Tomista* 128 (2001) 277–15.

C. Dogniez and M. Harl (edd.), *La Bible des Septante: Le Pentateuque d'Alexandrie* (Paris 2001).

L. E. Galloway, *Freedom in 1 Corinthians 9: Paul in Conversation with Epictetus and Philo* (diss. Emory University 2001).

P. von Gemünden, 'La figure de Jacob dans l'époque hellénistico-romaine: l'exemple de Philon d'Alexandrie', in J.-D. Macchi and T. Römer, *Jacob commentaire à plusieurs voix de Gen 25-36: Mélanges offerts à Albert de Pury* (Paris 2001) 358-370.

V. Guignard, 'L'interprétation de l'année jubilaire chez Philon', in L.-J. Bord and D. Hamidovic (edd.), *Jubilé ... Jubilés. Actes du colloque tenu à Angers les 1er, 2 et 3 mars 2000* (Paris 2001) 101–105.

L. Gusella, 'Esseni, comunità di Qumran, terapeuti', *Materia Giudaica. Rivista dell'associazione per lo studio del giudaismo* 6 (2001) 223–246.

D. M. Hay, 'Philo', in D. A. Carson, P. T. O'Brien and M. Seifrid (edd.), *Justification and Variegated Nomism: A Fresh Appraisal of Paul and Second Temple Judaism. Vol. 1, The Complexities of Second Temple Judaism*, WUNT 2.140 (Tübingen 2001) 357–379.

E. Hilgert, 'The Philo Institute, Studia Philonica and their *Diadochoi*', in D. T. Runia and G. E. Sterling (edd.), *In the Spirit of Faith: Studies in Philo and Early Christianity in Honor of David Hay [= The Studia Philonica Annual 13 (2001)]*, Brown Judaic Studies 332 (Providence RI 2001) 13–24.

D. R. Johnson, *Herod Agrippa's Letter to Gaius (Caligula): A Manifesto for Peace in Judaea* (M.A. thesis, California State University at Fresno 2001).

A. Kamesar, 'Ambrose, Philo, and the Presence of Art in the Bible', *Journal of Early Christian Studies* 9 (2001) 73–104.

U. Kellerman, 'Der Dekalog in den Schriften des Frühjudentums: ein Überblick', in *Wesiheit, Ethos und Gebot* (2001) 147–226.

M. Kister, "Leave the Dead to Bury their own Dead", in *Studies in Ancient Midrash* (2001) 43–56.

J. Klawans, *Impurity and Sin in Ancient Judaism* (Oxford 2001), esp. 64–66.

J. Leonhardt, *Jewish Worship in Philo of Alexandria*, TSAJ 84 (Tübingen 2001).

Y. D. Matusova, 'Philo of Alexandria and Greek Doxography (Russian)', *Vestnik Drevnej Istorii* 1 (2001) 40–52.

W. B. McNutt, *Philo of Alexandria: an Exegete of Scripture* (diss. University of Missouri, Kansas City 2001).

A. Nagy, 'A Timaiosz recepciója Philónál: *De opificio mundi* [The Reception of the Timaeus in Philo of Alexandria: *De opificio mundi*]', *Filozófiae Folyórat [Pécs]* 3 (2001) 134–151.

M. R. Niehoff, *Philo on Jewish Identity and Culture*, TSAJ 86 (Tübingen 2001).

M. Osmanski, *Logos i stworzenie. Filozoficzna interpretac;ja traktau De opificio mundi Filona z Aleksandrii [Logos and creation. Philosophical Interpretation of the 'De opificio mundi' of Philo of Alexandria]* (Lublin 2001).

A. Paul, 'Les «Écritures» dans la societé juive au temps de Jésus', *Recherches de Science Religieuse* 89 (2001) 13–42.

F. Petit, *La Chaîne sur l'Exode. IV Fonds caténique ancien (Exode 15,22–40,32)*, Traditio Exegetica Graeca 11 (Louvain 2001).

T. E. Phillips, 'Revisiting Philo: Discussions of Wealth and Poverty in Philo's Ethical Discourse', *JSNT* 83 (2001) 111–121.

R. Plunkett-Dowling, *Reading and Restoration: Paul's Use of Scripture in 2 Corinthians 1–9 (Saint Paul)* (diss. Yale University 2001).

P. H. Poirier, 'Gnosis and Patristics: Regarding Two Attestations of Interior Discourse', *Laval Theologique et Philosophique* 57 (2001) 235–241.

F. Raurell, 'La recerca sobre els LXX', *Estudios Franciscanos* 102 (2001) 1–52.

J. Riaud, 'La célébration de chaque septième sabbat dans la communauté des Thérapeutes d'Alexandrie', in L.-J. Bord and D. Hamidovic (edd.), *Jubilé ... Jubilés. Actes du colloque tenu à Angers les 1er, 2 et 3 mars 2000* (Paris 2001) 107–123.

J. R. Royse, 'Philo's Division of his Works into Books', in D. T. Runia and G. E. Sterling (edd.), *In the Spirit of Faith: Studies in Philo and Early Christianity in Honor of David Hay [= The Studia Philonica Annual 13 (2001)]*, Brown Judaic Studies 332 (Providence RI 2001) 59–85.

A. Runesson, *The Origins of the Synagogue. A Socio-Historical Study*, Coniectanea Biblica New Testament Series 37 (Stockholm 2001).

D. T. Runia, 'Eudaimonism in Hellenistic-Jewish literature', in J. L. Kugel (ed.), *Bar-Ilan and Harvard Conferences* (Leiden 2001).

D. T. Runia, *Philo On the Creation of the Cosmos according to Moses*, Philo of Alexandria Commentary Series 1 (Leiden etc. 2001).

D. T. RUNIA, 'Philo's Reading of the Psalms', in D. T. RUNIA and G. E. STERLING (edd.), *In the Spirit of Faith: Studies in Philo and Early Christianity in Honor of David Hay [= The Studia Philonica Annual 13 (2001)]*, Brown Judaic Studies 332 (Providence RI 2001) 102–121.

D. T. RUNIA, 'Philon d'Alexandria devant le Pentateuque', in C. DOGNIEZ and M. HARL (edd.), *La Bible des Septante: Le Pentateuque d'Alexandrie* (Paris 2001) 99–105.

D. T. RUNIA, E. BIRNBAUM, A. C. GELJON, H. M. KEIZER, J. P. MARTÍN, R. RADICE, J. RIAUD, T. SELAND, D. SATRAN and D. ZELLER, 'Philo of Alexandria: an Annotated Bibliography 1998', *The Studia Philonica Annual* 13 (2001) 250–290.

D. T. RUNIA and G. E. STERLING (edd.), *In the Spirit of Faith: Studies in Philo and Early Christianity in Honor of David Hay [= The Studia Philonica Annual 13 (2001)]*, Brown Judaic Studies 332 (Providence RI 2001).

K.-G. SANDELIN, 'Philo's Ambivalence towards Statues', in D. T. RUNIA and G. E. STERLING (edd.), *In the Spirit of Faith: Studies in Philo and Early Christianity in Honor of David Hay [= The Studia Philonica Annual 13 (2001)]*, Brown Judaic Studies 332 (Providence RI 2001) 122–138.

G. SCHÖLLGEN, *Reallexikon für Antike und Christentum*, Lieferungen 154–155 (Stuttgart 2001).

H. Ohme, art. 'Kanon I (Begriff)', 1–28, esp. 7–8 (Canon I, as concept).

T. SELAND, 'πάροικος καὶ παρεπίδημος: Proselyte Characterizations in 1 Peter?', *Bulletin for Biblical Research* 11 (2001) 239–268.

A. M. SERRA, 'La 'spada': simbolo della 'parola di Dio', nell'Antico Testamento biblico-guidaico e nel Nuovo Testamento', *Marianum* 63 (2001) 17–89.

Y. SHIBATA, 'On the Ineffable. Philo and Justin', *Patristica. Proceedings of the Colloquia of the Japanese Society for Patristic Studies. Suppl. vol.* 1 (2001) 19–47.

R. DE SMET and K. VERELST, 'Newton's Scholium Generale: The Platonic and Stoic Legacy — Philo, Justus Lipsius and the Cambridge Platonists', *History of Science* 39 (2001) 1–30.

H. J. SPIERENBURG, *De Philonische geheime leer: de Kabbala van Philo van Alexandrië* (Deventer 2001).

G. E. STERLING (ed.), *The Ancestral Wisdom: Hellenistic Philosophy in Second Temple Judaism. Essays of David Winston*, Studia Philonica Monographs 4, Brown Judaic Series 331 (Providence RI 2001).

G. E. STERLING, 'Judaism between Jerusalem and Alexandria', in J. J. COLLINS and G. E. STERLING (edd.), *Hellenism in the Land of Israel*, Christianity and Judaism in Antiquity Series 13 (Notre Dame 2001) 263–301.

G. E. STERLING, 'A History of the Philo of Alexandria Program Units in the Society of Biblical Literature', in D. T. RUNIA and G. E. STERLING (edd.), *In the Spirit of Faith: Studies in Philo and Early Christianity in Honor of David Hay [= The Studia Philonica Annual 13 (2001)]*, Brown Judaic Studies 332 (Providence RI 2001) 25–34.

G. E. STERLING, 'Ontology versus Eschatology: Tensions between Author and Community', in D. T. RUNIA and G. E. STERLING (edd.), *In the Spirit of Faith: Studies in Philo and Early Christianity in Honor of David Hay [= The Studia Philonica Annual 13 (2001)]*, esp. 199–204, Brown Judaic Studies 332 (Providence RI 2001) 190–211.

J. TAYLOR, 'The Community of Goods among the First Christians and among the Essenes', in D. GOODBLATT, A. PINNICK and D. R. SCHWARTZ (edd.), *Historical Perspectives; from the Hasmoneans to Bar Kokhba in Light of the Dead Sea Scrolls* (Leiden etc. 2001) 147–161.

J. E. TAYLOR, 'Virgin Mothers: Philo on the Women Therapeutae', *Journal for the Study of the Pseudepigrapha* 12 (2001) 37–63.

N. H. TAYLOR, 'Popular Opposition to Caligula in Jewish Palestine', *JSJ* 32 (2001) 54–70.

C. TERMINI, 'La creazione come APXH della legge in Filone di Alessandria (*Opif.* 1–3)', *Rivista Biblica* 49 (2001) 283–318.

T. H. TOBIN, 'The Jewish Context of Rom 5:12–14', in D. T. RUNIA and G. E. STERLING (edd.), *In the Spirit of Faith: Studies in Philo and Early Christianity in Honor of David Hay [= The Studia Philonica Annual 13 (2001)]*, Brown Judaic Studies 332 (Providence RI 2001) 159–175.

S. TORALLAS TOVAR, 'El libro de los sueños de Sinesio de Cirene', in R. TEJA (ed.), *Sueños y visiones en el paganismo y el cristianismo* (Santa María la Real 2001) 69–81.

A. TRIPOLITIS, *Religions of the Hellenistic-Roman Age* (Grand Rapids 2001), esp. 77–85.

L. TROIANI, 'Filone alessandrino e il cristianesimo delle originie', in D. AMBAGLIO (ed.), *Materiali e appunti per lo studio della storia e della letteratura antica* (Como 2001) 157–172.

E. VILLARI, *Il morso e il cavaliere. Una metafora della temperanza e del dominio di sé*, Università 52 (Genua 2001).

D. VOLGGER, 'Die Adressaten des Weisheitsbuches', *Biblica* 82 (2001) 153–177.

H. C. WAETJEN, 'Logos pros ton Theon and the Objectification of Truth in the Prologue of the Fourth Gospel', *Catholic Biblical Quarterly* 63 (2001) 265–286.

R. WEBER, *Das 'Gesetz' bei Philon von Alexandrien und Flavius Josephus: Studien zum Verständnis und zur Funktion der Thora bei den beiden Haupt-*

zeugen des hellenistischen Judentums, Arbeiten zur Religion und Geschichte des Urchristentums 11 (Frankfurt am Maim 2001).
J. WEINBERG, *Azariah de' Rossi, The Light of the Eyes* (New Haven 2001).
D. WINSTON, *The Ancestral Wisdom: Hellenistic Philosophy in Second Temple Judaism. Essays of David Winston, edited by G. E. Sterling*, Studia Philonica Monographs 4, Brown Judaic Series 331 (Providence RI 2001).
D. WINSTON, 'Philo of Alexandria and Ibn al-'Arabi', in D. T. RUNIA and G. E. STERLING (edd.), *In the Spirit of Faith: Studies in Philo and Early Christianity in Honor of David Hay [= The Studia Philonica Annual 13 (2001)]*, Brown Judaic Studies 332 (Providence RI 2001) 139–155.
B. W. WINTER, *Philo and Paul among the Sophists* (Grand Rapids 2001, 2nd edition).
D. ZELLER, 'Die angebliche Enthusiastische oder spiritualistische Front in 1 Kor 15', in D. T. RUNIA and G. E. STERLING (edd.), *In the Spirit of Faith: Studies in Philo and Early Christianity in Honor of David Hay [= The Studia Philonica Annual 13 (2001)]*, Brown Judaic Studies 332 (Providence RI 2001) 176–189.

2002

J. R. BARTLETT (ed.), *Jews in the Hellenstic and Roman Cities* (London 2002).
L. BAYNES, 'Personification, and the Transformation of Grammatical Gender', *The Studia Philonica Annual* 14 (2002) 31–47.
K. BERTHELOT, 'Philo and Kindness towards Animals (*De Virtutibus* 125–147)', *The Studia Philonica Annual* 14 (2002) 49–65.
G. BOHAK, 'Ethnic Continuity in the Jewish Diaspora in Antiquity', in J. R. BARTLETT (ed.), *Jews in the Hellenstic and Roman Cities* (London 2002) 175–192.
G. BOHAK, 'The Ibis and the Jewish Question: Ancient 'Anti-Semitism' in Historical Perspective', in M. MOR and A. OPPENHEIMER (edd.), *Jewish-Gentile Relations in the Periods of the Second Temple, the Mishna and the Talmud* (Jerusalem 2002).
F. CALABI, 'Conoscibilità e inconoscibilità di Dio in Filone di Alessandria', in F. CALABI (ed.), *Arrhetos Theos: l'ineffabilità del primo principio nel medio platonismo* (Pisa 2002) 35–54.
F. CALABI, 'Filone di Alessandria tra Bibbia e filosofia', in *Due grandi sapienze: Bibbia ed ellenismo* (Florence 2002) 231–260.
F. CALABI, 'Il governante sulla scena. Politica e rappresentazione nell'*In Flaccum* di Filone Alessandrino', in F. CALABI (ed.), *Immagini e rappresentazione. Contributi su Filone di Alessandria*, Studies in Philo of Alexandria & Mediterranean Antiquity (Binghamton–New York 2002) 45–57.

F. CALABI (ed.), *Immagini e rappresentazione. Contributi su Filone di Alessandria*, Studies in Philo of Alexandria & Mediterranean Antiquity (Binghamton–New York 2002).

F. CALABI, 'Sovranità divina, regalità umana in Filone di Alessandria', in P. BETTIOLO and G. FILORAMO (edd.), *Il dio mortale: Teologie politische tra antico e contemporaneo* (Brescia 2002) 63–77.

N. G. COHEN, 'Context and Connotation. Greek Words for Jewish Concepts in Philo', in J. L. KUGEL (ed.), *Shem in the Tents of Japheth: Essays on the Encounter of Judaism and Hellenism*, Supplements to the Journal for the Study of Judaism 74 (Leiden etc. 2002) 31–61.

J. M. DILLON, 'The Essenes in Greek Sources: Some Reflections', in J. R. BARTLETT (ed.), *Jews in the Hellenstic and Roman Cities* (London 2002) 117–128.

H. DÖRRIE and BALTES M., 'Die philosophische Lehre des Platonismus: Von der »Seele« als der Ursache aller sinnvollen Abläufe', in 2 vols., Der Platonismus in der Antike 6 (Stuttgart-Bad Cannstatt 2002).

J. E. DYCK, 'Philo, Alexandria and Empire: the Politics of Allegorical Interpretation', in J. R. BARTLETT (ed.), *Jews in the Hellenstic and Roman Cities* (London 2002) 149–174.

L. FELDMAN, 'Philo's Version of the 'Aqedah', *The Studia Philonica Annual* 14 (2002) 66–86.

L. H. FELDMAN, 'The Death of Moses, according to Philo', *Estudios Bíblicos* 60 (2002) 225–254.

L. H. FELDMAN, 'The Plague of the First-born Egyptians in Rabbinic Tradition, Philo, Pseudo-Philo, and Josephus', *Revue biblique* 109 (2002) 315–346.

L. H. FELDMAN, 'The Portrayal of Phinehas by Philo, Pseudo-Philo, and Josephus', *Jewish Quarterly Review* 92 (2002) 403–421.

C. B. FORBES, 'Pauline Demonology and/or Cosmology? Principalities, Powers and the Elements of the World in their Hellenistic Context', *JSNT* 85 (2002) 51–73.

F. FRAZIER, 'Les visages de Joseph dans le *De Josepho*', *The Studia Philonica Annual* 14 (2002) 1–30.

A. C. GELJON, 'Mozes als Platoonse Stoïcijn', *Hermeneus* 74 (2002) 344–353.

A. C. GELJON, *Philonic Exegesis in Gregory of Nyssa's De vita Moysis*, Brown Judaic Series 333 Studia Philonica Monographs 5 (Providence RI 2002).

U. GERSHOWITZ and A. KOVELMAN, 'A Symmetrical Teleological Construction in the Treatises of Philo and in the Talmud', *Review of Rabbinic Judaism* 5 (2002) 228–246.

P. GRAFFIGNA, 'L'immagine della bilancia in Filone d'Alessandria', in F. CALABI (ed.), *Immagini e rappresentazione. Contributi su Filone di Alessandria*,

Studies in Philo of Alexandria & Mediterranean Antiquity (Binghamton–New York 2002) 27–44.

E. GRUEN, *Diaspora: Jewish amidst Greeks and Romans*, esp. chap. 2 (Cambridge MA–London 2002).

L. R. HELYER, *Exploring Jewish Literature of the Second Temple Period. A Guide for New Testament Students*, esp. pp. 311–335 (Downers Grove, Ill 2002).

A. VAN DEN HOEK, 'Assessing Philo's Influence in Christian Alexandria: The Case of Origen', in J. L. KUGEL (ed.), *Shem in the Tents of Japheth: Essays on the Encounter of Judaism and Hellenism*, Supplements to the Journal for the Study of Judaism 74 (Leiden etc. 2002) 223–239.

A. KAMESAR, 'Writing Commentaries on the Works of Philo: Some Reflections', *Adamantius* 8 (2002) 127–134.

J. L. KUGEL (ed.), *Shem in the Tents of Japheth: Essays on the Encounter of Judaism and Hellenism*, Supplements to the Journal for the Study of Judaism 74 (Leiden etc. 2002).

J. P. MARTÍN, 'Historiografía, religión y filosofía en el siglo II', in J. FERNÁNDEZ SANGRADOR and S. GUIJARRO OPORTO (edd.), *Plenitudo Temporis, Miscelánea Homenaje a R. Trevijano Etcheverría* (Salamanca 2002) 313–332.

J. P. MARTÍN, 'Religión y teología', in F. DIEZ DE VELASCO and F. GARCÍA BAZÁN (edd.), *El estudio de la religión*, Enciclopedia IberoAmericana de Religiones 1 (Madrid 2002) 227–255.

A. MAZZANTI, 'L'identità dell'uomo in Filone di Alessandria', in F. CALABI (ed.), *Immagini e rappresentazione. Contributi su Filone di Alessandria*, Studies in Philo of Alexandria & Mediterranean Antiquity (Binghamton–New York 2002) 7–26.

D. A. NIELSEN, 'Civilizational Encounters in the Development of Early Christianity', in A. J. BLASI, J. DUHAIME and P.-A. TURCOTTE (edd.), *Handbook of Early Christianity. Social Sciences Approaches* (Walnut Creek, CA 2002) 267–290, esp. 269–278.

T. H. OLBRICHT, 'Greek Rhetoric and the Allegorical Rhetoric of Philo and Clement of Alexandria', in S. E. PORTER and D. L. STAMPS (ed.), *Rhetorical Criticism and the Bible*, JSNT.SS 195 (Sheffield 2002) 24–47.

R. PASSARELLA, 'Medicina in allegoria: Ambrogio, Filone e l'arca di Noè', in *Tra IV e V secolo: Studi sulla cultura latina tardoantica*, Quaderni di Acme 50 (2002) 189–252.

A. PASSONI DELL'ACQUA, 'I LXX nella Biblioteca di Alessandria', *Adamantius* 8 (2002) 114–126, esp. 125f.

R. RADICE, 'Filone Alessandrino e la tradizione platonica. Il caso di Seneca', in F. CALABI (ed.), *Immagini e rappresentazione. Contributi su Filone di*

Alessandria, Studies in Philo of Alexandria & Mediterranean Antiquity (Binghamton–New York 2002) 58–69.

G. REYDAMS-SCHILS, 'Philo of Alexandria on Stoic and Platonist Psycho-Physiology: the Socratic Higher Ground', *Ancient Philosophy* 22 (2002) 125–148.

D. T. RUNIA, 'Eudaimonism in Hellenistic-Jewish and Early Christian Literature', *Iris (Journal of the Classical Association of Victoria)* 15 (2002) 63–72.

D. T. RUNIA, E. BIRNBAUM, A. C. GELJON, K. A. FOX, H. M. KEIZER, J. P. MARTÍN, R. RADICE, J. RIAUD, T. SELAND, D. ZELLER, 'Philo of Alexandria: an Annotated Bibliography 1999', *The Studia Philonica Annual* 14 (2002) 141–179.

D. T. RUNIA, 'Philo of Alexandria and the End of Hellenistic Theology', in A. LAKS and D. FREDE (edd.), *Traditions of Theology: Studies in Hellenistic Theology, Its Background and Aftermath*, Philosophia Antiqua 89 (Leiden 2002) 281–316.

D. T. RUNIA, 'Eudaimonism in Hellenistic-Jewish Literature', in J. L. KUGEL (edd.), *Shem in the Tents of Japheth: Essays on the Encounter of Judaism and Hellenism*, Supplements to the Journal for the Study of Judaism 74 (Leiden etc. 2002) 131–157.

D. T. RUNIA, 'One of Us or One of Them? Christian Reception of Philo the Jew in Egypt', in J. L. KUGEL (ed.), *Shem in the Tents of Japheth: Essays on the Encounter of Judaism and Hellenism*, Supplements to the Journal for the Study of Judaism 74 (Leiden etc. 2002) 203–222.

S. RUZER, 'From 'Love your Neighbour' to 'Love your Enemy'. Trajectories in Early Jewish Exegesis', *Revue Biblique* 109 (2002) 371–389.

K. O. SANDNES, *Belly and Body in the Pauline Epistles*, Society for New Testament Studies Monograph Series 120 (Cambridge 2002), esp. 108–135.

K. L. SCHENCK, 'Philo and the Epistle to the Hebrews: Ronald Williamson's Study after Thirty Years', *The Studia Philonica Annual* 14 (2002) 112–135.

G. SCHIMANOWSKI, 'Philo als Prophet, Philo als Christ, Philo als Bischof', in F. SIEGERT (ed.), *Grenzgänge. Menschen und Schicksale zwischen jüdischer, christlicher und deutscher Identität: Festschrift für Diethard Aschoff*, Münsteraner Judaistische Studien 11 (Münster 2002) 36–49.

G. SCHÖLLGEN, Reallexikon für Antike und Christentum, Supplement-Lieferung 9 (Stuttgart 2002).

K. Thraede, art. 'Blutschande (Inzest)' 37–85, esp. 51–52 (Blood scandal (Incest)).

I. W. SCOTT, 'Is Philo's Moses a Divine Man?', *The Studia Philonica Annual* 14 (2002) 87–111.

T. SELAND, 'Saul of Tarsus and Early Zealotism. Reading Gal 1.1314 in Light of Philo's Writings', *Biblica* 83 (2002) 449–471.

G. Theissen, 'Zum Freiheitsverständnis bei Paulus und Philo. Paradoxe und kommunitäre Freiheit', in H.-J. Reuter (ed.), *Freiheitverantworten.* FS W. Huber (Gütersloh 2002) 357–368.

D. Winston, 'Philo and the Wisdom of Solomon on Creation, Revelation, and Providence: The High-Water of Jewish Hellenistic Fusion', in J. L. Kugel (ed.), *Shem in the Tents of Japheth: Essays on the Encounter of Judaism and Hellenism*, Supplements to the Journal for the Study of Judaism 74 (Leiden etc. 2002) 109–130.

2003

D. E. Aune, T. Seland and J. H. Ulrichsen (edd.), *Neotestamentica et Philonica: Studies in Honor of Peder Borgen*, Supplements to Novum Testamentum 106 (Leiden–Boston 2003).

K. Berthelot, *Philanthropia judaica: Le debat autour de la 'misanthropie' des lois juives dans l'antiquite*, Supplement Series to the Journal for the Study of Judaism (Leiden–Boston 2003).

E. Birnbaum, 'Allegorical Interpretation and Jewish Identity among Alexandrian Jewish Writers', in D. E. Aune, T. Seland and J. H. Ulrichsen (edd.), *Neotestamentica et Philonica: Studies in Honor of Peder Borgen*, Supplements to Novum Testamentum 106 (Leiden–Boston 2003) 307–329.

T. Engberg-Pedersen, 'Paraenesis Terminology in Philo', in D. E. Aune, T. Seland and J. H. Ulrichsen (edd.), *Neotestamentica et Philonica: Studies in Honor of Peder Borgen*, Supplements to Novum Testamentum 106 (Leiden–Boston 2003) 371–392.

K. Fuglseth, 'Common Words in the New Testament and Philo: Some Results from a Complete Vocabulary', in D. E. Aune, T. Seland and J. H. Ulrichsen (edd.), *Neotestamentica et Philonica: Studies in Honor of Peder Borgen*, Supplements to Novum Testamentum 106 (Leiden–Boston 2003) 393–414.

D. M. Hay, 'Foils for the Therapeutae: References to Other Texts and Persons in Philo's *De vita contemplativa*', in D. E. Aune, T. Seland and J. H. Ulrichsen (edd.), *Neotestamentica et Philonica: Studies in Honor of Peder Borgen*, Supplements to Novum Testamentum 106 (Leiden–Boston 2003) 330–348.

H. Jacobson, 'φαραν or βαραδ in Philo's *QG*', *Journal of Theological Studies* 54 (2003) 158–159.

D. T. Runia, 'Philo of Alexandria, *Legatio ad Gaium* 1–7', in D. E. Aune, T. Seland and J. H. Ulrichsen (edd.), *Neotestamentica et Philonica:*

Studies in Honor of Peder Borgen, Supplements to Novum Testamentum 106 (Leiden–Boston 2003) 349–370.

D. T. RUNIA, 'Plato's *Timaeus*, First Principle(s) and Creation in Philo and Early Christian Thought', in G. REYDAMS-SCHILS (ed.), *Plato's Timaeus as Cultural Icon* (Notre Dame 2003) 133–151.

D. T. RUNIA, 'The King, the Architect, and the Craftsman: a Philosophical Image in Philo of Alexandria', in R. W. SHARPLES and A. SHEPPARD (edd.), *Ancient Approaches to Plato's Timaeus*, Bulletin of the Institute of Classical Studies Supplement 78 (London 2003) 89–106.

D. T. RUNIA, 'Theodicy in Philo of Alexandria', in A. LAATO and J. C. DE MOOR (edd.), *Theodicy in the World of the Bible* (Leiden etc. 2003).

P. SCHÄFER, *Mirror of His Beauty: Feminine Images of God from the Bible to the Early Kabbalah. Jews, Christians, and Muslims from the Ancient to the Modern World*, (Princeton–Oxford 2002), esp. 39–57.

S. TORALLAS TOVAR, 'Philo of Alexandria on Sleep', in T. WIEDEMANN and K. DOWDEN (edd.), *Sleep*, Nottingham Classical Studies 8 (Bari 2003) 41–52.

BOOK REVIEW SECTION

Y. AMIR [עמיר .י] (ed.), פילון האלכסנדרוני. כתבים [Philo of Alexandria: *Writings*]: vol.4, part 1. *Allegorical Exegesis (Genesis 1–5)*. Jerusalem: Bialik Institute and Israel Academy of Sciences and Humanities, 1997. ISBN 965-342-673-7. Price $65.

As every student of Philo knows, the allegorical commentaries on scripture constitute the very heart of his literary legacy. They are at once the most difficult, the most rewarding and the most revealing of his writings. They are also, somewhat paradoxically, often among the first of Philo's works encountered by his modern readers, whether in anthological collections or in the standard editions and translations. The new five-volume presentation of the (Greek) Philonic corpus in modern Hebrew translation, under the general editorship of S. Daniel-Nataf, determined, as one of its overarching aims, to rectify this common error and the resultant frustration and misunderstanding. (On this question, see *SPhA* 2 [1990] 182–184.) Indeed, only now, with the appearance of the fourth volume of the series — following the translations of the historical/apologetic works (vol. 1) and the exposition of the Law (vols. 2–3) — does the Hebrew reader come face-to-face with the allegorical core of Philo's exegesis and thought.

This volume, the handiwork of the late Yehoshua Amir, the acknowledged doyen of Philonic studies in Israel, accordingly presents the initial portion of the great allegorical commentary on Genesis: *Legum allegoriae* 1–3, *De Cherubim*, *De sacrificiis Abelis et Caini*, *Quod deterius potiori insidiari soleat*, *De posteritate Caini*. Amir himself was responsible for the introductions, Hebrew translations and notes for all the treatises, with the exception of *Cher.* which has been contributed by C. Shur. In terms of general design and presentation, the volume adheres largely to the format of the three earlier volumes in the series. Each of the treatises is prefaced by a brief introduction, offering a succinct account of the composition's basic structure and progression. The translations reflect these structural analyses, bearing titles and subtitles which highlight the exegetical basis and thematic content of Philo's discussion for the convenience of the reader. The translations themselves are accompanied by copious notes which, in accord with the guidelines of the series, refer only occasionally to current Philonic research but offer a wealth of reference to ancient sources.

There is much, however, that sets this volume apart from its predecessors, both in terms of outlook and approach. In contrast to the positive view of the series' general editor regarding the scope of Philo's knowledge of Hebrew, Amir assumes no such familiarity. He opens the general introduction to the volume with a brief (9–10) yet acute discussion of the Greek Scriptures as the unwavering focal point of the Philonic enterprise. This theme is maintained throughout: the rich textual notes reveal a constant concern with the precise dynamic of the Greek scriptural citations as the point of origin of Philo's exegetical flights. Amir devotes the major portion of the introduction (11–22) to an examination of the character of Philo's allegorical exegesis and its complex relationship to the use of allegory in the wider Greco-Roman world; once again, while the discussion is brief, Amir returns to and illustrates many of his observations in his notes to the text of the treatises. Indeed, the general quality of the notes is both so attentive and detailed that this volume might be described more accurately as a commentary than as an annotated translation.

Amir's translation is expert and elegant. A generation of Hebrew readers is already familiar with his painstaking yet almost poetic rendering of the selections from Philo's writings chosen by Yohanan (Hans) Lewy (R–R 3012). It is with the same clarity and unfailing precision that Amir has translated here the allegorical treatises. Further, though this may not be the proper forum for a detailed discussion of the literary merits of the translation, a few words should be said. Amir's prose is straightforward yet deeply informed by the vocabulary and the cadences of classical Hebrew, from the Bible itself through the medieval philosophic literature. One might hope that these literary qualities would encourage additional readers, with a background in biblical and post-biblical Hebrew, to enjoy the riches of this new translation.

This first volume of the allegorical commentaries, sadly, is the only one that Yehoshua Amir lived to see in print. His death last year marked the end of a remarkable career of scholarship spanning seven decades of teaching and research dedicated to both ancient and modern Jewish thought. His innate sensitivity as a translator enriched not only students of Philo but equally readers of Rosenzweig and Buber as well. Actively involved in scholarship to the day of his death, his ninety-first birthday, Amir had only weeks earlier submitted to the publisher the completed manuscript of the next volume of the commentaries in Hebrew translation. May this and the succeeding volume stand as a fitting memorial for that wisest and most modest of men. [On Yehoshua Amir see further the biographical notice by A. Kamesar in News and Notes, p. 184. EDITORS]

David Satran
Hebrew University
Jerusalem

Cristina TERMINI, *Le potenze di Dio. Studio su δύναμις in Filone di Alessandria*. Studia Ephemeridis Augustinianum 71. Rome: Institutum Patristicum Augustinianum, 2000. 306 pages. ISBN 884-7961-023-6. Price € 33.50.

Although every comprehensive study on Philo's thought has to deal with the theme of the divine powers, the work under review is to my knowledge the first separate monograph devoted to the subject. This excellent study has its origin in a doctoral dissertation prepared at the University of Rome, 'La Sapienza,' under the direction of Prof. Clara Kraus Reggiani. It is yet another demonstration of the vitality of research in Classics, Judaism and Patristics in Italy at the present time.

The book divides, appropriately enough for a monograph on Philo, into seven parts (though strangely they are not numbered). In the Introduction the methodology to be used and reflections on previous research are set out. It is argued that the quest to find a philosophical background which will explain Philo's doctrine has proven a failure. The approach through comparative studies in the history of religions has also lacked focus and not been very successful. In line with much recent research Termini regards the role of exegesis in Philo's thought as not merely passive or offering pretexts for discussion, but rather as giving significant impulses towards the elaboration of specific doctrines. Moreover Philo's exegesis does not occur in a vacuum, but must be seen against the background of Hellenistic-Jewish tradition. The conceptual framework within which Philo's theology should be read is the strong affirmation of divine sovereignty and unicity. Any reading of Philonic theology which emphasizes the hypostasization or the mediatory role of divine attributes is strongly opposed. From the Jewish perspective transcendence does not mean separation in religious terms. This differs markedly from what we find in a philosophical treatise such as the *De mundo*. Next a thorough lexical and linguistic analysis is given of Philo's theological use of the term δύναμις. It occurs no less than 187 times. Unlike other Jewish authors writing in Greek (including Josephus) there are more instances in the plural (108) than in the singular (79). A telling result of the analysis is that verbs of action are seldom used with the divine powers as their subject. God remains the chief protagonist and the primary role of the divine powers is to act as his instruments.

In the first chapter of the main body of the work, Termini argues that the main role of the powers is *theophanic* in nature, i.e. to express the manifestation of the divine attributes and excellences (ἀρεταί) in the cosmos and in relation to human beings. The main method used here and in the other chapters is the close reading of central texts, e.g. *Spec.* 1.209, 32–50, 307, *Mut.* 7–29, *Plant.* 85–92, *Abr.* 119–132. The divine names and the powers associated with those names express aspects of divine revelation and as such have a functional role. The frequent reference to a plurality of powers is likely to be a concession to Hellenism. Termini notes the link to be made with the polyonomy found, for example, in pagan hymns to Isis and in Stoic philosophical theology. At the same time, however, she notes the strong parallelism with various Hellenistic-Jewish texts which emphasize divine action. Philo shares their ideological context, but expresses his theology in a philosophically more sophisticated way.

The next chapter has as its heading 'The theological value of δύναμις as instrument of reflection on God'. In fact, however, it primarily treats a more specific aspect of the functional role of the powers, namely its use in dealing with the thorny exegetical and doctrinal problem of theological anthropomorphism. Termini sees important connections with the rabbinic doctrine that links divine names in scripture and divine characteristics in dealing with human beings. The rabbis use the term *middah*, 'measure' instead of 'power', and this is particularly interesting in relation to the Philonic text at *Sacr.* 59–60, in which the 'three measures' of Gen. 18:6 are interpreted in terms of the theophanic role of God and his powers are called 'measurers'.

In the next chapter Termini zooms in on a group of texts in which the theophanic role of the powers is linked to the Cherubim of the Hebrew Bible. Here we are given very fine and detailed analyses of *QG* 1.57, *Cher.* 1–39 (esp. 27–30), *Fug.* 94–105 and *QE* 2.59–68. This allows the author to confront the Philonic phenomenon of multiple exegesis. She surmises that the interpretation of the ark of the covenant may have provided an important stimulus for Philo's doctrine of the powers, since the two Cherubim provide a basis for the binary emphasis on two chief powers. But at the same time we observe the flexibility of the doctrine, with various hierarchical schemes attached to different exegetical starting-points. In each case, however, the powers express and define the aspectual character of the divine manifestation. The same applies to the divine Logos, which is placed beside or in relation to the powers.

In the fifth and longest chapter the author tackles the difficult subject of the role played by the powers in the creation of humanity. The four main texts here are *Opif.* 69–75, *Conf.* 168–182, *Fug.* 65–74, and *Mut.* 30–31. The chief theological issue is theodicy and the problem of evil. Exegetical considerations (notably the controversial plurals in Gen. 1:26, 3:22 and 11:7) allow Philo to 'insinuate' (the author's term, p. 138) the doctrine of the powers into these contexts and so arrive at a solution. Only by recognizing Philo's flexible hermeneutics and by allowing the texts to speak for themselves will we be able to do justice to Philo's deeper theological intentions, which focus on the problem of theodicy. For Philo ethical considerations far outweigh the ontological concerns that have preoccupied most of his modern interpreters. On this basis we are presented with excellent readings of these central texts (I wish I could have used them for my commentary on *Opif.*). Termini interprets the plurality of creators invoked by Philo as 'virtual' (emphasized by the expression ὡς ἄν, cf. *Opif.* 75, *Conf.* 168, *Fug.* 68, 71), or perhaps even as fictional (cf. p. 186). On the correlation between a multiplicity of creators and the differing parts of the human being that are created (body, rational soul or mind, irrational soul) Philo remains deliberately vague, refusing a direct imposition of the scheme of Plato's *Timaeus* on his exegesis. His purpose is primarily theological and ethical. The language of alterity and subordination which is used of the powers in creationistic contexts reflects the extraneous nature of evil and wicked behaviour in relation to God (cf. the conclusion on p. 188).

The sixth and last substantial chapter of the monograph may come as a surprise. It is devoted to the theme of the divine powers as 'bonds' (δεσμοί). Here the main texts are *Her.* 22–23, *Migr.* 136, 179–183, *Conf.* 162–167, *Abr.* 58–59. The philosophical origins are to be found in Plato's *Timaeus*, some Stoic texts and allegorical exegesis of the Homeric 'golden chain' motif. But Termini finds them inadequate for the purpose of explaining their theological use in Philo, and speculates that the emphasis on the theme may have a Jewish origin. The theme of the powers (and the Logos) as bonds can be seen as an extrapolation from the famous text in *Tim.* 41a, but it seems that Philo gives it an added ethical and religious weight. The themes of binding and adherence can be linked to that of stability in God, which is a theological metaphor — encouraged by a number of Pentateuchal texts — for the ethical and religious notions of faith and trust in God.

A final brief chapter outlines the main conclusions that Termini has reached in the course of her research. The notion of δύναμις as an expression of God's manifestation in the cosmos and to humanity is inherited from Hellenistic Judaism. The preference for the plural over the singular shows how Philo has adapted the doctrine for the purposes of a more sophisticated theology. He can thus do justice to the diversity of divine manifestation in scripture and also accommodate his thought to universalistic religious developments outside Judaism. Plurality of manifestation may appear to occur at the cost of divine unity, but this is not the case. It is in fact tied to the limited perspective of human thought, for which accommodation is made in scripture. This conclusion is reinforced by an examination of the functionality of the doctrine of the powers. The final sentences of the book are worth quoting in full (p. 238, my translation):

> Philo has a strong preference for the term δύναμις because of the extent of the cultural connections that distinguish it, but the doctrine of the powers, even in its binary

structure, does not finish up being dangerous for Jewish monotheism because the triangulation with God is always explicit. If there is a feature of the Philonic system which is potentially risky, it resides in the doctrine of the Logos, as the trajectory followed by Christianity demonstrates. Philo takes precautions against this risk by depriving the Logos and the powers of autonomy and by continually varying his theological schemes. The multiplicity and fluidity of articulations safeguard the unicity of God because the refusal to concentrate functions in a single figure does not allow a turn in a binitarian direction. For this reason the Logos and the powers manifest only those aspects of God which are knowable to humankind in a rational process or through revelation, but they do not exhaust the profoundity of the divine mystery.

The summary of the contents of the book that I have just given is sufficient to show that it represents a significant step forward in research on its theme. It has many strengths, including its strong philological basis, its focus on the role of exegesis, and the careful and detailed analysis that it gives of central Philonic texts. The link that it makes between the doctrine of the powers and the theme of divine theophany is, I think, fundamentally valid, provided 'theophany' is taken in the broadest possible sense. The book is particularly strong on the biblical and Jewish roots of Philo's thought. This will come as no surprise, given the research background of the author. In the case of the philosophical background of the doctrine, Termini has done her research conscientiously enough. Most of the important texts are cited, but in the course of the work their role remains secondary. This applies in particular to texts from the Platonist tradition (rather than from Plato himself).

Termini prides herself on using an inductive method. She wants the texts to speak for themselves, rather than have a philosophical or theological system imposed on them. The method is admirable, but there are limits to what it can achieve. I agree with many of her interpretations which argue that Philo does not wish to establish a clear ontological separation between God and his powers. But to argue that the separation is 'virtual' or 'fictional', as in the case of the powers assisting God in the creation of humankind, is to introduce an element of interpretation which cannot be fully resolved by the analysis of texts. The use of the phrase ὡς ἄν is a fascinating example of the issue at stake. If we translate it by 'as if' or 'as though', then it would indicate a 'virtual' separation. But the parallelism in *Fug.* 71 between ὡς ἄν ἐπὶ πλήθους and ὡς ἄν ἐπὶ ἑνός shows that the issue is one of perspective (i.e. plurality and unity) rather than that the one is privileged above the other (i.e. virtual plurality opposed to real unity; note that Colson's Loeb translation is quite unhelpful here). Termini argues that multiplicity is introduced from a human perspective, and in a sense this is true. The perspective of human reason exploits the distinctive tools of conceptual analysis and so, encouraged by the biblical text, reaches a partial solution to the problem of theodicy. It is precisely Philo's use of philosophical conceptuality that makes his thought so distinctive in the Jewish context. The author's recognition of this aspect of his thought is somewhat grudging, and it is easy to see why. Its presence is responsible for an element of tension which both sides of the interpretative divide, i.e. those who privilege the Judaic religious aspect and those who favour the Hellenic philosophical side, would rather see removed.

A possible criticism of the book is that it takes into account too little the context of the Philonic texts it studies. Texts from the three main commentaries are freely mingled, in marked contrast to the important monograph on Philo's theology published by Christoph Noack in the same year (see the review by Dieter Zeller in *SPhA* 12 (2000) 199–205). An interesting example of a text where recognition of the context might have induced the author to come to a slightly different view is the very first text analysed in the book, *Spec.* 1.209. Here Philo in a symbolic interpretation of the division of the sacrificial victim into its parts, exhorts the soul to honour God by the use of reason and science, and this involves making the right division into each of the divine powers and excellences (καθ' ἑκάστην τῶν θείων δυνάμεων καὶ ἀρετῶν). Termini argues that the terms δύναμις and ἀρετή are practically synonymous. But the fact that Philo speaks here of God's ἀρεταί is in fact nothing short of remarkable. The only other texts to do so are *Contempl.* 26 and *Mos.* 2.189. In fact Philo almost always speaks of excellences in relation to human beings and not God. Why this hesitation? A possible reason might be that God's excellences, e.g. goodness and righteousness, could easily be taken to be essential attributes, indicative of what he is in himself and not in relation to creation and humanity. So Philo almost always prefers to speak of his powers, i.e. the manifestation of those attributes in the cosmos and in God's dealings with humankind. A synoptic view of Philo's entire corpus might thus lead us not to place too much weight on the text at *Spec.* 1.209. We need to take into account why he refers to 'divine excellences' so rarely in his works, and never in his allegorical commentaries.

In her introduction Termini cites a number of recent scholars who have pronounced the origin and scope of Philo's doctrine of the powers to be 'mysterious' or 'far from clear'. Her monograph has done an enormous amount to clarify this essential part of Philo's theological thought. The book is clearly organized and well-written. To a non-Italian reader its style seemed literary and quite erudite, making it not always so easy to read. The publication of an English translation would be an excellent initiative, enabling its contents to become available to a larger international reading public. The mystery of Philo's doctrine may not be entirely resolved in its pages, but that certainly cannot be held against the author. It is caused by the mystery of Philo himself, Jew and Hellenist at the same time, which will long continue to intrigue us.

> David T. Runia
> Queen's College
> University of Melbourne

Manuel ALEXANDRE, Jr., *Rhetorical Argumentation in Philo of Alexandria*. Brown Judaic Studies 322. Studia Philonica Monographs 2. Atlanta: Scholars Press, 1999. xx + 302 pages. ISBN 0-78-850582-3. Price $34.95.

This volume seems to have had an interesting and long period of gestation before emerging in its published English version. It began with research in the late 1970s and early 1980s (probably a doctoral dissertation, researched at Claremont), and then first appeared in 1990 in a Portuguese edition, and now in an English one. At the least, it appears to have some of the characteristics of a doctoral dissertation, including a detailed survey of literature at the beginning, and some apparent concessions to what appears to be a doctoral supervisor, or at least an influential senior scholar, especially in reference to *chreia* material. None of this is necessarily deleterious, of course, but it does help to explain some of the characteristics of this work, even though it comes from a senior scholar later in his career.

The volume begins with a general introduction that gives an overview of Philo studies, outlines the author's method and defends reading Philo from a rhetorical standpoint. The survey of research is helpful and is generally brought up to the present in both Philo and rhetorical studies (with some major omissions, nonetheless). However, the defence for reading Philo from a rhetorical standpoint is clearly forced. The author wants to utilize the categories of ancient rhetoric, but does not show why this is better than using the New Rhetoric or something else. He invokes precedent found in several scholars—such as Hughes and Kennedy—for application of the categories of ancient rhetoric to authors other than those of the New Testament, without differentiating which categories and which forms of literature. He also does not address scholarly opinion to the contrary. To my mind, this is not an adequate method for proceeding, and it calls into question some of the rest of the enterprise.

Chapter one is a lengthy survey of the nature of argumentation in Greco-Roman rhetoric. He treats both the Greek and the Latin rhetorical traditions, and concludes with a synoptic chart that outlines various structures of argumentation, compared to the formal structures of an idealized speech. This is a very useful and detailed treatment of the topic, and one that can be returned to for insight even if one is not pursuing rhetoric in Philo.

Chapter two discusses what access Philo would have had to theories of argumentation. In essence, this is a discussion of the role of rhetoric in the Greco-Roman world, especially that of Alexandria. It also usefully includes a recognition of the interplay of Judaism and Hellenism. As the author acknowledges, we in fact know so little about Philo himself, that much of the discussion must proceed by inference. Even if one accepts that rhetorical studies have proven insightful into the work of Philo, this does not necessarily mean that Philo was drawing on ancient rhetoric, whether he follows the handbook tradition or not. There may have been functional similarities between his literary forms and the conventions of rhetoric. The question that is not answered clearly and fully to my satisfaction, therefore, is whether the categories of rhetoric that Alexandre wishes to invoke can be drawn upon for analysis of some of the kinds of material that Philo wrote.

The next three chapters apply the categories of ancient rhetoric to Philo's writings. Chapters three and four utilize the categories of arrangement to examine several complete works and embedded discourses, and the structures of several complete arguments. Overall, the argumentation here is not persuasive. Nevertheless, in some instances—for example, for some of the embedded speeches and for some instances of elaboration—Alexandre is convincing that rhetoric was on Philo's mind. However, since no clear foundation has been laid for this extensive application, I cannot be sure whether I am reading Philo or Alexandre in many of the instances. His treatment of *De Vita Mosis* proposes a five part arrangement of the argument that seems to me to be imposed from without. There is the further problem that in many instances Alexandre seems simply to engage in labelling, rather than explaining how these categories are arrived at or useful for interpretation. Also, Alexandre makes phenomenal use of chiasm to explain the organization of various lengths of discourse. I find most if not virtually all of his examples here unconvincing—not only because of my doubts regarding the use of chiasm by the ancients (and I think that Alexandre wants us to believe that this was conscious on Philo's part) but because the instances themselves are less than evident.

Chapter five deals with rhythmic and periodic structures. In the use of style, I believe that Alexandre is on his firmest footing in seeing rhetoric at work in Philo. He deals with Philo's periodic style and the shape of his cola. However, when he invokes chiasm here also, I must confess to being unconvinced. The book concludes with a brief summary of rhetorical argumentation in several of its dimensions, and a detailed and useful bibliography that provides much helpful material on Philo and work on argumentation.

No doubt Alexandre has performed an exhausting labor on behalf of rhetoric and Philo. I think, however, that there is probably less formal and grand-scale rhetorical influence on Philo at a number of these places than Alexandre believes. This does not mean that some of the categories of rhetoric cannot be profitably used (such as style), but I believe that the claims for any such findings need to be tempered by the secure basis on which such assertions or arguments are made. My impression is that there is more functionalism that is confused with conscious utilization of rhetoric than is often realized, especially in terms of grand schemes for the argumentative structures of entire discourses.

Stanley E. Porter
McMaster Divinity College
Hamilton, Canada

Jutta LEONHARDT, *Jewish Worship in Philo of Alexandria*. Text and Studies in Ancient Judaism 84. Tübingen: Mohr Siebeck, 2001. xiv + 347 pages. ISBN 3-16-147597-6. Price € 79.

This is a revised and expanded version of a 1999 doctoral dissertation written at Cambridge University under the supervision of William Horbury. It is the first comprehensive study of Philo's descriptions and interpretations of Jewish worship laws and practices. The bibliography and indices indicate that the author has read widely in primary and secondary sources.

The organization of the book is straightforward. A brief introduction is devoted to matters of definition and method and Philo's use of the term λατρεία which Dr. Leonhardt considers to be of special importance for specifically Jewish worship (although Philo uses it only seven times). Philo uses θεραπεία far more often (99 times, according to the Borgen Index), but mainly with reference to worship in general or to philosophical veneration of God. Leonhardt takes the following as a working definition of worship: 'the formal expression of religious adoration; rites, prayers, etc.' (p. 8). A two-paragraph 'survey of scholarship' mentions that important contributions to this field of study have been made by Isaac Heinemann, Harry Wolfson, E. R. Goodenough, and Samuel Belkin.

Chapter Two discusses all the Jewish festivals mentioned by Philo and what he has to say about outward observances and their meanings (noting, e.g., that he calls the Sabbath 'the birthday of the world' — *Mos.* 1.205–207). From Philo's apparent surprise at the presence of women in the Sabbath meetings of the Therapeutae (*Contempl.* 32–33), Leonhardt infers that in other Jewish communities those meetings were restricted to men (p. 86). Here and elsewhere in the book the author discusses major Greek terms Philo employs and presents exegetical analyses of key passages in his writings. She maintains that Philo's habit of referring to Greek philosophers and other writers in his exposition of the Jewish scriptures probably was common practice in the synagogues of his time (p. 91).

There follows a chapter on prayer (solitary and communal), Philo's references to biblical psalms and hymns, and his concept of thanksgiving. Leonhardt's discussion of Philo's nineteen quotations from the Book of Psalms is particularly interesting. She maintains that he considered that Book virtually equal in authority to the Pentateuch. Although Philo ignored context in his interpretations of the psalms, those interpretations reveal a 'traditional Jewish approach' (p. 172).

Next comes a lengthy chapter on Philo's statements about temple worship, sacrifices and rituals of purification. Leonhardt urges that the taxes paid to the temple demonstrate from Philo's perspective how Jews residing all over the Mediterranean world shared in the ongoing worship at the temple (p. 275). For a thinker famously keen on understanding religion and philosophy in relation to immaterial realities, Philo writes a good deal about outward religious observances. He gives quite detailed accounts of some aspects of the communal practices of Essenes and Therapeutae, and Leonhardt is happy to analyze those accounts when they bear on worship. She also notes Philo's descriptions of Jews at prayer as they celebrate the Septuagint's translation (*Mos.* 2.41–44) and the arrest of a malicious Roman governor (*Flacc.* 121–22), and she emphasizes the importance for Jews everywhere of Caligula's attempts to desecrate the temple in Jerusalem (*Legat.* 214–15). But much of her detailed analysis of Philo on worship hinges on the *Special Laws*, which offers numerous interpretations of Pentateuchal regulations regarding worship. She argues that his exegesis of these laws regularly reflects, though often abstractly or incompletely, Jewish worship in his own time. In that exegesis Philo typically does not distinguish the tabernacle of Moses from the temple of Herod (e.g., pp. 32, 130, 222). The fact that only a single passage (Prov. 2.107 [64]) in all his writings mentions that Philo has personally gone to worship at that temple is irrelevant (p. 253). Leonhardt argues that the institution was of fundamental importance for him and his intended audience. Though Philo's 'personal preferences' lay with spiritual worship, he stresses the value of the physical cult since human beings have bodies as well as souls (pp. 254–55). In general, Leonhardt insists, Philo assumes the necessity of the literal observance of ritual laws, including those of sacrifice, while using allegory to explore their moral and spiritual meanings. She often cites *Migr.* 89–93 to support this claim.

The book's concluding chapter summarizes the preceding chapters and goes on to discuss some general issues. As a source of information about Jewish worship in the first century C.E., Philo is 'more frustrating than helpful' because he tends to focus on interpreting biblical texts in abstract terms and often fails to furnish concrete information about worship practices he must have often experienced. Nevertheless, his descriptions of biblical worship customs imply that Jews followed them everywhere in his own day (pp. 278–79). Philo often writes about Jewish worship as a Hellenistic cult in line with pagan philosophical ideals, above all those of Plato. He may even consciously employ Plato's Laws as his primary model for describing Jewish worship in Greek terms (p. 292). Philo claimed that Hellenistic religious ideals were so fully realized in the Jewish worship of his day that that worship constituted in his eyes 'the ultimate Hellenistic cult' (pp. 294–95).

As a collection and exegetical analysis of major Philonic passages dealing with Jewish worship practices, this volume will be a fine resource for years to come. Scholarly caution and good attention to salient details usually mark the author's interpretations of particular Philonic passages. Her footnotes offer illuminating though very concise indications of how her interpretations compare with those of other scholars. She frequently finds herself in agreement with Belkin (on links with rabbinic traditions), Jean LaPorte (on thanksgiving as the basis of prayer and worship), and Valentin Nikiprowetzky (on spiritualization). She often disagrees with Heinemann and Wolfson. She recognizes that Philo uses mystery terminology to explain spiritual dimensions of worship, but quickly dismisses Goodenough's theory of Jewish mystery rites.

A number of previous investigators have suggested that communal Jewish ceremonies were not of high importance to Philo since he preferred to concentrate on the spiritual experiences of individuals. Leonhardt offers a helpful balance by stressing the frequency and detail with which he speaks of laws and practices related to the material cult. While she regularly reports Philo's spiritualizing interpretations of the cult, she does not attempt to show how his statements about outward worship fit into his personal religious outlook as a whole. One might wish that Leonhardt had more systematically compared her approach and conclusions with those of previous scholars who have dealt with her topic. Likewise it would have been helpful to have had more discussion of the methodological problems involved in drawing plausible inferences about worship in Philo's day from his exegesis of Pentateuchal narratives and commandments.

Although this book does not resolve all the important questions it raises, we must be grateful to the author for a sophisticated and insightful examination of Philo's numerous statements about Jewish worship.

David M. Hay
Coe College
Cedar Rapids, Iowa

D. T. RUNIA, *Filone di Alessandria nella prima letteratura cristiana*. A cura di R. Radice. Centro di Ricerche di Metafisica dell'Università Cattolica del Sacro Cuore, Vita e Pensiero, Milano 1999. xxix + 507 pages. ISBN 8-83-430004-1. Price € 33.57.

What is immediately striking about this study is its organic quality. The framework, the methodological premises, and the evaluations are all clearly expressed, and the various themes are developed according to a rational and comprehensive process, with ample recourse to a comprehensive bibliography.

The book opens with the reconstruction of the historical data on Philo's life and work. The information provided by the Fathers and the earliest Christian writers, who affirmed the existence of the Alexandrian's contacts with the Christian community, can be contrasted to the influence, not easily brought out, on Plotinus' ideas via Numenius, as well as the silence of the Judaic sources. The deep link with Christianity was further accentuated by the fact that the survival of his writings was determined entirely by the intervention of Christian writers. It was only from the seventeenth century onwards that the recognition of the Platonic influence on Philo's thought led to an interest in an interpretation that gradually meant thinking of him in terms of his belonging to Jewish culture, and from the twentieth century he has been the object of special attention in the realm of Jewish studies.

There follows a complex analysis of the reception given to Philo's work among early Christian writers, here examined one at a time according to a diachronic order. Runia emphasizes the need to confront the problematic subject of the transmission of texts, the emerging conversation with the world of Judaism and the distinctive and varied theological developments of this period. Additionally, it is important to discern the context that is specifically Philonic and to compare that to characteristic Greek and Judaic ideas and to be fully aware of the work of each writer which has to be interpreted in light of Philo's exegetical and philosophical concerns. As a result there is the need to explore in detail both the meaning of these explicit references and to develop an adequate understanding of the formulations re-proposed. It is undoubtedly difficult to grasp each individual aspect and connect up the various data, as Runia clearly recognises while attempting to do so. There is confirmation of this in the conflicting opinions reached by some scholars in their analysis of the relationship between Philo and some Christian writers, or the extensive scholarship that Runia cites with his characteristic thoroughness and breadth.

The studies that examine the presence of Philo's ideas in early Christian literature offer another, though in some respects limited, chance to uncover influences. In this case the recognition of conceptual and exegetical analogies, of the presence of similarities and differences in the doctrines of the various authors, becomes clearer. It is enough to mention the emblematic notion of 'double creation' that runs through the various ways the anthropological conception was formed. The risk remains, however, that the reader is left with a fragmentary understanding of the writer being referred to, and occasionally of stressing some not really essential aspects in order to create continuity. The author's frequently expressed recognition in this context that there is a limited intersection at work, within a divergent background, is significant. He repeatedly makes use of it in the formulation of his conclusions: for in seeking a tradition which for some writers is not linked to contexts of direct sharing but is justified by evaluation, or is directly transmitted and attributed a positive value, to the extent in some cases of assimilation (e.g. calling Philo a Christian), it is almost inevitable that a distorted frame of reference, resulting in a different identity, emerges. The significant and clearly emerging impact of a Philonic tradition in the first place in Alexandria, then in Palestine, and in the West limited to certain Fathers, shows a prevailing interest in both the exegetical and conceptual modes that Philo developed, taking on *topoi* and forms of classical philosophical thought.

Angela Maria Mazzanti
University of Bologna
Italy

F. PETIT, *La Chaîne sur l'Exode. I Fragments de Sévère d'Antioche.* Traditio Exegetica Graeca 9. Louvain: Peeters, 1999. xxvii + 209 pages. ISBN 90-429-0736-3. Price € 50.

F. PETIT, *La Chaîne sur l'Exode. II Collectio Coisliana. III Fonds caténique ancien (Exode 1,1–15,21).* Traditio Exegetica Graeca 10. Louvain: Peeters, 2000. xxxi + 357 pages. ISBN 90-429-0893-9. Price € 95.

F. PETIT, *La Chaîne sur l'Exode. IV Fonds caténique ancien (Exode 15,22–40,32).* Traditio Exegetica Graeca 11. Louvain: Peeters, 2001. xiv + 359 pages. ISBN 90-429-0993-5. Price € 95.

In two previous reviews readers of this Annual have been able to follow the progress of Françoise Petit's magisterial edition of the *Catenae*, that vast anonymous compilation of brief excerpts from the early tradition of biblical exegesis up to the 5th century C.E. The four volumes of her edition of the *Catena on Genesis* were reviewed in *SPhA* 5 (1993) 229–232 and 11 (1999) 113–120. In the present volumes under review she continues her work by presenting a complete edition of the *Catena on Exodus* in three volumes.

Philo plays a more modest role in this work than he did in the *Catena on Genesis*. Nevertheless it is a contribution that will certainly be of interest to Philonists, and especially those who are interested in the transmission of his corpus.

The three volumes are divided into four parts. The reason for this has to do with the complex manner in which the original work has been embedded in a gradually accumulated corpus of exegetical material. The first part, occupying the first volume, gives a separate edition of the excerpts ascribed to Severus of Antioch (c. 465–538). Petit gradually came to realize during her work on the *Catena on Genesis* that these excerpts form a foreign body in the whole which was added later. It was no longer possible to edit them separately for that work. But in the present case, she argues (vol. 9, p. xi), 'it would be absurd to persevere in the error.' This volume is of no relevance for Philonic studies, since there is no direct connection between Severus and the Philonic tradition. In the second part the excerpts on Exodus — only 26 in number — found in the *Collectio Coisliana* are edited. These were originally attached to another work, the *Questions on the Octateuch* by Theodoret of Cyrrhus (393–460), but have obtained an integral place in the tradition of the *Catenae*. Many of these rather long excerpts are derived from the Antiochene exegete Diodore of Tarsus. No material is directly taken from Philo (but there is one extract from Josephus, no. 24). It is noteworthy that no. 23 on Ex. 25:8 is an extract from Clement of Alexandria, *Stromateis* 5.34–35, which is based on Philo's description of the tabernacle furnishings in *Mos.* 2.97–104.

Part three presents the edition of the 'Fonds caténique ancien' (i.e. the Ancient corpus of *Catenae*) for Exodus up to the Song of Miriam in Ex. 15:21. There is a very good reason for breaking up the corpus at this point, which will be discussed below. The method followed is the same as in the edition of the excerpts from Genesis: location of the excerpt in the mss. together with the superscription indicating the author (if present), the edited text, critical apparatus, attribution (if possible) and some very brief comments (nearly always on the transmission, not the content). A constant complicating factor is the presence of Procopius of Gaza (c. 475–538), who in his *Commentary* paraphrases and rewrites the original *Catena* to a remarkable degree, sometimes even including material that has otherwise been lost. Petit includes his evidence where possible, which is all the more necessary because his *Commentary* is one of the very few major works from antiquity that has as yet never been properly edited. In this part there are 466 excerpts (minus 27 imported from Severus). Five of these (nos. 51, 199, 240, 246, 370) come from the first book of Philo's *De vita Moysis*. In all cases the lemma is prefixed with the title Φίλωνος Ἑβραίου. C-W refer to them in their apparatus, but do not print them out in full. Petit makes the full text available, as well as Procopius' paraphrase. As she notes in her Avant-propos, the Catenist apparently had fewer commentaries and technical exegetical works available, and so resorted to more literary works such as the lives of Moses by Philo and Gregory of Nyssa. A further interesting text is no. 437 on Ex. 15:1. Petit has observed that the first two lines are taken almost word for word from Philo *Agr.* 80, except that the allegorical identifications of Moses as perfect mind and Miriam as purified sense-perception have been dropped. The allegorical interpretation of the timbrel (τύμπανον) given in the fragment is not found in Philo. A similar interpretation of the timbrel as symbolizing the mortification of the body is found in fragments of Origenian exegesis (*Frag. in Ps.* 80:3, *Sel. in Psalmos* PG 12.1680), so it seems to me quite plausible that this fragment is derived from Origen or his tradition, which would explain the borrowing from Philo quite neatly.

Part four commences at Ex. 15:22 and goes through to the end of the book. Its transmission is considerably inferior to that of the first part. The primary tradition of the *Catena* in fact discontinues, but traces of it have remained in a secondary tradition. This tradition is less reliable and often paraphrases and modifies the text of the original source, a practice which can only be detected if the original is still extant. The evidence of Procopius does continue and is even more valuable in this part, since it derives its material from the original version of the *Catena*. In this part there are 606 excerpts (minus 53 imported from Severus). The use of Philonic material is both extensive and limited at the same time. Between no. 618 (on Ex. 20:25) and no. 750 (on Ex. 24:18) the *Catena* cites Philo no less than 20 times, all the excerpts being drawn from *QE* 2.1–49. In most cases the lemmata are prefixed with the title Φίλωνος Ἑβραίου, although sometimes Φίλωνος alone is found. 19 of these excerpts had already been included by Petit in her splendid edition of the Fragmenta Graeca of the *Quaestiones*, published in the French edition of Philo's works 25 years ago (PAPM 33). The present edition adds very little to what was already included there, with one striking exception. No. 669 is recorded under the title Ἰσιδώρου, i.e. Isidore of Pelusium, but Petit has discovered that the excerpt is really a combination of the last part of *QE* 2.11 and the first words of *QE* 2.12. These four lines of text thus constitute a new Greek fragment of Philo's *Quaestiones* missing in her earlier volume.

The end result of Petit's researches, as far as the presence of Philo in the *Catena on Exodus* is concerned, is quite intriguing. There are two distinct group of texts. The first group of five all come from *Mos.*, the second group of twenty all come from the first half of *QE* book 2. It is intriguing to conclude that the Catenist, who in Petit's view in all likelihood compiled his work in the second half of the 5th century, had a limited range of Philonic works at his disposal. Many years ago James Royse suggested that it be concluded on the basis of this evidence that these first 49 sections of the present *QE* book 2 originally constituted a separate book on their own, which may have been the fourth of six original books (*SPh* 4 (1976–77) 56–57). There are arguments for and against this proposal, but they should not be entered into here.

Thanks to Petit's tireless labours we are now in a position to see with full clarity how Philo the Hebrew obtained a limited but noteworthy place in this remarkable exegetical work. We should be most thankful to her, but also to the publisher, Peeters of Louvain, who has had the courage to take on this highly specialized piece of scholarly research and distil it in three beautifully produced volumes.

David T. Runia
Queen's College
University of Melbourne

Folker SIEGERT, *Zwischen Hebräischer Bibel und Altem Testament: Eine Einführung in die Septuaginta. Register zur „Einführung in die Septuaginta": Mit einem Kapitel zur Wirkungsgeschichte*. Münsteraner Judaistische Studien 9 and 13. Münster, Hamburg, London: Lit Verlag, 2001 and 2003. viii + pages 1–340 + 2 and 16* + pages 341–464. ISBN 3-8258-5012-9 and 3-8258-5785-9. Price € 25,90 and 20,90.

Folker Siegert, the director of the Institutum Judaicum Delitzschianum in Münster, is well known to readers of this journal for his careful studies of the Philonic fragment *De Deo* and of the pseudo-Philonic *De Jona* and *De Sampsone*. In the two-volume work under review he calls upon a wide range of further interests and displays admirable scholarship to produce the first introduction to the LXX in German.[1] These volumes provide much

---

[1] See 20–22. Siegert observes that introductions have recently appeared in English, French, and Spanish, but criticizes (21 n. 11) that of Natalio Fernández Marcos: *Introducción a las versiones griegas de la Biblia* (Madrid 1979); *The Septuagint in Context: Introduction to the Greek Version of the Bible*, tr. Wilfred G. E. Watson (Leiden 2000). However, his objections are perhaps unduly harsh. The alleged confusion of the satirist Lucian of Samosata with the martyr Lucian of Antioch apparently rests on the statement by Fernández Marcos that the latter was born in Samosata; but, while the details of the martyr's life are obscure, standard reference works often say that he was born in Samosata. The antiquated term 'Suidas (Lexicographus)' is found only in the English translation (224), which is often inaccurate; the original has 'Y según la Suda' (214). Fernández Marcos's citation of παταχρον (instead of παταχρα) follows LSJ and *PGL* in taking παταχρα as being from the neuter singular παταχρον. And, although γλυπτόν is the

of value and stimulation to anyone who is interested in the transmission of the Biblical text.

The scope of Siegert's work can be judged from the index of citations, where there are some 1600 references to verses (or passages) in the LXX or MT, as well as about 300 from the NT. Some of these are simply mentioned, of course, but many passages receive detailed attention. Certainly a strength of the work is the continual interaction with the text, and the complexities of the material are covered under various headings, with frequent cross-references. The LXX and the MT are often compared word for word, as well as book by book. We find discussions of the individual fates of the books of the LXX, and of groups of books. Textual variants are frequently handled, within LXX manuscripts, within the discoveries at Qumran and related sites, and within versional evidence and later citations. The reader is informed about the various editions and their critical apparatuses, the lexica and grammars, the use of the LXX in the NT and in early Christianity (including the further translations into Latin and other languages), and the later translations by Aquila, Symmachus, and Theodotion. Naturally, Philo, Josephus, and Hellenistic Judaism appear prominently throughout. Siegert manages to compress the studies of scores of scholars into his pages, while adding the fruits of his own research at every turn. And, while much of the discussion is appropriately exacting, Siegert presents the material in a clear and even lively style.

Siegert classifies the relations found between the LXX and the Hebrew into precise categories and gives clear examples, with due attention to all the uncertainties; e.g., does the LXX reading reflect a scribal error in the Hebrew *Vorlage* or a misreading by the translators? One will find details on the translational tendencies of the LXX, with many comparisons of the Hebrew and Greek concepts involved. Siegert also presents what he calls a 'Kleine Septuaginta-Grammatik,' to which he frequently refers in subsequent discussions. The reader will find in these pages a multitude of examples, clearly organized and discussed, with references to material found elsewhere, but with fresh insights.

Siegert (133) states as the commonly accepted view that the LXX should be understandable without reference to the Hebrew.[2] And certainly most of his analyses follow this principle.[3] Yet later (282) he accepts that there is

---

form actually found in the LXX, it does not seem incorrect to cite γλυπτός, under which again LSJ cites the LXX instances.

[2] Siegert was able to cite only in his additions (9*) the first volume of the NETS, Albert Pietersma's translation of the Psalms (New York and Oxford 2000). But there (see pp. ix–x) we find a quite different perspective, namely that the Greek 'can only be understood in its entirety with the help of the Hebrew.'

[3] See, e.g., his comment on p. 162 (next to last paragraph of section 3.3.3).

in some sense a kind of 'Jewish Greek,' and explains this as a language that would have been familiar, not to the 'Literaten,' but to 'Synagogenbesuchern.' This issue of a 'Jewish Greek' is, of course, very controversial, but a few specific places where it may play a role may be mentioned.

Siegert (279) notes that many words once thought to be peculiar to the LXX (or to 'Jewish Greek') have been shown by the papyri to be elements of the Koine, and discusses (279–82) alleged neologisms in the LXX.[4] But Siegert later (286) cites παταχρα (Aramaic for 'idols') in Isa 8:21 as providing 'ein wertvoller Hinweis auf die Zwei- (oder besser: Drei-)sprachigkeit der Septuaginta-Übersetzer und ihre Beziehungen zur Umgangssprache des Mutterlandes.' But then were the readers of the LXX of Isa, even if they went to synagogue, assumed also to be trilingual? In contrast, Katz sees the translator in his use of this word as 'taking from his idiomatic Greek a word which here was borrowed from Aramaic.'[5] On this view the readers would presumably also have known the word from their idiomatic Greek. This example may be compared with γιώρας another borrowing from Aramaic (see Siegert 128 and 281).[6] Philo uses this word at Conf. 82 with no suggestion that it is foreign, and certainly Philo did not know Aramaic.[7]

Of course, lexical borrowings are different from syntactical influence. Siegert also perspicuously displays what may be seen as peculiar features of LXX syntax. But one of the examples (159–60) is Gen 6:12, which is cited as a lack of congruence where the LXX does violence to Greek syntax with its: κατέφθειρεν πᾶσα σὰρξ τὴν ὁδὸν αὐτοῦ. Siegert does not mention the possibility of taking αὐτοῦ as referring to God, but Philo does mention this possibility at Deus 140–44 and QG 1.99 (ad fin., in Armenian only). Indeed, at Deus 140 Philo rejects the interpretation of those who would see a solecism here. This interpretation of the LXX is found as well in Origen, who could compare the Hebrew, and who evidently follows Philo's interpretation: a citation in the catena reads τὸ δὲ κατέφθειρε τὴν ὁδὸν τοῦ θεοῦ,[8] and

---

[4] At 257 (and n. 40) he cites ἀσυνθετεῖν and εὐσυνθετεῖν as having been adopted from Stoicism; however, at p. 279 both these words are cited as neologisms of the LXX.

[5] Peter Walters (Katz), The Text of the Septuagint: Its Corruptions and their Emendation, ed. D. W. Gooding (Cambridge 1973) 175.

[6] Katz, ibid., 33–34, argues that the usual γειώρας is simply an itacism. At Isa 14:1 Ziegler edits γιώρας, and at Exod 12:19 Wevers edits γιώραις.

[7] Philo is citing Ex 2:22, where all the other witnesses read πάροικος, and Mangey thus proposed to emend Philo to read the same. But Katz, Philo's Bible: The Aberrant Text of Bible Quotations in Some Philonic Writings and its Place in the Textual History of the Greek Bible (Cambridge 1950) 73–74, argues that Philo's γιώρας should be viewed as the authentic LXX, since this rare word would not have replaced πάροικος, which would moreover have suited Philo's context better. (Unfortunately, Philo does not use παταχρα.)

[8] Françoise Petit, ed., La chaîne sur la Genèse, Édition intégrale, 2 (chapitres 4 à 11) (Louvain 1993) 95–96 (# 653); one manuscript conforms to the LXX in reading αὐτοῦ for θεοῦ. The fragment is ascribed to Origen, and is thus found in PG 12:105A.

in his *De principiis* 1.3.7 (surviving only in a Latin translation), we read 'cum omnis caro corrupisset uiam dei,' obviously reflecting the same Greek.[9] Didymus similarly understands αὐτοῦ as referring to God.[10] Not only is this a possible interpretation of the LXX, but the LXX may not even be incorrectly interpreting the Hebrew; for the MT is in fact ambiguous, since the masculine suffix on דרכו can refer either to the flesh or to God.[11]

Siegert's bibliographical references provide sound guidance to much of the literature. However, with respect to Philo specifically, it would be useful to have some reference to the assistance to be found in R-R and RRS, to *Biblia Patristica: Supplément* (especially at 342–43), and to Katz's invaluable *Philo's Bible*. The neglect of the latter leads to imprecision when Siegert (105) refers to Barthélemy's theory about the interpolator in the manuscripts of Philo as allaying the suspicion that Philo used another (Siegert says 'ältere') translation. Katz was clear that Philo used the LXX, and thus that the interpolations occurred later within the tradition. What Barthélemy attempts is to go beyond Katz and to identify this later interpolator.[12]

A few further points were noted:

127: קשׂיטה occurs at Gen 33:19.

230–31: In fact, οἰκέτης occurs more than 30 times in the Pentateuch.

303: The Greek of 4 Kgdms 9:3, 6, 12 has κέχρικά σε εἰς, which seems to represent precisely משחתיך ל. The misspelling κέκρικά has caused an entry in the index under κρίνειν instead of χρίειν.

307: Only ἀναστάσεως of the superscription to Ps 66(65) was excluded by Rahlfs, as Siegert notes at 323 n. 24.

The helpful cross-references are occasionally off by a section; I found (with the help of the indexes) the following larger differences: 133 and 149 n. 19 (1.6.4 should be 2.4.4), 179 (5.3.4 should be 5.5.4), 211 (5.7.4 should be 5.7.1), 253 (1.7.6 should be 2.5), 285 (4.7 should be 4.8.2), 291 (2.5.3 should be 3.5.3), 303 (3.7 should be 4.8.2), 308 (2.3.1 should be 3.3.1), 315 (4.8.2 should be 5.7.1). Further, besides the errors in Scriptural references that are noted at 15*–16*, at 320 l.16 read Ps 122(121) and 124(123). Finally, the extensive and well-organized indexes are quite accurate; but I noticed that the citations of Ps 115:14 (113:22 LXX) and 115:3 (113:11 LXX) at 178–79 are not in

---

[9] Ed. Henri Crouzel and Manlio Simonetti (SC 252; 1978) 156.

[10] But later he also interprets it as referring to σάρξ since that is used for ἄνθρωπος. See his *Comm. in Gen.* 11.7–8 (p. 167 l. 25 – p. 168 l. 1), ed. Pierre Nautin with Louis Doutreleau (SC 244; 1978) 62, and the note to p. 168 l. 1.

[11] See John William Wevers, *Notes on the Greek Text of Genesis* (SBLSCS 35; Atlanta, 1993) 82.

[12] *Philo's Bible*, 114–21. For some details see my 'The Text of Philo's *Legum Allegoriae*,' *SPhA* 12 (2000) 17–22.

the index; at 441 βωμός on 209 should be 229; at 443 εἴδωλον is listed twice; and at 452 παράνομος is also on 75.

It should be noted, however, that the aforementioned errors do not diminish the significance of this work, as they are perhaps inevitable when producing a volume so rich in details in multiple languages. Siegert's work will doubtless take its place as a trusted guide to the LXX, at once a reliable introduction and a source of provocative insights.

James R. Royse
San Francisco

Joan E. Cook, *Hannah's Desire, God's Design: Early Interpretations of the Story of Hannah*. Journal for the Study of the Old Testament: Supplement Series 262. Sheffield: Sheffield Academic Press, 1999. 134 pages. ISBN 1-85-075909-X. Price $65.

Cook's book is to be commended for drawing our attention to a neglected topic: the story of Hannah and its reinscription in early Judaism and Christianity. While various monographs have appeared in recent years that treat the interpretation of Adam and Eve, David, Solomon, and other biblical figures, Hannah has been left largely alone. Now we have a book that can begin to fill the void. An outgrowth of her 1989 dissertation under Walter Harrelson at Vanderbilt University, the work's six chapters examines the treatment of Hannah in 1 Samuel, *Pseudo-Philo*, the *Targum of the Prophets*, and Luke's infancy narrative. Her stated aim is to develop three interweaving issues: the literary issue of 'barren mother' type scene, the theological theme of divine guidance and human initiative, and the historical question of early biblical interpretation.

Her introductory chapter lays out her approach and the scope of the volume. She discusses the 'barren mother' type scene and its variations in the Hebrew Bible, coming to the conclusion that the story of Hannah uniquely includes elements of promise, competition with others, and human initiative in relation to her plight. Chapter Two provides a thoughtful treatment of 1 Samuel 1–2, which includes a consideration of the ambiguous effect of 'canonical shape' in relationship both to the story's position between Judges and Samuel-Kings and to the more limited canonical question of the prose narrative-poetic song dynamic. The third chapter considers the heightened role of women in *Biblical Antiquities* and Hannah in particular. Picking up on David Jobling's assessment of 1 Samuel 1–2 as having a private and public plot, she applies the same analysis to *Pseudo-Philo* 49–51 with good result. Cook sees Hannah's character as both diminished (in relation to Eli) and expanded (as a wisdom voice who utters a testament). In Chapter 4, she discusses the expansion of the story in the *Targum of the Prophets* in which the hymn's genre is transformed to apocalypse. Hannah now speaks in 'a spirit of prophecy,' which for Cook raises the intriguing question of the public role of women in community and synagogue at this time. The fifth chapter turns to Luke's infancy narrative. While the gospel does not draw on the Hannah story explicitly, Cook, following many others, sees allusions to 1 Samuel 1–2 imbedded in the 'barren mother' type scene and the patterning of the Magnificat after Hannah's prayer. She sketches Luke's dependence on the Hebrew Bible for values, motifs, and vocabulary, pointing in particular to the shared view of poverty and wealth offered in Hannah's prayer and Luke's gospel overall. The final chapter concludes by summarizing the variations of 'barren mother' type reviewed in the book, the various degrees to which divine or human initiative is emphasized, and what she views as the major interpretive thrust of each retelling. She concludes by articulating her hope that these models for interpreting the story of Hannah might inspire contemporary retellings.

Because of its brevity, Cook's work leaves a number of questions unanswered. One example is her treatment of Hannah in the *Targum of the Prophets*. Cook adopts the approach of classical form-criticism and takes seriously the often omitted final step of identifying the social setting after doing the formal literary analysis. Yet this way is fraught with challenges. Cook describes the *Sitz im Leben* of the *Targum of the Prophets* thus: 'like all the Targums, it translates and expands the Hebrew Bible in order to interpret it for a postexilic synagogue community'(p. 77). This is a fair assessment of the probable use of the targums, although the origins and functions of such synagogue communities remain shrouded. She then goes on further to specify the genre of Hannah's song in the targum as an 'apocalypse' suggesting 'its provenance within a community ravaged by destruction and demoralization' (p. 90). This leaves two problems. First is the widely recognized difficulty, thanks to John Collins and Adela Yarbro Collins, in making a firm connection between the apocalypse as a genre and the social matrix which may give rise to such literature. But assuming one could make such a firm assessment, the question of the redactional history of the targum remains.

There are also a number of bibliographical oversights which could have enriched her discussion. While she has clearly updated references to scholarship in some areas since completing the dissertation in 1989, notably in her treatment of 1 Samuel and feminist approaches to scripture, there are holes in other areas. Her characterization of early Jewish biblical interpretation in the first chapter mentions five characteristics: 'free midrashic development, insertion of theological views, avoidance of anthropomorphic references to the Deity, respect for Israel and its elders, and use of contemporary geographical names for ancient places' (p. 25). Her approach to assessing the history of interpretation might have been considerably broadened and deepened if she had engaged the articles of the *Mikra* volume of CRINT or James Kugel's *Traditions of the Bible*. In chapter 4 she points to the significance of the divine warrior, without a reference to Patrick Miller's seminal work on that topic. Nor has she wrestled with Howard Jacobson's weighty 1996 two-volume translation and commentary on Pseudo-Philo. Although Jacobson's work was published well after completion of her dissertation, its importance surely merited inclusion in her discussion of Pseudo-Philo. But such is the challenge of writing a book with a broad reach. In any case, Cook's book cuts a welcome swath through the variegated jungle of ancient biblical interpretation.

Judith H. Newman
General Theological Seminary
New York

John David DAWSON, *Christian Figural Reading and the Fashioning of Identity*. Berkeley: University of California Press, 2002. x + 302 pages. ISBN 0-520-22630-5. Price $50.

Intriguing, dense and difficult, this book begins as a response to a question that strongly challenges the entire history of Christian thought. It asks whether the rabbinic scholar Daniel Boyarin is right in asserting that the allegorical interpretation found in the letters of Paul, and in the exegetical works of Philo and Origen is destructive of Judaism. Does it spiritualize the Old Testament to the severe detriment of its literal interpreters, the Pharisees and rabbis — and their heirs, the ancient and modern Jewish community? More pointedly, when those three allegorical interpreters relegated the literal meaning of biblical texts to a lower level, or even referred to the letter as 'fatal,' as Paul did, in order to transfer by means of allegory the meaning, validity and authority of its words to the realm of the spiritual, or contemplative level found in Christianity, did they undermine Jewish identity as the heirs of the covenant of which the Bible speaks? Does the early Christian insistence that the new revelation, the Gospel, is the new covenant flatly replace and evacuate the old covenant and with it eliminate, at least in theory, the people who still adhere to it? Is allegorical interpretation ineluctably supersessionist and the chief source of all subsequent Christian supersessionism?

Against this proposal an initial difficulty arises right at the outset: because Dawson is interested mainly in the modern, scholarly discussion of allegory (and the modern version of supersessionism), he does not address a fundamental error of Boyarin's. The latter judges that Paul's thought represents a sharp opposition between spiritual Christianity and carnal Israel, where Paul conceives of himself and his followers as spiritual and, of course, Christian. In the fifties of the first century, as even more the case during Philo's career, there was little opposition between literalist Jews and spiritual Christians — no Gnostics had yet begun to write, and many followers of Christ apparently still thought of themselves as Messiah-followers among a Jewish community allowing differing interpretations of Law, righteousness and cult. Boyarin has himself proposed that there were no separate bodies 'Judaism' and 'Christianity' in the first century, and many would accept that this was the case before 70.

After all, Paul's question in Romans 9 is a Jewish one: 'how are children of the promise born' (9:6–13 e.g.)? Philo and Paul are not outside the main stream of Jewish thought, most of which is highly 'Hellenized' in one way or another in the first century, but within it. They do not make Jewish 'identity' carnal and inferior; in Paul there is a strongly literal law and a spiritual experience based in it, which is largely how Paul was interpreted in the early Christian branch of Israel. But a different view of Paul, as a Marcionite *avant la lettre*, prevails when he is contrasted with a rabbinic Judaism that develops a century and a half after Paul's career.

These remarks, however, illustrate a difficulty for the reviewer: whom does Dawson wish to address? If he wanted to enter the historians' discussion of ancient Judaism, biblical interpretation, and Christian beginnings, he would have broadened his research into the period. Thus if he had integrated the studies of E. P. Sanders, N. T. Wright, David Flusser, B. F. Meyer, John Collins or Martin Hengel with the views of Daniel Boyarin, his judgements about allegorical (i.e. Hellenistic, contemplative and mystagogic) interpretation, and Jewish reinterpretations of religious practice, would have shifted and been deepened.

On the other hand, Christian supersessionism would not have disappeared. For to Dawson's worry that allegorical reading generated a supersessionist view, many historians of early Christianity would respond that supersessionist rhetoric did not depend on an allegorical interpretation, controversial in the early church as it is now (except perhaps among literary theorists) for its allegedly arbitrary and subjective interpretation. Allegory was neither sufficient nor necessary to prove to Christian eyes the failure of Judaism. The proof from prophecy and well-known historical occurrences — the actual destruction of Jerusalem with its Temple and sacrifices, the conquest of Palestine in 70 by a triumphant Roman army, the slaughter of thousands of Jews and the consequent inability of Jews to fulfill their cultic obligations including perhaps most seriously the Day of Atonement — were enough to convince most Christian writers and many (not all) Christian believers that Judaism was finished, despite its stubborn persistence in practice. Uninterested in allegory, the fourth-century authors Aphrahat of Persia, Ephrem the Syrian, and John Chrysostom, in different ways treated the Old Testament as a literally and often factually true account of Israel's past. They were all convinced from their own Christian view of history that God had turned against the Jews as a result of the death of the messiah, and that God's punishment had as usual followed swiftly upon Israel's crime. This literalist interpretation of the Old Testament they learned from the prophetic books themselves. Furthermore, many early Christians understood Israel's downfall to be potentially their own: such was, in their view, the consequence of having 'become' Israel.

But this book avoids considering the historical development of a church that separated from Judaism and developed its own *adversus Judaeos* interpretation. Thus the book was not written for historians, although those with a sympathy for Origen may find some of its passages evocative or convincing. Dawson is not interested in giving a full account of Christian supersessionism and placing Origen's views in that larger mentality. It is important to understand that his interest is not in history or in ancient exegesis or text-criticism; instead, it is to make an assertion about the relationship of hermeneutics to Christian life and (strangely) to reveal the uncovered motivations of the three modern interpreters whom he sets in conversation with Origen's figural reading. Therefore Dawson's interest is in theology — theology influenced by literary theory. He writes (p. 214):

> Where Origen most excels, though, and where each of our three modern thinkers falls short, is in his awareness that classical Christian life is a life of continual transformation of what already is into something different. In their varying but related repudiations of Origenist allegorical reading, Boyarin, Auerbach, and Frei manifest a common fear of 'making all things new'.

What Dawson is talking about here, though, is not the relationship between (old) Judaism and (new) Christianity; he is talking about Origen's (and Alexandria's) fascination with mystagogy, the *itinerarium mentis ad deum* that begins in religious cult, whether that of Temple or church, and ends in the angelomorphic moment where the mystic initiant passes beyond the veil, becoming someone different from what he previously was, fit for the heavenly court. Mystagogy does not require supersessionism, because after Second Temple Judaism discovered the means for such transformation, it required only the appearance of Jesus and the reinterpretation of Jewish traditions of ascent to the heavenly throne to relocate mystagogy in the imitation of the messiah in cult, life and thought. In Origen, allegory is not the servant of supersession, it is the servant of mystagogy, and it can never escape the letter it inhabits. If Dawson had made this clear, his readers could have understood how and where the church remains Israel and does not supersede it. Yet because he focuses his study upon the disputed act of interpreting (in the modern, twentieth-century sense) he does not make prominent the reason why the ancients were interested in interpreting at all: to draw and be drawn close to God.

So the distracting problem remains whether allegory is anti-Jewish. According to Dawson, Origen represents a still-barely-realized Christian view that 'requires the Christian to embrace as Christianly significant the concrete bodily and historical practices of Judaism precisely in ways that do not undermine but respect their bodily and historical integrity: the letter must remain in the spirit' (p. 217). Origen's views allow Christian 'meaning' in the Old Testament that 'extends without supplanting the former Jewish meanings — that the spirit does not undermine but instead draws out the fullest meaning of the letter; the letter must remain in the spirit because the spirit is the letter fully realized' (p. 217). Once again, Dawson invokes a concept called 'classical Christianity' to show that 'figural' reading represents that paradox or antithesis lying at the center of the religion. Thus it is worth quoting his last lines in full (p. 218):

> Those familiar with a religion that affirms that submission to God's agency constitutes human freedom, or that Jesus of Nazareth is no less human for being divine, or that divine power is manifested as divine suffering, or that wholly historical action is the realization of a transcendent divine intention, will not be surprised by the equally unexpected claim that fulfillments are more, and yet again are not more, than their figures.

For Dawson, 'classical Christianity' is the neo-orthodox theology that emphasizes existential and even (latterly) psychological states with respect to God, based in a strongly narrative interpretation of the Bible understood as revelation-in-history. As such, this 'classical' theology tends simultaneously to de-emphasize the weight of the church as interpreter through its varying forms of juridical authority — which is why Origen (many of whose writings were condemned or suppressed at an early ecumenical council) can here be the inspiration for a non-supersessionist Christianity. Perhaps this is the reason why the abstract quality of theological expression here belies the book's stated ambition to retain the literal, concrete and specific meaning of scripture.

So Dawson's interest is not in history, but in modes of interpretation — 'readings' of texts — and their moral consequences. If he makes the common mistake of scholars in thinking that textual interpretation was the preoccupation of early Christians, it damages his argument only slightly; his real interest is in whether 'figural' interpretation can be held as accountable for supersessionism as allegorical interpretation can. In connecting Origen (and two other modern interlocutors) with the former, he believes that he has shown how the Christian interpretation of Israel's history can with figural interpretation preserve the historicity of the Old Testament to such an extent that the ongoing life of Judaism can be endorsed as true and valid while the Christian meaning of the Old Testament can remain stable and at the same time grounded in the bodily meaning. The moral aspect of Dawson's project is clearly a preservationist program, then, because it believes that certain kinds of interpretation are more likely to damage the living community of the Jews and the meaning that it discerns in the biblical texts; it is just these kinds of interpretation that are to be avoided. Instead, Dawson wants to discover a 'kind of Christian figural reading that can remain true to its vocation of fashioning Christian identity while simultaneously cherishing human diversity'(p. 7). Becoming a Christian, though (if that is what 'fashioning identity' means) has been held traditionally to be a matter of ritual far more than of reading, if ritual includes both the sacraments communally performed, prayers personally prayed, the performance of good works and obedience to laws of conduct. The reason for this is, of course, that most Christians until recently could not read — and how they understood what was read to them is hard to gauge.

As in his previous two books, Dawson is interested largely in the reading and interpretation of texts, mainly biblical texts. The logic of reading, the assumptions behind it, and the construction of meaning all fascinate him. In *Allegorical Readers and Cultural Revision in Ancient Alexandria*, Dawson examined the interpretive programs of Philo, Valentinus and Clement. In *Literary Theory*, he engaged DeMan, Bloom, Luther and Bakhtin to show how contemporary literary theory offered resources to theologians in their traditionally Christian aim of addressing 'the whole of reality.'

Therefore it is not surprising that Dawson, who credits Boyarin for waking him from his 'modest anti-dogmatic slumber' (p. x), approaches a theological issue — right interpretation — by means of a close reading of the texts of three modern thinkers, by setting each beside a close reading of a few texts by Origen.

Dawson divides the book into three parts. The first looks at Daniel Boyarin's *Carnal Israel* and *A Radical Jew: Paul and the Politics of Identity*. The second discusses Erich Auerbach's *Mimesis* and his famous article 'Figura.' The third discusses the two early works of Hans Frei, *The Eclipse of Biblical Narrative: A Study in Eighteenth-and Nineteenth-Century Hermeneutics* and *The Identity of Jesus*. The first chapter in each part discusses the modern author in question, and the second sets that author's views beside those of Origen. Each author was chosen because each proposes that figural reading preserves the history of a described event, although the arguments of each are different. Because Origen is usually identified with 'fanciful' allegory, a close reading of certain texts by Origen is shown to have more to do with the typological reading than with the figurative or allegorical reading, and thus to be a suitable respondent to Boyarin, Auerbach and Frei. The objections of each one are matched and answered by an Origen whom Dawson interprets as a paradoxically literal allegorizer.

Origen by Dawson's account is not really an allegorist, though. He is really dependent upon typological (which Dawson calls 'figural,' preferring the Latin *figura* to the Greek *typos*) interpretation that sees past events as pointing to and being fulfilled by present or future events. Proving this is an uphill battle, and not only because in his *Commentary on John* Origen speaks openly of *allegoria*. Boyarin and others have misunderstood Origen as a thinker imbued with the binary opposition coming from Paul's agitated attempts to persuade by contrast, expressed in particular by the opposition between letter and spirit. But this is not true, and the consequences of this kind of reading make it important to show that it is not true. Origen, in his *Commentary on the Song of Songs* leaves, according to Boyarin, 'a telling example of the way post-Pauline Christian allegorical reading perpetuated the disembodying consequences of Pauline allegory' (p. 47). To come back to the point anticipated above, then, allegorical reading of scripture thus becomes not only a conceptual but a moral error: its practitioners not only distort the meaning of the text under consideration, but they also ignore or refute the very community for which the literal meaning was binding — in this case, rabbinic Judaism. Allegorical reading, therefore, is the foundation of supersessionism, and as the foundation of early Christian self-understanding as *verus* Israel — and spiritual Israel — it allows Marcionism to affect the entire theology of the church, dissenting traditions within Christianity notwithstanding.

Dawson wants to show that Boyarin has got the right worry but the wrong villain: Origen honors the flesh and the spirit of Jesus and therefore must be seen to honor both the past and the present of Israel by honoring its future reality, a reality signified by the 'eternal Gospel' of which Moses (Origen says) was just as aware as were the most privileged of apostles, those who witnessed the Transfiguration. And yet, theological objections might be raised to Dawson's theological argument: any comprehensive view of Origen's allegorical interpretation of the past of Israel must take account of his views in the *Contra Celsum*. There he defends ancient Jewish practice against a pagan philosopher for precisely the allegorical reason that Dawson wishes to avoid. In Judaism the truth was preserved until its true heirs arrived and discerned the real meaning of the Old Testament. Such passages must be read against Dawson's more conciliatory and optimistic portrait.

Robin Darling Young
University of Notre Dame

Peter SCHÄFER, *Mirror of His Beauty: Feminine Images of God from the Bible to the Early Kabbalah.* Jews, Christians, and Muslims from the Ancient to the Modern World. Princeton/Oxford: Princeton University Press, 2002. xviii + 306 pages. ISBN 0-691-09068-8. $29.95.

The similarities between Philo and the kabbalah have struck a significant number of scholars. There is a consensus that Philo's works did not directly influence the kabbalists of the twelfth and following centuries; however, the phenomenological similarities have forced students of the kabbalah to note the works of Philo (for a summary of earlier scholarly views see E. Wolfson, 'Traces of Philonic Doctrine in Medieval Jewish Mysticism: A Preliminary Note', *SPhA* 8 [1996] 99–106). Peter Schäfer has done so in his study of the emergence of the feminine manifestation of God in the earliest kabbalistic treatise, the *Bahir*.

Schäfer's monograph is a History of Religions effort to understand the appearance of the Shekhinah in the *Bahir*. He sets up his work in two parts. In part one, he sketches the varied constructions of feminine manifestations of God in Judaism from the Hebrew Bible to the *Bahir*. His treatment is in the form of a survey of significant texts. In chapter one he examines the place of Lady Wisdom in the Hebrew Bible and related texts: Job 28; Prov 8; Sirach 24; and Wis 7. In chapter two he explores the Philonic material (see below). He considers the Gnostic material in chapter three. He correctly — in my view — includes this material not only because of its importance in the history of scholarship on this question, but because some forms of Gnosticism had Jewish roots. He considers the wisdom myth in the *Apocryphon of John* and Irenaeus' summary of the Valentinian myth. He scans the rabbinic understanding of the Shekhinah in chapter four, pointing out that while the Shekhinah was initially identified with God it gradually became personified by the rabbis, although they did not develop the feminine aspect. Thinkers such as Saadia Gaon, Judah ben Barzillai, Judah Ha-Levi, and Maimonides, who laid the foundation of Jewish medieval philosophy, eschewed gender since they rejected any notion of divine corporeality (chapter five). This changed with the appearance of the *Bahir* that considered the Shekhinah to be the tenth *sefirot* (chapter six). As the tenth *sefirah*, the Shekhinah is on the borderline between God and humanity. She has a double-function: on the one hand, she relates to the third *sefirah* ('understanding' [*binah*]); on the other hand, she represents God on earth. Schäfer is most interested in the Shekhinah's latter role as *mediatrix*. 'Through her God enters the world, and her only task is to unite Israel with God' (p. 134).

The suddenness of such an important feminine manifestation of God requires an explanation. Schäfer attempts to provide an explanation in part two. He begins by considering Gershom Scholem's thesis that the ultimate origin is Gnosticism (chapter seven). Scholem's case rests on the parable of the king's daughter who corresponds to the 'daughter of light' in the bridal hymn of the *Acts of Thomas* or the Hymn of the Pearl and, more importantly, on Irenaeus' summary of the Valentinian myth that presents the 'fall of Sophia' and her exile in the lower, material world. Schäfer criticizes Scholem's reading (and by extension H. Jonas' reading) of the Gnostic material — aided by the presence of texts such as the *Apocryphon of John*: he does not find any evidence for the 'fall' and 'exile' of Sophia. He admits that 'there are some stunning and rather unexpected similarities' between the Gnostic myth and the Shekhinah of the *Bahir* (p. 142); however, there are also real differences, e.g., the Shekhinah does not create the material world. Unlike the Gnostic myth, the *Bahir* does not associate evil with the feminine, but rather with the fifth *sefirah*. This leads Schäfer to consider a more contemporary nexus for the emergence of the Shekhinah: Christianity in southern France. He argues that the development of the salvific functions of Mary as *mediatrix* and *interventrix* forms one of the poles creating a dialectic that brought the Shekhinah into the *Bahir* (chapter eight). He surveys the development of Mariology and then compares Mary to the Shekhinah. The closest phenomenological similarity is their common function as *mediatrices* between heaven and earth. Most importantly, this assignment to the feminine manifestation of God took place in the same time and place for Christianity and Judaism, twelfth century Provence in southern France — a coincidence that Schäfer suggests is not accidental. Schäfer considers the counter-arguments in chapter nine: Christian anti-Jewish legends and images as well as Jewish polemics against Mary. He concludes with a methodological chapter (see below).

Schäfer should be congratulated for providing a sweeping overview of a great deal of complicated material. It is a daunting task, one that he handles quite well. He writes clearly and covers the major texts. At the same time, specialists will undoubtedly point to the limits of his treatment of specific material. For example, Schäfer does not appear to know the bulk of recent work on Philo. His failure to interact with this scholarship restricts his interpretation of some important texts. He opens with a citation of *Ebr.* 30–31, a most appropriate text for his purposes. Unfortunately, he does not engage the extended discussion of this text among Philonists who have pointed out the importance of the Platonic background (e.g., D. T. Runia, *Philo of Alexandria and the* Timaeus *of Plato*, PhilAnt 44 [Leiden 1986] 283–91, esp. 284–86). A knowledge of these discussions would enrich his analysis by helping him to understand the possibilities and constraints that confronted a thinker like Philo who was attempting to relate Wisdom to the receptacle of Plato's *Timaeus*. Another significant gap is the absence of discussions of gender in Philo (e.g., R. A. Baer, *Philo's Use of the Categories Male and Female*, ALGHJ 3 [Leiden 1970]; D. Sly, *Philo's Perception of Women*, BJS 209 [Atlanta 1990]; and the article of L. Baynes that appeared too late for Schäfer's work, 'Philo, Personification, and the Transformation of Grammatical Gender', *SPhA* 14 [2002] 31–47). It is difficult to address the gender of Sophia adequately without also taking into account the larger issue of gender in Philo. A similar point might be made with respect to larger discussions of gender and God, an area in the notes that is surprisingly absent. Schäfer's basic point would still stand if he had interacted with this literature, but his treatment would look different.

The thesis of the book depends to a great extent upon the methodology that he offers to sustain it. He rejects a historicist perspective that attempts to trace the development of a concept back to its original form (Scholem). He also critiques functionalist approaches that bracket the historical question and concentrate on the role of ideas within specific texts (E. Wolfson, 'Hebraic and Hellenic conceptions of Wisdom in *Sefer ha-Bahir*', *Poetics Today* 19 [1998] 147–76). Instead he adapts H. Bloom's 'anxiety of influence' model to argue that 'historical influence is a creative and mutual process that affects both partners, so that neither is simply "source" or "recipient"' (p. 232; cf. also p. 13). He is trying to create a dynamic model that avoids 'proof' in the sense of a direct link and phenomenological similarities between ideas or structural parallels as evidence for dependency. Instead he wants to consider both religions as active partners in a common religious discourse. Schäfer clearly recognizes the difficulties that any attempt to explore the origins of the Shekhinah in the *Bahir* faces.

Does his model work? He demonstrates that the Shekhinah in the *Bahir* and the elevation of Mary in Christianity took place in Provence at the same time. He has further shown that both the Shekhinah and Mary have salvific functions. At this point the parallels begin to wane. I must confess that as intriguing as I found Schäfer's analysis, I was still scratching my head at the end of the book. How do we know that it was not a common *Zeitgeist* that led both traditions to develop their concepts independently from their own or from other traditions? At this point I begin looking for 'proof' or at least striking phenomenological parallels. To his credit,

Schäfer recognizes their absence and states so candidly (p. 238). Without them I think that Schäfer has a provocative hypothesis but no more.

I do not want to suggest that the work fails to make a contribution. It simply struggles with the same limitations of evidence that Scholem and Wolfson encountered. While some might find this disconcerting, I find it intriguing. It is one of the reasons that I keep reading Philo and the kabbalists. I am grateful to Schäfer for providing a competent summary of the evidence and a fresh way to reflect on it.

Gregory E. Sterling
University of Notre Dame

NEWS AND NOTES

Philo of Alexandria Group of the Society of Biblical Literature

The Philo of Alexandria Group of the Society of Biblical Literature convened for two sessions on November 24, 2002, in Toronto, Canada, at the Annual Meetings of the AAR and SBL. The first session was devoted to the issue of the relationship of two later thinkers to Philo of Alexandria. The session, which was presided over by Thomas Tobin, S.J. (Loyola University of Chicago), included two papers and was followed by a discussion. The two papers were by David Winston (Professor emeritus, Graduate Theological Union) on 'Philo and Maimonides,' and by Cyril O'Regan (University of Notre Dame) on 'Hegel's Retrieval of Philo and the Curing of Judaism.'

The second session, which was presided over by David Runia (University of Melbourne), was devoted to a presentation by Pieter van der Horst (Utrecht University and the Netherlands Institute for Advanced Study) of material from the commentary he is preparing on Philo's treatise *In Flaccum*. The title of Professor van der Horst's paper was 'Philo's *In Flaccum*: Problems and Perspectives.' This was followed by a panel discussion. The three panellists were: Sarah Pearce (University of Southampton), Ellen Birnbaum (Brandeis University), and John Barclay (University of Glasgow).

In the annual business meeting, David T. Runia presented a report on *The Studia Philonica Annual*; David M. Hay provided an update of The Studia Philonica Monograph Series; and Gregory E. Sterling reported on the progress of the Philo of Alexandria Commentary Series. One session at next year's meeting of the Group at the Annual Meetings of the AAR and SBL in Atlanta, Georgia will be devoted to two papers on the question of how original a thinker Philo of Alexandria actually was. The other session will be devoted to a paper by David M. Hay on issues connected with the interpretation of Philo's treatise *De vita contemplativa*.

Thomas H. Tobin, S.J.
Loyola University
Chicago

First International Symposium of the research project Corpus Judaeo-Hellenisticum Novi Testamentum (CJHNT) held in Eisenach and Jena

Philo and the New Testament – The New Testament and Philo. Mutual Perceptions

This Symposium connected to the Corpus Judaeo-Hellenisticum Novi Testamenti (CJHNT), organized by Prof. Karl-Wilhelm Niebuhr (University of Jena), with emphasis on the work of Philo, was held in Eisenach and Jena on May 1–4, 2003. The basic idea of the conference was the attempt to look at the relevant sources from the double perspective of New Testament and Philonic studies, aiming at a better integration of both fields.

Prof. Gregory E. Sterling (University of Notre Dame/Indiana) gave the opening lecture on 'The place of Philo of Alexandria in the study of Christian origins'. His advice for the audience and the further CJHNT-project was: 'We should not use Philo's works without first listening to his own voice'. Following his lecture the participants of the symposium were invited to a reception sponsored by the Thüringen Protestant church, represented by its bishop Prof. Christoph Kähler, who addressed the audience with a word of greeting, mentioning the shameful role of the so-called 'Entjudungsinstitut' during the time of Nazism in Germany, which was located in Eisenach.

On Friday and Saturday six 'twin-lectures' were held, each dealing with a related topic from both a more Philonic and a more New Testament perspective. The first pair, Prof. Folker Siegert (University of Münster) and Prof. Jens Herzer (University of Leipzig), discussed the phenomenon of inspiration in Philo and 2 Timothy 3:16. The second pair, Prof. Dieter Zeller (University of Mainz) and Prof. Gerhard Sellin (University of Hamburg), focused on the possible influence (or relevance) of Philonic thoughts on the conflict mentioned in 1 Corinthians 1–4. The third pair, Dr. Naomi Cohen from Haifa (who was unfortunately not personally present, but her paper was read) and Prof. Bernhard Heininger (University of Würzburg), were involved in the question of mystical terminology and mystical experiences in Philo and Paul. The fourth pair were Prof. Torrey Seland (University of Volda, Norway), who offered a stimulating 'Philonic Reading of 1 Peter', and Dr. Karl-Heinrich Ostmeyer (University of Leipzig), who compared the understanding of suffering in Paul and Philo. The following 'twin-lectures' were given by Prof. David Hay (Coe College, Cedar Rapids) and Prof. Berndt Schaller (University of Göttingen). In these, the focus again was 1 Corinthians, but this time chapter 15, and the question was whether Philo's statement about the double creation of humanity in his exegesis of Genesis 1–2 is comparable to Paul's Adam-Christ-typology. The final pair was comprised by Prof. Pieter van der Horst (University of Utrecht) and Prof. Friedrich Avemarie (University of Marburg), treating Philo's *In Flaccum* in comparison to the Acts of the Apostles, with a special eye on the conflict-stories in both books. Besides these 'twin-lectures', two more papers were read, one by Dr. Christian Noack (University of Frankfurt) on 'Haben oder Empfangen', dealing with the difference between ego-centred and God-centred knowledge in Philo and Paul, and one by Dr. Cana Werman (Jerusalem) on 'God's House: Temple and Universe', dealing with the different concepts of human vs. divine building of God's House.

On Friday evening a public lecture at the University of Jena was given by Prof. George W. E. Nickelsburg (University of Iowa), incorporating Philo into the broader context of the Jewish-hellenistic literature. This was followed by a reception at the Theological faculty, which was sponsored by the publishing house of Mohr Siebeck (Tübingen), who have agreed to publish both the CJHNT-Commentary series as well as the conference volume in the WUNT-series. Prof. Larry Hurtado (Edinburgh) brought the symposium to a close with a lecture under the title: 'Does Philo help explain early Christianity?' Besides these papers, three simultaneous workshops were offered, in which under the guidance of Prof. Jürgen Hammerstaedt, Dr. Rosa Maria Piccione (both University of Jena) and Dr. Jutta Leonhardt-Balzer (University of Munich) sections from Philo were read and discussed together.

This conference feature was very well received by the participants. The location of conference in the beautiful environs at the foot of the Wartburg, the famous castle where Martin Luther as 'Junker Jörg' translated the New Testament from Greek into German 1521/22, as well as bright sunshine and a discussion-provoking atmosphere all contributed to the symposium, which was deemed a great success by the participants.

As organizers of the symposium it is our duty to thank with great pleasure all participants and guests for their contributions. As editors of the symposium-volume we are proud to get the chance to make the results of the meeting available for a wider readership in the field of Philonic and New Testament studies.

Roland Deines and Karl-Wilhelm Niebuhr
University of Jena
Germany

In memoriam

Yehoshua Amir (1911–2002)

It is with sadness that we learned of the death of Yehoshua Amir, which occurred in Jerusalem on December 1, 2002, his ninety-first birthday. From the time of his Würzburg dissertation, *Die Verwendung griechischer und jüdischer Motive in den Gedanken Philons über die Stellung Gottes zu seinen Freunden*, published in 1937 under his earlier name Hermann Neumark, up until his most recent contributions in the new annotated Hebrew translation of Philo's works, he has left an important mark on Philonic scholarship.

Amir was born in the German city of Duisburg in 1911, of a family that had its roots in the eastern city of Posen, which later became part of Poland. His father was a rabbi. He spent his formative years in Germany during the period of the Weimar Republic and the Nazi regime. He studied classical philology at the universities of Bonn and Berlin, where Elias Bickermann and Eduard Norden were still teaching, and at Würzburg. At the latter institution he studied under Friedrich Pfister, among others. He also came under the strong influence of Isaak Heinemann, who helped him with the formulation of the topic of his doctoral dissertation. Amir was able to complete his doctorate in 1937, just weeks before a Nazi edict barring Jews from that degree would go into effect. In the same period, he was also a student at the liberal Jewish seminary in Berlin, where he was guided by scholars such as the philosopher Julius Guttmann, the historian Ismar Elbogen, and the theologian Leo Baeck. He finished his rabbinical studies at the seminary before emigrating to Israel in 1939.

Amir worked for many years as a teacher in the newly established *ulpanim* (Hebrew language schools) for new immigrants, before securing an appointment at the University of Tel Aviv in 1966, where he taught Jewish-Hellenistic as well as modern Jewish thought. He did many translations, especially of German works. He prepared Hebrew versions of works by Martin Buber and Franz Rosenzweig, and of Elbogen's history of Jewish liturgy. His translation of Rosenzweig's *The Star of Redemption* is something of a classic in its own right. In addition, he worked in the opposite direction, producing a German version of A. Schalit's Hebrew study of Herod the Great. In the present context, one may note his Hebrew edition of Hans Lewy's anthology of Philo's writings, published in 1964.

Amir began to publish regularly on Philo again in the 1960s and 70s. Of particular importance in this period are his essays, 'Ha-allegoria shel Filon be-yahasah la allegoria ha-homerit', *Eshkolot* (1970–71), on the allegorical method, and 'Philo and the Bible', *Studia Philonica* 2 (1973). He later published a collection of his articles on Philo in a work entitled *Die hellenistische*

Gestalt des Judentums bei Philon von Alexandrien (1983). Of later publications, his survey of Philo's biblical interpretation that appeared in the volume *Mikra* (ed. M.J. Mulder, 1988), may be mentioned. Amir believed, as did most German scholars of the earlier generation, that Philo's writings need to be evaluated primarily on the basis of Greek categories, and Amir was quite sensitive to the influence of Stoic *allegoresis* and philosophy. Especially insightful is his differentiation of Philo's concept of the Mosaic authorship of the Pentateuch from that of the Rabbis. For Philo, Moses' personal role as writer takes on much greater significance than in rabbinic literature. Amir was skeptical of attempts to link Philo with Palestinian *halakhic* traditions. On the other hand, he did recognize that there were important connections between Philo's biblical exegesis and Palestinian *aggada*, and did much to illuminate them in his writing, although these connections are more often limited to isolated themes and motifs than indicative of extensive correspondence in exegetical method.

In recent years, Amir dedicated his primary energies to the preparation of a complete Hebrew edition of Philo's works, which is being published under the editorial supervision of Suzanne Daniel. He has been responsible for much of the *Allegorical Commentary*, the first volume of which appeared in 1997 (vol. IV of the complete works). In the volume are included the allegorical treatises from the first book of the *Allegory of the Law* through *On the Posterity of Cain*. The annotations to this volume constitute a major contribution to the understanding of the treatises, and contain much philological in addition to philosophical learning. They go well beyond just aids to the Hebrew reader. Just weeks before his death Amir delivered to the publisher the completed manuscript of the next volume of treatises, all edited by him, although some of them have been translated by others. We look forward to the publication of this volume.

Amir represented an important generation of scholars of classical and Judaeo-Hellenistic literature, those trained in Germany who brought their approaches and traditions of learning to Israel. As Amir himself rendered Philo's words, 'the form of wisdom in which they engaged will live on' (*Quod deterius*, § 75).*

Adam Kamesar
Hebrew Union College
Cincinnati, USA

---

* I wish to thank my Jerusalem colleague, Dr. Yehoyada Amir, the son of Yehoshua Amir, for his help with the preparation of this note. [For a review of the first volume of Yehoshua Amir's translation of the Allegorical Commentary, see pp. 149–150 in this volume. EDITORS]

Philo Hispanicus Project

Since 2001 a number of scholars working in the Spanish language area have pointed out the lack of an academically sound translation of Philo of Alexandria. It was recalled that the critical edition by Cohn and Wendland (1896–1915) and the subsequent English, French and (partially completed) Italian editions have given a vital impulse to Philonic studies in their respective linguistic areas. On one hand we knew that many colleagues specializing in Greek language and culture, Hellenistic philosophy, Judaism, Biblical Studies, Patristics, Ancient history and other disciplines, strongly regretted the lack of a suitable instrument for coming closer to Philo. But on the other hand we were unable to envisage the day approaching in which the conditions were right for undertaking a Spanish translation of the extensive and complex Corpus Philonicum.

Now, I am pleased to report, the situation has changed. Our project was formed by moving from the particular toward the universal. The first stage began when some scholars thought it would be valuable to translate specific texts of Philo which were of particular relevance to their research. In 2001 Marcelo Boeri, now Professor in the Universidad de Los Andes (Chile), expressed to me his interest in translating *De aeternitate mundi* in connection with research on Aristotelian and Stoic physics. I responded that my own interest was in translating *De posteritate Caini* in connection with research on the transformation that Philo introduces in his use of Platonic dialectical language. In 2002 I met at a conference Marta Alesso, Professor in the Universidad Nacional de la Pampa (Argentina), who told me that, after studying Heraclitus rhetor on the method of allegory, she intended to translate the *Legum allegoriae* of Philo as a further step toward a systematic study of the allegory in the first century C.E. Having being informed about these projects in particular fields, we wondered if it was not an auspicious hour for organizing a project which would undertake the translation of the entire Philonic corpus. With this in mind I took up contact with Dr. Sofía Torallas, of the Research Council of Spain (Madrid), who had already published the translation of three Philonic works with the Publishing House Gredos, and with Francisco Lisi of the Universidad Carlos III (Madrid), who had published in Spanish the platonic *Timaeus* and was interested in its relationship with *De opificio mundi*. On April 19 2003 I sent a letter to all those I could think of who might be interested in the project. The letter concluded with the following words: 'We have now two difficult tasks. First, To close ranks among us (. . .) Second, to maintain together the virtue that is the specifically human according to Philo, namely *elpis*, hope. In our case that is more specifically to maintain the hope of a finding a publisher.' Our hope was quickly realized. On June 5 Editorial Trotta of Madrid, one of the most important publishing houses in Spanish language, communicated to us its firm interest in carrying out the project. At this time we have entered in a discussion with Trotta for the organization of the edition.

Besides the scholars mentioned so far, others have shown interest in contributing to the translation as well. In fact, José María Zamora (Madrid) is working on *De Cherubim*. Lena Balzaretti of the Universidad Nacional de Rosario (Argentina) is committed to *De ebrietate* and *De sobrietate*. Patricia Ciner of the Universidad Nacional de San Juan (Argentina) is working on the translation of *De vita contemplativa*.

During 2003, the Publishing house Trotta and the provisional editorial board will make the basic decisions in order to establish the number of volumes, the order of books and other criteria for the translation. It is our sincere hope that, as has happened in other linguistic areas, our initiative will promote a further revival of the Philonic studies in the Ibero-American world. We will keep readers of this Annual informed about our progress. Any person who wishes to contribute or give advice is asked to take up contact with the undersigned (details are found in the section Notes on Contributors).

> José Pablo Martín
> Argentinian Research Organization (CONICET)
> Buenos Aires

Philo in the Far East (continued)

In an earlier note in this section (vol. 9, 1997, p. 371) I mentioned rumours that a Chinese translation of Philo's works was in preparation. I can now report that a first volume was in fact published already in 1998. This first translation of Philo into Chinese was produced by the Institute of Sino-Christian studies in Hong Kong. Its full title is: *Lun chuangshiji: yuyi de jieshi* (Chinese = *On Genesis: Allegorical Interpretation*). The translators are Wang Xiaochao and Dai Weiqing, who were assisted by Sze-kar Wan in an editorial capacity. My information about this volume comes from Sze-kar Wan. He informs me that the works translated are *De opificio mundi* and *Legum Allegoriae*, i.e. the contents of the first volume of the Loeb Classical library. The translation is in fact made primarily on the basis of the English translation found there and some of the notes are translated as well. An introduction has been contributed by Wang. For further details of the contents of the volume see the bibliographical notice on p. 137 of this volume. I am sure that all Philonists will join me in expressing the hope that the publication of this volume will be an encouragement for Philonic studies in the most populous country on our globe.

Prof. Gohei Hata, whose volume of Philo translations was reported in these pages in vol. 13 (2001, pp. 291–292), has kindly sent me three subsequent volumes published in Japanese. These are the first three volumes of his Japanese translation of the Septuagint, covering the first three books of the Pentateuch. He tells me that the notes in these volumes make reference to Philo. I have no reason to doubt this whatsoever, but unable to verify this myself. We congratulate the author on his achievement and wish him every success in the continuation of his project. It will surely be of immense importance for the study of Greek-speaking Judaism in Japan.

David Runia
Queen's College
Melbourne

NOTES ON CONTRIBUTORS

Ellen BIRNBAUM has recently taught and conducted postdoctoral research at both Harvard and Brandeis University. Her postal address is 78 Porter Road, Cambridge, MA 02140, USA; her electronic address is ebirnbaum@comcast.net.

KENNETH A. FOX is Assistant Professor of Biblical Studies and New Testament at Canadian Theological Seminary. His postal address is 630-833 4th Avenue SW, Calgary AB, CANADA T2P 3T5; his electronic address can be obtained from the editors.

Albert C. GELJON teaches classical languages at the Christelijke Gymnasium in Utrecht. His postal address is Gazellestraat 138, 3523 SZ Utrecht, THE NETHERLANDS; his electronic address is geljon@ixs.nl.

David M. HAY is McCabe Professor of Religion Emeritus, Coe College, Cedar Rapids, Iowa. His postal address is 1428 Airline Road McDonough, GA 30252, USA; his electronic address is DavidMcKec@aol.com.

Brad INWOOD is Canada Research Chair in Ancient Philosophy and Chair of the Department of Classics at the University of Toronto. His postal address is University of Toronto, 97 St. George St., Toronto, M5S 2E8, CANADA; his electronic address is brad.inwood@utoronto.ca.

Heleen M. KEIZER is Dean of Academic Affairs at the Istituto Superiore di Osteopatia in Milan, Italy. Her postal address is Via Guerrazzi 3, 20052 Monza (Mi), ITALY; her electronic address is h.m.keizer @hetnet.nl.

Jose Pablo MARTÍN is Director of Studies at the Universidad Nacional de General Sarmiento, San Miguel, Argentina, and Senior Research fellow of the Argentinian Research Organization (CONICET). His postal address is Azcuenaga 1090, 1663 San Miguel, ARGENTINA; his electronic address is fmk@ciudad.com.ar.

Angela Maria MAZZANTI is Research Assistant Professor of History of Religions in the Department of Paleography and Medieval History at the University of Bologna. Her postal address is Department of Paleography and Medieval History, Piazza S. Giovanni in Monte 2, 40124 Bologna ITALY; her electronic address is angelamaria.mazzanti@unibo.it.

NOTES ON CONTRIBUTORS

Phillip MITSIS is A.S. Onassis Professor of Hellenic Culture and Civilization and Director of the Onassis Center for Hellenic Studies. His postal address is New York University, 726 Broadway, New York, NY 10003, USA; his electronic address is phillip.mitsis@nyu.edu.

Hindy NAJMAN is Assistant Professor in Judaism, Department of Theology, University of Notre Dame. Her postal address is Department of Theology, University of Notre Dame, Notre Dame, IN 46556, USA; her electronic address is Najman.1@nd.edu.

Judith H. NEWMAN is Associate Professor of Old Testament and Director of the Center for Jewish-Christian Studies and Relations at General Theological Seminary. Her postal address is General Theological Seminary, 175 Ninth Avenue, New York, NY 10011, USA; her electronic address is newman@gts.edu.

David K. O'CONNOR is Associate Professor of Philosophy and Concurrent Associate Professor of Classics at the University of Notre Dame. His postal address is Philosophy Department, 100 Malloy Hall, University of Notre Dame, Notre Dame, IN 46556-4619, USA. His electronic address is doconnor@nd.edu.

Stanley E. PORTER is President, Dean and Professor of New Testament at McMaster Divinity College, Hamilton, Ontario, CANADA. His postal address is McMaster Divinity College, 1280 Main St. W., Hamilton, ON, CANADA, L8S 4K1; his electronic address is princpl@mcmaster.ca.

Roberto RADICE is Professor of Ancient Philosophy at the Sacred Heart University, Milan. His postal address is Via XXV Aprile 4, 21016 Luino, ITALY; his electronic address is rradice@iol.it.

Tessa RAJAK is Professor of Ancient History, University of Reading and Director of the AHRB Parkes Project on the Greek Bible in the Graeco-Roman World. Her postal address is Department of Classics, University of Reading, Whiteknights, Reading RG6 6AA, UK; her electronic address is T.Rajak@reading.ac.uk.

Jean RIAUD is Professor in the Institut de Lettres et Histoire, Université Catholique de l'Ouest, Angers. His postal address is 24, rue du 8 mai 1945, Saint Barthélemy d'Anjou, FRANCE; his electronic address is jean.riaud@wanadoo.fr.

James R. ROYSE is a software engineer specializing in real-time financial applications. His postal address is P. O. Box 16700, San Francisco CA 94116-0700, USA; his electronic address is jamesrroyse@hotmail.com.

DAVID T. RUNIA is Master of Queen's College and Professorial Fellow in the School of Fine Arts, Classics and Archaeology at the University of Melbourne. His postal address is Queen's College, College Crescent, Parkville 3052, AUSTRALIA; his electronic address is runia@queens.unimelb.edu.au.

David SATRAN is Senior Lecturer in the Department of Comparative Religion, Hebrew University, Jerusalem. His postal address is Department of Comparative Religion, Hebrew University, Mt. Scopus, Jerusalem 91905, ISRAEL; his electronic address is Satran@h2.hum.huji.ac.il.

David SEDLEY is Laurence Professor of Ancient Philosophy in the University of Cambridge, where he is also a Fellow of Christ's College. His postal address is Christ's College, Cambridge, CB2 3BU, UK; his electronic address is dns1@cam.ac.uk

Torrey SELAND is Professor in Biblical Studies at the Volda University College, Volda, Norway, and presently Dean of the Department of Social Sciences. His postal adress is Gamletunveien 5, 6100 Volda, NORWAY; his electronic address is ts@hivolda.no

Gregory E. STERLING is Associate Dean of the Faculty, College of Arts and Letters and Professor in New Testament, Department of Theology, University of Notre Dame. His postal address is Department of Theology, University of Notre Dame, Notre Dame IN 46556, USA; his electronic address is gregory.e. sterling.1@nd.edu.

Paul VAN DER WAERDT is principal in a consulting firm that provides planning, intervention design and evaluation, and fund development assistance to nonprofit health and human service agencies in the San Francisco Bay Area. His postal address is 257 Oak Street, San Francisco, CA 94102, USA; his electronic address is paulvw1@mac.com.

David WINSTON is Emeritus Professor of Hellenistic and Jewish Studies, Graduate Theological Union, Berkeley. His postal address is 1220 Grizzly Peak, Berkeley CA 94708, USA; his electronic address is dwinston@jps.net.

Robin Darling YOUNG is Associate Professor of Theology at the University of Notre Dame. Her postal address is Department of Theology, Malloy Hall, University of Notre Dame, Notre Dame, Indiana 46556, USA; her electronic address is ryoung@ nd.edu.

Dieter ZELLER is Professor für Religionswissenschaft des Hellenismus at the Johannes-Gutenberg University of Mainz and Honorar-Professor at the Ruprecht-Karls University of Heidelberg. His postal address is Schillerweg 4, 65346 Eltville (Erbach), DEUTSCHLAND; his electronic address is dzeller@mail.uni-mainz.de.

INSTRUCTIONS TO CONTRIBUTORS

Authors and Book reviews can only be considered for publication in *The Studia Philonica Annual* if they rigorously conform to the guidelines established by the editorial board. For further information see also the website of the Annual:

http://www.nd.edu/~philojud

1. *The Studia Philonica Annual* accepts articles for publication in the area of Hellenistic Judaism, with special emphasis on Philo and his *Umwelt*. Articles on Josephus will be given consideration if they focus on his relation to Judaism and classical culture (and not on primarily historical subjects). The languages in which the articles may be published are English, French and German. Translations from Italian or Dutch into English can be arranged at a modest cost to the author.

2. Articles and reviews are to be sent to the editors as email attachments. For the formatting of submitted material the following formats can be accepted:

(a) Apple Macintosh, formatted preferably in MS-Word, using Greekkeys or SuperGreek and SuperHebrew;

(b) Microsoft Windows formatted in Word or Word Perfect. Users of Nota Bene are requested to submit a copy exported in a format compatible with Word.

In all cases it is **imperative** that authors give **full details** about the word processor and foreign language fonts used and that, if their manuscript contains Greek or Hebrew material, a hard copy be sent by mail or by fax. This is not required if authors are able to send pdf versions of their manuscripts to the editors. No handwritten Greek or Hebrew can be accepted. Authors are requested not to vocalize their Hebrew (except when necessary) and to keep their use of this language to a reasonable minimum. It should always be borne in mind that not all readers of the Annual can be expected to read Greek or Hebrew. Transliteration is permissible for incidental terms.

3. With regard to the citation of scholarly references the Annual employs the conventions embodied in the following examples (note (i) that no publishers' names are given, (ii) for articles single quotation marks are used, and (iii) that books and journals are italicized, series are not):

   A. Mendelson, *Secular Education in Philo of Alexandria,* Monographs of the Hebrew Union College 7 (Cincinnati 1982) 15–27.
   Y. Amir, 'The Transference of Greek Allegories to Biblical Motifs in Philo', in F. E. Greenspahn, E. Hilgert, B. L. Mack (edd.), *Nourished with Peace: Studies in*

Hellenistic Judaism in Memory of Samuel Sandmel, Scholars Press Homage Series 9 (Chico, California 1984) 15–25.

J. P. Martín, 'El encuentro de exégesis y filosofía en Filón Alejandrino', *Revista Bíblica* 46 (1984) 199–211.

Mendelson *op. cit.* (n. 0) 23ff.

Amir, *art. cit.* (n. 0) 16–18 **or** Martín 'El encuentro' 199–201.

It is also possible to give references by author and date in the footnotes only, with full details presented in a bibliography at the end of the article, as in the following example:

In notes:

See Kraemer (1989) 351; Mangey (1742) 2.134; Nikiprowetzky (1977) 251.

In bibliography;

R. S. Kraemer, 'Monastic Jewish Women in Greco-Roman Egypt: Philo Judaeus on the Therapeutrides', *Signs (Chicago)* 14 (1989) 342–370.

T. Mangey, *Philonis Judaei opera quae reperiri potuerunt omnia*, 2 vols. (London 1742).

V. Nikiprowetzky, *Le commentaire de l'Écriture chez Philon d'Alexandrie: son caractère et sa portée; observations philologiques*, ALGHJ 11 (Leiden 1977).

For the abbreviations to be used, see further below. A sound guide to the way that Philonic scholarship should be cited will be found in D. T. Runia, *Philo of Alexandria: an Annotated Bibliography 1987–1996*, VCSup 57 (Leiden 2000). Note that with regard to the use of capitals in citing English references, both English-American and continental European conventions are permissible.

4. The following abbreviations are to be used in both articles and book reviews.

(a) Philonic treatises are to be abbreviated according to the following list. Numeration is according to Cohn and Wendland's edition, using Arabic numbers only (e.g. *Spec.* 4.123). Note that *De Providentia* should be cited according to Aucher's edition, and not the LCL translation of the fragments by F. H. Colson.

Abr.	*De Abrahamo*
Aet.	*De aeternitate mundi*
Agr.	*De agricultura*
Anim.	*De animalibus*
Cher.	*De Cherubim*
Contempl.	*De vita contemplativa*
Conf.	*De confusione linguarum*
Congr.	*De congressu eruditionis gratia*
Decal.	*De Decalogo*
Deo	*De Deo*
Det.	*Quod deterius potiori insidiari soleat*
Deus	*Quod Deus sit immutabilis*
Ebr.	*De ebrietate*

Flacc.	In Flaccum
Fug.	De fuga et inventione
Gig.	De gigantibus
Her.	Quis rerum divinarum heres sit
Hypoth.	Hypothetica
Ios.	De Iosepho
Leg. 1–3	Legum allegoriae I, II, III
Legat.	Legatio ad Gaium
Migr.	De migratione Abrahami
Mos. 1–2	De vita Moysis I, II
Mut.	De mutatione nominum
Opif.	De opificio mundi
Plant.	De plantatione
Post.	De posteritate Caini
Praem.	De praemiis et poenis, De exsecrationibus
Prob.	Quod omnis probus liber sit
Prov. 1–2	De Providentia I, II
QE 1–2	Quaestiones et solutiones in Exodum I, II
QG 1–4	Quaestiones et solutiones in Genesim I, II, III, IV
Sacr.	De sacrificiis Abelis et Caini
Sobr.	De sobrietate
Somn. 1–2	De somniis I, II
Spec. 1–4	De specialibus legibus I, II, III, IV
Virt.	De virtutibus

(b) Standard works of Philonic scholarship are abbreviated:

Aucher	*Philonis Judaei sermones tres hactenus inediti* (Venice 1822), *Philonis Judaei paralipomena* (Venice 1826)
G-G	H. L. Goodhart and E. R. Goodenough, 'A General Bibliography of Philo Judaeus', in E. R. Goodenough, *The Politics of Philo Judaeus: Practice and Theory* (New Haven 1938, reprinted Hildesheim 1967^2) 125–321
PCH	*Philo von Alexandria: die Werke in deutscher Übersetzung*, edited by L. Cohn, I. Heinemann *et al.*, 7 vols. (Breslau, Berlin 1909–64)
PCW	*Philonis Alexandrini opera quae supersunt*, ediderunt L. Cohn, P. Wendland, S. Reiter, 6 vols. (Berlin 1896–1915)
PLCL	*Philo in Ten Volumes (and Two Supplementary Volumes)*, English translation by F. H. Colson, G. H. Whitaker (and R. Marcus), 12 vols., Loeb Classical Library (London 1929–62)
PAPM	*Les œuvres de Philon d'Alexandrie*, French translation under the general editorship of R. Arnaldez, J. Pouilloux, C. Mondésert (Paris 1961–92)
R-R	R. Radice and D. T. Runia, *Philo of Alexandria: an Annotated Bibliography 1937–1986*, VCSup 8 (Leiden 1988)
RRS	D. T. Runia, *Philo of Alexandria: an Annotated Bibliography 1987–1996*, VCSup (Leiden 2000)
SPh	*Studia Philonica*
SPhA	*The Studia Philonica Annual*

(c) Biblical books, Pseudepigraphical, Qumran, Rabbinic and Gnostic literature are to be abbreviated as recommended in the *SBL Handbook of Style* Peabody Mass. 1999 (published by Hendrickson) §8. Note that biblical books are not italicized and that between chapter and verse a colon is placed (placement of a full stop after the abbreviation is optional, provided the author is consistent). Authors writing in German or French should follow their own conventions for biblical citations.

(d) Classical and Patristic authors should be cited in the manner recommended by the three Oxford lexica:

H. G. Liddell, R. Scott , H. S. Jones (edd.), *A Greek-English Lexicon* (Oxford 1940[9]);
P. G. W. Glare (ed.), *The Oxford Latin Dictionary* (Oxford 1982);
G. W. H. Lampe (ed.), *A Patristic Greek Lexicon* (Oxford 1961).

Preferred abbreviations for Josephus, however, are *AJ*, *BJ*, *c. Ap.*, and *Vita*, but English abbreviations (*Antiquities*, *War*, etc.) are permitted. Once again consistency is the first requirement.

(e) Journals, monograph series, source collections and standard reference works are to be be abbreviated in accordance with the recommendations listed in *The SBL Handbook of Style*, Peabody Mass. 1999 (published by Hendrickson) §8. The following list contains a selection of the more important abbreviations (adding a few abbreviations of Classical and philosophical journals and standard reference books not furnished in the list mentioned above. (Note that some of these differ from the above-mentioned list in order to attain consistency with the bibliographies R-R and RRS.)

ABD	*The Anchor Bible Dictionary*, 6 vols. (New York etc. 1992)
AC	*L'Antiquité Classique*
ACW	Ancient Christian Writers
AGJU	Arbeiten zur Geschichte des antiken Judentums und des Urchristentums
AJPh	*American Journal of Philology*
AJSL	*American Journal of Semitic Languages*
ALGHJ	Arbeiten zur Literatur und Geschichte des hellenistischen Judentums
ANRW	*Aufstieg und Niedergang der römischen Welt*
APh	*L'Année Philologique (founded by Marouzeau)*
BAGD	*A Greek-English Lexicon of the New Testament and other Early Christian literature*, edited by W. Bauer, W. F. Arndt, F. W. Gingrich, F. W. Danker (Chicago 1979[2])
BDB	*Hebrew and English lexicon of the Old Testament*, edited by F. Brown, S. R. Driver, C. A. Briggs (Oxford 1952)
BibOr	Bibliotheca Orientalis
BJRL	*Bulletin of the John Rylands Library*
BJS	Brown Judaic Studies

BMCR	*Bryn Mawr Classical Review* (electronic)
BZAW	Beihefte zur Zeitschrift für die alttestamentliche Wissenschaft
BZNW	Beihefte zur Zeitschrift für die neutestamentliche Wissenschaft
BZRGG	Beihefte zur Zeitschrift für Religions- und Geistesgeschichte
CAH	*The Cambridge Ancient History*, edited by J. B. Bury *et al.*, 16 vols. (Cambridge 1923–)
CBQ	*The Catholic Biblical Quarterly*
CBQ.MS	The Catholic Biblical Quarterly. Monograph Series
CChr	Corpus Christianorum, Turnhout
CIG	*Corpus Inscriptionum Graecarum*, edited by A. Boeckh, 4 vols. in 8 (Berlin 1828–77)
CIJ	*Corpus Inscriptionum Judaicarum*, edited by J. B. Frey, 2 vols. (Rome 1936–52)
CIL	*Corpus Inscriptionum Latinarum* (Berlin 1862–)
CIS	*Corpus Inscriptionum Semiticarum* (Paris 1881–1962)
CPh	*Classical Philology*
CPJ	*Corpus Papyrorum Judaicarum*, ed. by V. Tcherikover and A. Fuks, 3 vols. (Cambrige Mass. 1957–64)
CQ	*The Classical Quarterly*
CR	*The Classical Review*
CRINT	Compendia Rerum Iudaicarum ad Novum Testamentum
CPG	*Clavis Patrum Graecorum*, edited by M. Geerard, 5 vols. (Turnhout 1974–87)
CPL	*Clavis Patrum Latinorum*, edited by E. Dekkers (Turnhout 1954)
CSCO	Corpus Scriptorum Christianorum Orientalium
DA	Dissertation Abstracts
DBSup	*Dictionnaire de la Bible*, Supplément (Paris 1928–)
DSpir	*Dictionnaire de Spiritualité*
EncJud	*Encyclopaedia Judaica*, 16 vols. (Jerusalem 1972)
EPRO	Études préliminaires aux religions orientales dans l'Empire romain
FrGH	*Fragmente der Griechische Historiker*, edited by F. Jacoby
GCS	Die griechischen christlichen Schriftsteller, Leipzig
GLAJJ	M. Stern, *Greek and Latin authors on Jews and Judaism*, 3 vols. (Jerusalem 1974–1984)
GRBS	*Greek, Roman and Byzantine Studies*
HKNT	Handkommentar zum Neuen Testament, Tübingen
HNT	Handbuch zum Neuen Testament, Tübingen
HR	*History of Religions*
HThR	*Harvard Theological Review*
HUCA	*Hebrew Union College Annual*
JAAR	*Journal of the American Academy of Religion*
JAOS	*Journal of the American Oriental Society*
JbAC	*Jahrbuch für Antike und Christentum*
JBL	*Journal of Biblical Literature*
JHI	*Journal of the History of Ideas*
JHS	*The Journal of Hellenic Studies*
JJS	*The Journal of Jewish Studies*
JQR	*The Jewish Quarterly Review*
JR	*The Journal of Religion*
JRS	*The Journal of Roman Studies*
JSHRZ	Jüdische Schriften aus hellenistisch-römischer Zeit
JSJ	*Journal for the Study of Judaism (in the Persian, Hellenistic and Roman*

	Period)
JSNT	Journal for the Study of the New Testament
JSNT.S	Journal for the Study of the New Testament. Supplement Series
JSOT	Journal for the Study of the Old Testament
JSOT.S	Journal for the Study of the Old Testament. Supplement Series
JSP	Journal for the Study of the Pseudepigrapha and Related Literature
JSSt	Journal of Semitic Studies
JThS	The Journal of Theological Studies
KB	L. Koehler and W. Baumgartner, Lexicon in Veteris Testamenti libros, 3 vols. (Leiden 1967–83^3)
KJ	Kirjath Sepher
LCL	Loeb Classical Library
LSJ	A Greek-English lexicon, edited by H. G. Liddell, R. Scott, H. S. Jones (Oxford 1940^9)
MGWJ	Monatsschrift für Geschichte und Wissenschaft des Judentums
Mnem	Mnemosyne
NCE	New Catholic Encyclopedia, 15 vols (New York 1967)
NHS	Nag Hammadi Studies
NT	Novum Testamentum
NT.S	Supplements to Novum Testamentum
NTA	New Testament Abstracts
NTOA	Novum Testamentum et Orbis Antiquus
NTS	New Testament Studies
OLD	The Oxford Latin dictionary, edited by P. G. W. Glare (Oxford 1982)
OTP	J. H. Charlesworth (ed.), The Old Testament Pseudepigrapha, 2 vols. (New York-London 1983–85)
PAAJR	Proceedings of the American Academy for Jewish Research
PAL	Philon d'Alexandrie: Lyon 11–15 Septembre 1966 (Paris 1967)
PG	Patrologiae cursus completus: series Graeca, edited by J. P. Migne, 162 vols. (Paris 1857–1912)
PGL	A Patristic Greek lexicon, ed. by G. W. H. Lampe (Oxford 1961)
PhilAnt	Philosophia Antiqua
PL	Patrologiae cursus completus: series Latina, edited by J. P. Migne, 221 vols. (Paris 1844–64)
PW	Pauly-Wissowa-Kroll, Real-Encyclopaedie der classischen Altertumswissenschaft, Stuttgart
PWSup	Supplement to PW
RAC	Reallexikon für Antike und Christentum
RB	Revue Biblique
REA	Revue des Études Anciennes
REArm	Revue des Études Arméniennes
REAug	Revue des Études Augustiniennes
REG	Revue des Études Grecques
REJ	Revue des Études Juives
REL	Revue des Études Latines
RGG	Die Religion in Geschichte und Gegenwart, 7 vols. (Tübingen 1957–65^3)
RhM	Rheinisches Museum für Philologie
RQ	Revue de Qumran
RSR	Revue des Sciences Religieuses
SB	H. L. Strack and P. Billerbeck, Kommentar zum Neuen Testament aus Talmud und Midrasch, 6 vols. in 7 (Munich 1922–61)
SBLDS	Society of Biblical Literature. Dissertation Series

SBLMS	Society of Biblical Literature. Monograph Series
SBLSPS	Society of Biblical Literature. Seminar Papers Series
SC	Sources Chrétiennes
Sem	*Semitica*
SHJP	E. Schürer, *The History of the Jewish people in the Age of Jesus Christ*, revised edition, 3 vols. in 4 (Edinburgh 1973–87)
SJLA	Studies in Judaism in Late Antiquity
SNTSMS	Society for New Testament Studies. Monograph Series
SR	*Studies in Religion*
StUNT	Studien zur Umwelt des Neuen Testaments
SVF	Stoicorum veterum fragmenta, edited by J. von Arnim
TDNT	*Theological Dictionary of the New Testament*, 10 vols. (Grand Rapids 1964–76)
THKNT	Theologischer Handkommentar zum Neuen Testament, Berlin
TRE	*Theologische Realenzyklopädie*, Berlin
TSAJ	Texte und Studien zum Antike Judentum
TU	Texte und Untersuchungen zur Geschichte der altchristlichen Literatur, Berlin
TWNT	*Theologisches Wörterbuch zum Neuen Testament*, 10 vols. (Stuttgart 1933–79)
VChr	*Vigiliae Christianae*
VChr.S	Supplements to Vigiliae Christianae
VT	*Vetus Testamentum*
WUNT	Wissenschaftliche Untersuchungen zum Neuen Testament
ZAW	*Zeitschrift für die alttestamentliche Wissenschaft*
ZKG	*Zeitschrift für Kirchengeschichte*
ZKTh	*Zeitschrift für Katholische Theologie*
ZNW	*Zeitschrift für die neutestamentliche Wissenschaft*
ZRGG	*Zeitschrift für Religions- und Geistesgeschichte*

www.ingramcontent.com/pod-product-compliance
Lightning Source LLC
Chambersburg PA
CBHW020758160426
43192CB00006B/369